HISTORY AND
THE IDEA OF MANKIND

History and
the Idea of Mankind

edited by
W. WARREN WAGAR

ALBUQUERQUE
UNIVERSITY OF NEW MEXICO PRESS

TO THE MEMORY OF
HANS KOHN
(1891-1971)

Preface:
The Council for
the Study of Mankind

GERHARD HIRSCHFELD

Executive Director
Council for the Study of Mankind, Inc.

IN NO CENTURY BEFORE OURS HAVE SO MANY DELIBERATE EFFORTS been made by scholars and public men to address themselves to the cause of human peace and unity. Statesmen of all countries speak incessantly of the welfare of mankind. The League of Nations and the United Nations have attempted to act, with varying degrees of success, as the conscience and the forum of mankind. Innumerable programs for world-betterment, often well financed, have been set in motion by governments, international agencies, private foundations, religious bodies, and universities.

But in no century before ours has the need for human unity been so imperative. Indeed, mankind is already unified in a material sense. It is this very fact that renders higher orders of synthesis necessary, if mankind is to survive. The race has always existed, but its unity was in earlier times mostly a dream, a distant image. Now, almost suddenly, mankind has become an inter-communicating and inter-dependent whole in which every part is vulnerable to destruction by other parts. For the first time, our planet is living a single history. The material unity which already and irrevocably exists must be reinforced by legal, moral, and spiritual unity, which sadly—despite all our good intentions—still does not exist.

In past ages, one could deal with the idea of mankind however one pleased, or not deal with it at all. There was no inescapable need, obligation, or force of circumstance. Whether or not to think about mankind was a matter of choice. We have no such choice today. Instead, there is great urgency to think about mankind and its future, and to convert the idea of mankind into the reality of an orderly world. Short of a global holocaust, there is no alternative.

One organization which has worked persistently to develop and to broaden the idea of a unified mankind in the post-war world is the Council for the Study of Mankind, founded by a group of interested scholars in Chicago in 1952. With the Johnson Foundation of Racine, Wisconsin, the Council is co-sponsoring this book.

The original group consisted of Professors Adolf A. Berle (Law), Herbert Blumer (Sociology), Charles Morris (Philosophy), Richard P. McKeon (Philosophy), Robert Redfield (Anthropology), and Quincy Wright (Political Science). Preliminary discussions were held until August, 1958, when the informal group became an official organization.

Inasmuch as the Council for the Study of Mankind was organized to deal directly with the problem of understanding the idea of mankind, the reader may want to know more about the organization—how it began, how it approaches the concept, what its work has been, and what kinds of support it has attracted. Like many others, we were concerned with finding answers to certain questions, such as: What brought about the critical state of world affairs in the twentieth century? What specifically are our problems as a species? What can we do about them? What kind of knowledge do we need, and what kind of education? Obviously, there was need for inquiry.

But the members were also concerned about the size and depth of the task they were committed to undertake. Was a new group like the Council for the Study of Mankind really necessary? Many organizations have an expressed interest in mankind. But, as the members soon discovered, no existing organization deals exclusively with the study of the problems of mankind from the point of view of mankind as a whole. Man of today is neither intellectually nor spiritually prepared for the mankind age. The members hoped that the Council could help bring into being that essential requisite of all effective action—the intellectual and moral readiness to face and to meet the challenge of this age. Many of the issues confronting mankind are new; they require new approaches, new methods, perhaps a new faith. Here, the members felt, the Council could make an important contribution.

The great and urgent problems of our age, we agreed, are universal. The threat of nuclear global war, world poverty and population overgrowth, automation, the loss of values, and other major problems concern men everywhere. However, the proposed solutions are influenced, guided, even dominated by specific interests, loyalties, aspirations, environments.

They are American, Russian, Chinese, Christian, Buddhist, democratic, communist, capitalist, or, in other words, segmental, parochial, and partisan solutions. An important question emerges: Can we realistically hope to find solutions for the universal problems of men by insisting upon partisan approaches? The members did not think so. The need, they felt, was to understand mankind not only as a universal quality but as a new phenomenon. At first, we did not know what we meant by "new." Gradually, there came a realization that looking at things from a segmental point of view and again from the point of view of mankind involved a profound and basic difference.

Education in the American perspective, for example, emphasizes certain major problems—overcrowded classes, underpaid teachers, high school dropouts, desegregation, federal subsidies. Education in the mankind perspective would stress problems of a different sort—illiteracy, disease, poverty, very limited funds for any kind of organized education, virtually no funds for teacher training in many countries. In short, the needs of American education differ sharply from the needs of world education. Nor would the courses of action demanded by the one resemble the courses of action demanded by the other.

Looking at the achievements of medical science in the Western world, we are apt to admire the remarkable success in bringing under medical control one major disease after another. Looking at medical problems from the point of view of mankind, we speak accusingly of the seemingly incessant flow of new-born babies being added to the world's population, of ever more persons reaching a ripe old age which lacks many of life's necessities; we wonder about the survival not only of the fittest but of the least fit. In the one perspective, we see what is largely a medical problem; in the other, primarily a social problem aggravated by economic and political complications. Again, the remedies which fit the one perspective, do not fit the other. The prospect of good health for all is brighter than ever, but only if we are willing to view problems from the perspective of mankind.

Another example is automation. In the United States, the often poorly controlled application of the principles, methods, and devices of automation contributes to unemployment (if temporary), estranges persons from their jobs, confuses and undermines personal values, all of which may cause serious dislocations in the life of the individual and his family. In the newly developing countries, the problems are different: how to build an automated industry on top of a basically agricultural economy; how to make underdeveloped resources serve the rising expectations of the people; how to protect native traditions, beliefs, and values against the powerful impact of highly automated technological systems. The methods which work under American conditions are rarely successful when tried under entirely different conditions overseas. The prospects for infinitely spiralling affluence in the United States and a few other countries must be balanced against the likelihood of mass starvation and misery for the rest of the world, if drastic steps are not taken to plan economic progress for the good of all mankind.

This, we thought, is mankind understanding: not to judge problems in familiar and parochial terms, but to judge them by those characteristics that spell out their universal significance. Not to judge the concept of, let us say, freedom exclusively as the American citizen understands it, or as it is understood by the Chinese, or the South Africans, or the Swedes. Freedom in the mankind understanding would embrace all kinds of freedom. In a pluralistic society—which a mankind world-system by its very nature would have to be—there would be more than one interpretation of values and rights.

The Council for the Study of Mankind did not seek a concept of mankind in the sense of a rigid ideological program, but in the sense of a framework within which to discuss common attitudes, values, and formulas for action. The members did not want to become a pressure group, at one extreme advocating a unitary world society or government, or at the other a sect promulgating a dogma of salvation. They preferred to advance the discussion of common ends and to explore the possibilities of associated action.

The Council developed a program in which the idea of mankind was one pole; disciplines, institutions, nations, cultures, the individual person the other. The number of participants in the academic world grew; they were later joined by others in business and the professions. Exchanges of views led to research and education programs, conferences, seminars, and books, made possible by growing foundation support. Among the first to encourage and to support the work of the Council were Dr. Clarence Faust, President of the Fund for the Advancement of Education; Dr. Frederick Burkhardt, President of the American Council of Learned Societies; Dr. Leslie Paffrath, President of the Johnson Foundation; Professor Adolf A. Berle, Chairman of the Board, Twentieth Century Fund. Later, they were joined by the Rockefeller Foundation, the Corning Glass Works Foundation, the Kaufmann Foundation, and others. Individual sponsors, among them Fowler McCormick and Aaron Scheinfeld of Chicago, Peter Oser of Switzerland, and many others, played an important part in the growing activities of the Council. In 1968 the Board of Directors of the Council was enlarged to include several members from the non-Western countries.

The present work is the third in a series of symposia in various disciplines sponsored by the Council. Its predecessors were *Education and the Idea of Mankind*, edited by Robert Ulich (1964), and *Economics and the Idea of Mankind*, edited by Bert Hoselitz (1965). A fourth, *Technology and the Idea of Mankind*, will appear soon, edited by Leonard Reiffel.

None of these volumes has been easy to produce, but the problem of how to relate the study of history to the idea of mankind proved to be especially difficult, if only because history is so vast and so many promising possibilities offered themselves. Through the generosity of the Johnson Foundation, we were able to hold a conference of historians in Racine, Wisconsin, in May, 1962, where we considered at length the mankind perspective in the study of history. Among those attending the conference were Professors Cyril Black, Merle Curti, Lloyd Fallers, Louis Gottschalk, Mark Krug, Donald Lach, Theodore Marburg, William McNeill, Richard Morse, and Caroline Ware.

The conference was followed by two discussion meetings, in December, 1962, and in June, 1964, devoted chiefly to the planning of the present work. Some of the above mentioned scholars participated in one or both of these later meetings, and others were invited as well, including Professors Tom Jones, Hans Kohn, Melvin Kranzberg, Richard McKeon, George Mosse, Herbert J. Muller, and Leften Stavrianos. Three basic approaches were discussed: a universal history of mankind, a study of the idea of mankind found in the writings of the great historians, and a history of the idea of mankind. The first approach was rejected because it seemed to fall outside the scope of the Council's program, and did not deal with the *idea* of mankind. The second also met with disapproval. A majority of scholars in attendance favored the third suggestion, which occupied the middle ground between the immensity of the first and the much more specialized nature of the second.

The finished work, then, is in essence a symposium on the evolution of the idea of human unity, with special attention to the definitions of mankind offered by the major civilizations of the Eastern and Western worlds. Our authors do not attempt to deal with the whole history of mankind. Their concern is mankind as seen by mankind itself, in its search for unifying concepts and institutions, from antiquity to very recent times. We might have entitled our book "Mankind: A Self-Portrait."

The first five chapters trace the idea of mankind in five historic cultures: Indian, Chinese, Jewish, Muslim, and Helleno-Christian. The last four address themselves to the thought of the modern and present-day world in relation to the problem of the unity of mankind: the world of nationalism, science, racial conflict, and the decline of traditional systems of belief. Each writer was given the widest possible latitude in developing his ideas, so that the symposium lacks monolithic unity. We can only hope that it exhibits what so many thinkers have said mankind itself must strive for—unity in diversity. We also hope that it will throw new light on the idea of mankind, an idea that takes strength not only from its intrinsic value but also from its deep roots in the history of civilization.

Appreciation is due to our co-sponsors, the Johnson Foundation, whose support made this project possible, and to the many scholars who gave us the benefit of their advice in Racine. I also wish to thank the authors for their patience and good work, Professor Mark Krug for his services as editor during much of the history of the manuscript, and Professor Warren Wagar, who joined us later and finished the job.

Contents

PART 1

FIVE TRADITIONAL SOCIETIES

ONE

The Idea
of Mankind
in Indian Thought

KEES W. BOLLE

Department of History, University of
California at Los Angeles

I

Speaking of "Mankind"

A CONCERTED STUDY OF HUMAN CONCEPTS OF "MANKIND" IS A
novel enterprise. Even in studies of Indian culture, which has itself produced so much scholarship and has been the object of so many learned
treatises, the subject of man and mankind has been mainly a matter of
casual remarks and suggestions, revealing mostly the convictions and
biases of the student. Some popular ideas have nevertheless resulted from
these remarks and suggestions and are indeed known to all. It will be well
to state that some of these popular ideas about India will not take us very
far.

There is the very general notion of Hinduism as the paradigm of tolerance, indeed some sort of a super-Catholicity, embracing the confessions,
the freedom, and the ultimate goal of all men. Rightly or wrongly, some
great figures have come to be regarded as incorporations of such a super-
Catholicity: S. Radhakrishnan as its ideologist, Aurobindo as its thinker,
Nehru as its political exponent, and of course, Gandhi, the father of the
country, as its architect and symbol. There are also very negative reactions
to things Indian when the subject of "mankind" is broached. Is it necessary to recall the caste system—perennial source of indignation for so
many non-Indians? It seems to me that both types of reaction—an un-

critical enthusiasm for India's tolerance, and the hue and cry over her social injustices—are unfit as a starting point for a serious discussion. They both forget to ask what the Indian traditions themselves tell about man.

Furthermore, if I look at Indian documents with the idea of "mankind" in mind, it may be advisable to ask myself: what is this I am looking for? This step is principally a confession of my own uncertainties. If it is omitted—and one could omit it without evil intentions—the omission may cause the sort of popular and rather baseless notions that we have just summarily dismissed. Let me illustrate this.

One might be favorably inclined toward the notion of Hinduism as a super-catholic commodity in a discussion on mankind—in spite of my summary dismissal. And really, it would not be difficult to collect some texts as "evidence." One text is bound to be a crown text: Bhagavadgītā 9, 32. Kṛṣṇa, the representation of God, says there:

> . . . those who turn to Me, even though their birth may have been impure—women, vaiśyas and also śūdras—they too attain the supreme goal.[1]

And would not this text add considerably to the suggestion of a truly all-embracing catholic idea of man? It might—but only on condition that the eager defendant would be willing to accept some notions that are usually not connected with the English word "mankind," and to drop some others that are almost always appended to it. The text implies an understanding of a reliance on the supreme Viṣṇu; also, it does not reject, but actually presupposes the possibility of impure births. Its does not imply anything of a social equality in the sense that we usually take for granted. If the first step, the student's open-minded confession of uncertainty, is not omitted, these simple considerations will be made.

Is it not best to admit that we know of "mankind" mainly—if not exclusively—as a problem? Only, I believe that there is nothing to be ashamed of in this admission. If "mankind" were a simple, clearly definable concept, we should have no particularly interesting reason for our enquiry. There is no compelling reason to pin down one concept of "mankind" as the highest achievable. It may be underlined at the same time that there is no reason to believe that at one time in the past a clear concept existed and that our confusion is sadly unique. Really, what ground could there be to lament that we have no clear, unshaken idea of mankind anymore? As long as people and peoples have been living in harmony and in disharmony, the idea of man and mankind has been in flux. The most profound reason for the study of another culture is to expose ourselves to such harmony and disharmony, to offer our own ideas to revision. First and foremost this should be true of our idea of "mankind." In India we may find notions of man that are unlike our own and may provide incentives for correction.

II
Insiders and Outsiders

One of the most elementary notions we append to "mankind" presents itself for question immediately.

I think that the English word "mankind" has a nice ring for us because it refers to *all people*; referring to real people, it is more specific than "humanity." It suggests to us that all people can somehow really be viewed together, that for all their specificity they can be seen as equals, or even as one organic whole. A picture postcard I have seen showed a man with a bitter grimace saying: "It is not that I hate humanity—it's people I dislike." Our word "mankind" seems closer to *people*—even though they are referred to collectively, globally—than the word "humanity," and that is why it appeals to the peace-loving mentality we all hold at least publicly. And here the questions begin not only for cartoonists; for surely, everyone has always known that the real difficulties begin with specific people and that for that reason some practical distinctions must be made.

Like everyone else, all Indians have always known of the species of man (*manuṣyajāti*), but even in the earliest records, the Vedic texts, we hear of practical distinctions. As is well known, the people whose religious heritage we have before us in the Ṛgveda spoke of themselves as āryas, the noble or free men. There were many occasions—not in the last place on the battlefield—to refer to others, outsiders not belonging to the ārya traditions. Two conspicuous names for outsiders were mleccha and dasyu. These names did not just mean "non-Aryan" (anārya) and for that reason "outsider," "foreigner," or even "ignoble one" or "Barbarian." It is worth mentioning that they did not have strong racial connotations, in spite of the importance of "pure" origins. Mleccha is the more transparent of the two terms. It is obviously onomatopoeic and indicates first of all the speech of a person. The root mlecch means "to speak unclearly, indistinctly," and therefore in particular: "to speak a non-aryan language." Speech was a marked line of division between peoples, and for powerful reasons. It was not merely a matter of communication in general. To speak the ārya speech meant not in the last place *to participate in the religious rites*, and therefore to follow the right traditions. The word mleccha has always kept the connotation "marked by incorrect speech and therefore by unacceptable customs," and hence "barbaric." Many centuries later, after the

Vedic and Brahmanic periods were over, Buddhism had risen and begun to decay, the Indian world used the word again for the Muslim invader.

I have said that the word *mleccha* is transparent. Yet it is striking that we have no concept in our own vocabulary quite like it, for we do not have the awareness of specific sacred rites necessary for the civilized world, and even less an awareness of the sacred supremacy of a specific language. Even the most isolationist Midwesterner could not think of English, undisputedly one of the global languages, in quite those terms.

The other word indicating outsiders, *dasyu*, differs significantly from *mleccha*. We do know of the basic experience that is related to it, yet it is far from transparent. *Dasyu* is a word for enemies. However, not only foes of men are called *dasyu*, but also the foes of the gods. Indra, the warrior god, leads the warriors in battle and fights the *dasyus*, who are at the same time both "ordinary" enemies and demons. How can they be the two at once? It is necessary to realize that a distinction between enemy and demon—which goes without saying for us—does not apply here; we are not dealing with an ambiguous concept or an error of judgment. The very relationship of "insiders" and "outsiders" in ancient India differs from the terms we are used to, and, strangely enough, implies a unity which for us does not seem to exist. For the very fact that the foes can be devilish means that they are assigned a place in a total world-view; they are much more than belligerent outsiders. Behind the differences among mankind is the sacred world. In this sacred world struggles go on that justify men's wars.

Is this a glimpse of a dim, cruel past, in which Heaven participated in the divisions of man? The suggestion of a split through mankind, between a half truly civilized or even fighting on the side of the gods, and a half not quite human, even demonic, seems to belong to dark ages. However, before taking leave of this subject too hastily by calling a world-view "primitive," I would like to suggest that the idea of the *dasyu* is not wholly foreign to us. I am thinking of the many columns of newspaper writing that have been devoted for years now to descriptions of the Vietcong. If one could imagine oneself coming in from a part of the world unaffected by news bulletins, many of those reports must seem peculiar; it would appear in many cases that soldiers did not really have to deal with other people, not even with an "ordinary" type of enemy, but with an altogether different species, popping up and vanishing unexpectedly, or even with some dangerous vermin, unaffected by anything—yes, something demonic.

The simile does not go further than to serve as a warning against discarding ancient terms bearing on "mankind." Is it necessary to say that there are also differences between the ancient Indian and ourselves? Both examples, *mleccha* and *dasyu*, show that the most vehemently practical Indian antitheses between "insiders" and "outsiders" had a support, on one hand in the traditional religious practices, and on the other in the religious meaning given to the inevitable struggles of the day. That is more than we could say for our practical distinctions, I think.

III

Unity in Spite of Divisions

The Indian traditions have found various ways to speak of the unity of mankind concretely, but again, these ways differ from the ideas we are most familiar with. Profound Indian convictions concerning the unity of mankind come to the fore clearly in certain religious symbols.

According to the Vedic traditions Vivasvant is one of the great figures in the mythical age who is divine and human at the same time. Above all, he is called the first sacrificer, and this title reveals what was most important to the Vedic and Brahmanic thinkers when they considered the prototype of the human race. The ritual activity seems at least as crucial to the image of man as the fact itself of his beginnings. Another symbolic figure who is first mentioned in the Vedas and around whom many religious ideas crystallized is Manu, the "first man," or "the man." Like Vivasvant, he is particularly related to sacrifice.[2] According to one early text (Rgveda 5, 29, 7) Indra drinks from the *soma* juice of the sacrifice performed by Manu, and thus Indra is strengthened for the battle with the primordial monster Vrtra.

It is clear that in these and related imageries we are not dealing with a scientific theory about the genesis of the human race. No nation has ever presented its creation myth as a "scientific fact." The multiplicity of the Indian images of early beings underlines the necessity of seeing their sense rather than their factuality. With reference to our topic the sense of these images can be stated like this: in order to speak of mankind it is necessary not to make a formal statement about unity, but to focus on something of great value, of so great a value that it must be central to all we can see or imagine about human life. For the people of the Vedic and Brahmanic period that meant the primacy of the traditional ritual enactments.

It is in this light that we must see numberless other texts, all concurring in their vision of the ritual or the god called on as relevant to the whole world. Agni, the god who himself is the sacrificial fire, "is known to the seven races of peoples," (Rgveda 8, 39, 8). Elsewhere in a hymn Indra himself speaks:

The races of man call me like children call on their father. I give food to the sacrificer. (Rgveda 10, 48, 1)

The most famous and most precise image concerning mankind as a totality is that of the *Puruṣasūkta* (Ṛgveda 10, 90), the hymn chanting the sacrifice of the primal, man-like being (the *puruṣa*) by the gods at the beginning of time. To this sacrifice the whole world owes its origin. Among other things, the Vedas are mentioned, and they are the sine qua non of ritual activity. And then, specific mention is made of the four classes of men:

> The brahman was his [the sacrificial victim's] mouth, of his arms was made the warrior, his thighs became the vaiśya, of his feet the śūdra was born.

The chant enumerates all the important elements born from this mythical sacrifice and making up the world, and, significantly, what we would call "mankind," an unmistakable part of this world, is summed up in this manner. Mankind can be thought of meaningfully only as a fourfoldness: the "priestly" class (*brahmans*), the "warrior" class (*kṣatriyas*), the "third" class (*vaiśyas*: merchants, farmers); these three were known as the higher classes (*dvijas* or twice-born ones, since their ceremonial initiation and admission to the study of the Vedas amounted to a second birth); finally there were the "serfs" (*śūdras*), who were meant to serve the higher classes.

This division of human society into mutually complementary parts (which no doubt has its root in the ancient Indo-European concepts about a tripartition of society) became the pan-Indian tradition and the ideological basis of all Hindu speculation on mankind as a whole. The word "ideological" is appropriate for the peculiar nature of these thoughts about divisions and their unity. It would be a mistake to think of the divisional groups as if they were professions in an exceedingly simple society. Indeed, there is nothing to indicate that there ever was a society consisting in three (or four) precise groups, each with its precise socio-economic function: one complete group of priests, one of warriors only, and so on. No matter how much scholars disagree on the forms of life among the earliest Indo-European peoples or the sort of coherence the earliest Indo-European dialects may have provided in thought and social structure, they agree that these earliest communities were far from the stage of primitive "savages." Even at that early date society must have shown a great differentation of economic needs and specialized skills and professions. The division of society in three parts, or, in ancient India, in three plus the *śūdras*, was not the result of an empirical investigation. From the beginning, this manner of "summing up" the people as a whole must have had a religious intent; it was not an attempt at sociological description, but the symbolic undergirding of all social and economic norms.[3]

It will be useful to underline that in general in Hindu thought "mankind" has its sense not in its uniformity. The Hindu authorities seem to have cared only for such a concept of unity in mankind as would allow for the specificity of various groups. Nowhere does this become more evident to the "modern" man than in statements about the place of women. The famous Lawbook of Manu (Manusmṛti 5, 155) says:

> No sacrifice, no vow, no fast must be performed by women apart from their husband; if a wife obeys her husband, she will for that reason alone be exalted in heaven.

Similarly the classes have their distinct functions because only in that manner can they collectively form the wholeness meant by the creator. In the words of Manu's Lawbook, resuming the ancient imagery of the Puruṣa:

> . . . for the sake of the prosperity of the worlds, he caused the brahman, the kṣatriya, the vaiśya, and the śūdra to proceed from his mouth, his arms, his thighs, and his feet. (1, 31)
>
> . . . in order to protect this universe, He, the most resplendent one, assigned separate duties and occupations to those who sprang from his mouth, arms, thighs, and feet. (1, 87)

Without these divisions no world would be possible. There would be chaos. Needless to say the same ideology has its resonances in the Bhagavadgītā, when Kṛṣṇa admonishes Arjuna that it is better to do one's own duty poorly than the duty of another excellently.

With the central vision of the class system in mind, endeavors were made to view the whole of mankind together, including those who obviously stood outside the Brahmanic tradition. A first step had already been made by positing the fourth class, the śūdras. For no doubt in ancient days the Aryan invaders included among the śūdras many of the peoples and tribes among and around them who were not enemies, yet had no part in the Aryan heritage. The collective concept śūdra, subordinated as a group to the traditional classes, made it possible to expand and at the same time to preserve the social ideology. In the earliest text, the Rgveda, the word śūdra occurs only once, and it might be correct to think of a gradual historical development, in which the concept of śūdra came to serve as a bridge between a predominantly hieratic, "ideal-typical" stratification of society and the actual complexities of the world. This view is borne out by the tenth chapter of the Manusmṛti, which presents a whole web of relations and cross relations to account for different castes, tribes, peoples and functions. The manifoldness of the world is depicted as showing not just a differentiation but a certain hierarchy. The model for this hierarchic presentation is given with the four-class system. The peculiar ambiguity of the *śūdras*—on the one hand the servants of the twice-born ones and hence part of the structure and on the other hand a collective name for all "lower ones," outside the sacred order—helps a great deal in holding together the web of relationships. They demonstrate that there are degrees of excludedness all over.

However, the text does more than speak of generalities. A few samples will suffice to show how specificity and underlying unity were related and both done justice. The caste of the *sūtas* is said to have been born from the alliance of a *kṣatriya* man and the daughter of a *brahman* (10, 11). The *sūtas* form a social group traditionally employed as charioteers, heralds and royal bards. The rule given concerning their origin—just like the rules about the origin of many other castes—is obviously not a "true" historical statement. It disregards the fact that the parental *kṣatriya* and *brahman* must have had their own social and economic subdivisions (in addition to their "ideal-typical" names). Yet, by relating the *sūta* caste to the class system it accounts with one stroke for a specific social group that itself must have been large enough to have its own higher and lower members. We can understand the process exemplified in these texts best by saying: the ancient class system provided a permanent source of mythological concepts that could be drawn on to schematize men and groups of men in all specific, "historical" cases.

Specific social groups, castes, tribes, hereditary professions were grafted on a fixed symbolism, and it is only natural that these specific groups to some extent became "ideal-typical" themselves; they were given a mythological basis. Hence words for class (*varṇa*) and caste (*jāti*, literally "birth") came to be widely used as synonyms, both in India and in Western writings about India. However, in a history of ideas about mankind it is essential to see the distinction. I think that this problem of class or caste is crucial to the Indian ideas about man. It deserves some elaboration, the more so since it usually falls on the blind spot of Western perception.

The problem is not too severe perhaps as long as we speak about it in general terms, as I have done so far. We are ready to see, I think, that both words, class and caste, harbor as much relatedness as divisiveness. The class symbolism provided the basic unit of thought on which specific groups could be modeled—separate in their own social traditions, yet integrated through a general code of behavior. We are perhaps even ready to admit that here we are touching on the secret of the multicoloredness of Indian life, fascinating for every Western visitor. That visitor marvels at the number of very different individuals moving in the Indian market place. He see before his eyes the simultaneity of independence and interrelatedness.

Things seem to become much less marvelous when the Western observer is confronted with the specifics of the caste system. Then he is tempted to see only social divisions, without realizing that this vision is principally the product of his own underlying scale of values. He begins to pass judgments of what he sees from the perspective of an *ideal* of his own society; it is an ideal of equality of people, of which it is not so clear to him at that moment that it is rather an ideal that he fosters than an ideal that he has realized. He is shocked when he first hears that a traditional *brahman* cannot accept his clean linen from the washerman's hands. The washerman is to throw the clean laundry into the water. Then only can the *brahman* or the *brahman's* wife put their hands on it; they hang it in the sun to dry again. The observer is shocked again when he meets with similar, seemingly insulting rules governing the behavior of the twice-born ones towards barbers. For barbers, like washermen and many others, belong to the "low castes."

Is such behavior indeed "insulting," as one is inclined to believe? Certainly, the external, "sociological" indignation of the visitor does not go the whole way toward understanding. It is too obvious to be spelled out that *brahmans* have always needed washermen and barbers; they were and are needed not in the last place for prescribed cultic duties of the *brahmans* (including certain tonsures). An understanding must also involve the realization that such behavior toward lower castes emphatically guarantees the independence of groups. The *brahmans* themselves, all members of the same "class," are subdivided in castes with traditional patterns of behavior.

It is wrong to judge isolated parts of other societies on the basis of an overall ideal view of our own. We can only judge ideal forms on the basis of our ideal forms. If the intention of our own society is to be egalitarian (which is problematic enough as a thesis), we should make a serious effort to see the intention of the caste system. I shall always remember the lesson in the intentionality of the caste system I was given by a South-Indian schoolmaster. Invited for dinner, I was offered a chair, which made me feel very uncomfortable. It was the only chair in the house and in fact borrowed for the occasion. I was sitting up on that chair, while every one else sat on the floor; I felt uncomfortably unequal and could not help raising a question. Of course, I should not have raised a question about it, why this exceptional position had been created for me, for the answer my host gave was perfectly clear: I was used to chairs and therefore I should have one. It was his duty as host to see to that. Indeed, being embarrassed by being different would be giving up all civilized life.

Perhaps less humorous, the Hindu scriptures leave no doubt as to their intention with class and caste: to relate to the tradition as a whole and guarantee the individual at the same time. Returning to the Lawbook of Manu, we find an illuminating example in the caṇḍāla. The caṇḍāla is repeatedly called "the lowest of men," the "impurest of mortals." He owes his birth to a truly infamous alliance: a brahman mother and a śūdra father (Manusmṛti 10, 12). He may be called despicable, but the text does not leave it with that observation; the legendary mésalliance accounts for his existence and that is the main point for our author. It is not enough to foster an appealing ideal of mankind, of its unity, equality, homogeneity. There must be a basic imagery that speaks for the common sense knowledge that it takes many different people to make a world. Mésalliances are a standard device to relate lower social groups to the fundamental symbolism.

Even when all social groups are accounted for, through intermarriages, and because of their indispensable economic functions in society, there is still the problem of the obvious outsiders. The Manusmṛti solves the problem by assigning important ethnic groups—too large and impressive to be dealt with as castes—a place as "degraded twice-born ones." They are the descendants of vrātyas, who are defined as legitimately begotten twice-born ones, but who are excluded from full membership because of their neglect of their sacred duties (10, 20). Among such "degraded" ones are the Drāviḍas (occupying the greater part of South India!), the off-spring of a vrātya from the kṣatriya class (10, 20). This legendary descendancy from the warriors certainly accounts for such a formidable group. Because of their thoroughgoing negligence however, the text adds, the Drāviḍas, among many others, "have gradually sunk in this world to the condition of śūdras" (10, 43).

This whole system of legendary ancestries may seem too schematic and artificial. How could this manner of linking tribes and peoples to a religious structure be effective in the world?

These doubts on the part of anxious modern reformers are answered in one impressive chapter of human history. It is the history of the "Hinduization" of Southeast Asia: the gradual expansion from the beginning of our era well into the Middle Ages of Indian culture and Indian standards over the countries of Further India and Indonesia. For the examples I quoted from the Manusmṛti are not isolated phenomena of some strange jurist on the Indian subcontinent. Along with many authoritative

Hindu writings, they are symptoms of a mentality with which Indians participated in world affairs. Indian merchants established their trade-posts as far as Java and, curiously enough, without military intervention or any organized invasions, in several places Hindu kingdoms were born, modeled on the Indian pattern. The Indian way of accounting for new peoples and new circumstances was an irresistible civilizing force. Earlier customs and arts were not cut off; rather they continued and contributed to a new cultural unity. Thus the Indian relational schemes proved to guarantee the specificity of peoples on a grand scale.

It is easy to conclude from what we have seen so far that the underlying class system has a certain flexibility. But several authoritative texts make this point outright. The safety of the highest places depends at least in part on the fulfillment of the prescribed duties, and the effects of a certain birth do not determine a position for ever, whether high or low. By certain mésalliances twice-born ones can eventually enter the state of śūdras (Manusmṛti 10, 65), but reversely, the decendants of a brahman and a śūdra woman, through correct marriages reach the level of the highest class "within the seventh generation" (10, 64).

The fact that the brahman man is the one who profits most by this rule may make us raise the eyebrows. But the fact remains that there are ascending as well as descending lines, and the flexibility I mentioned shows itself in various ways.

In the epic (Mahābhārata, Vanaparva, chap. 177, Poona Edition) we hear the wise king Yudhiṣṭhira in discussion with the serpent prince Nahuṣa. It is a battle of words on which much depends, and Yudhiṣṭhira, questioned by Nahuṣa is faced with the troublesome suggestion: if you regard a man as a brahman only because of his work—as Yudhiṣṭhira seemed to do, thus "spiritualizing" the class system—then birth really means nothing! The wise Yudhiṣṭhira, the classical example of the dharmarāja, the righteous king, gives an elaborate reply. He shows himself well aware of the world's complexity and the sheer impossibility of seeing anything in black and white. It is a polite way of saying: it is wrong on a point like this, of vital concern for mankind, to raise such a simple either/or question! And thereupon he makes two points which are indeed no precise reply to the neat question, but are typical of the Hindu tradition. In the first place he quotes the Vedic word: "We [who are called on to do so] perform the sacrifice," thus reminding the questioner of the necessity of the Vedic practice; whatever one could bring in against the theory of brahman superiority, the performance of the right rituals on which the actual world depends must not be interrupted, and that means: there must be brahmans to perform the sacred acts. In the second place he quotes Manu (Manusmṛti 2, 172) to make clear that a brahman becomes *really* a *brahman* only through the prescribed rites: "Until [the *brahman*] is born in the Veda, he is on a level with the śūdra." No reasoning could have pinpointed the symbolic structure of the classes more precisely. This structure does not work as a static, definable system but preserves what is most essential in life. This symbolism is flexible because it is itself alive.

These very vital issues are never settled finally, but are illuminated ever anew in narratives. Elsewhere in the epic, in one of the many creation accounts (Mahābhārata, Śāntiparva, chap. 181, Poona Edition) it is stated: "There is no difference of classes. This world was first created by the god Brahmā entirely brahmanic, and became separated into classes later as a result of works." The story then continues to tell in detail how those original *brahmans* forsook their duty and some of them fell into the state of kṣatriyas and so on. In the same sequence of events demon-like classes of beings were born, and notably "various mleccha tribes." All in all, these traditions show an unmistakable realism and yet the creative ability to link the presence of peoples to a symbolic hierarchy dynamic enough to bear the weight of the very real and moving world.

IV

Greater Unity, More Divisions and Return of Hierarchy

The class system did not go unchallenged in India. The major challenge was presented by Buddhism from its beginning in the sixth century B.C.

It is perhaps not by chance that the word ārya has its widest use not as an epithet of peoples or languages, but of the truths discovered and taught by the Buddha—the "noble truths" (the ārya-satyas), independent of cultural superiority, not in need of a divine revelation and certainly not linked with one's birth. Buddhism seems to break through even the "practical" divisions of "insiders" and "outsiders."

When the prince Siddhārta was to become a Buddha, the Evil One made a final attempt to frustrate the attainment of enlightenment. At that moment the Earth herself raised her voice and bore witness on the future Buddha's behalf.[4] The way shown by the Buddha concerns the whole world and is never presented as the property of one group in particular. A Buddha is born "for the weal of the world."[5] Some unified idea of mankind seems implied, more profoundly than ever before.

In this light the brahmanic class-system seems quite entangled, lacking sense, and unnecessarily arrogant. The Buddhist statements about it are straightforward and sometimes devastating. One early Buddhist text (the

Tevijja Sutta of the *Dīghanikāya*) compares the reliance on the existence of Brahmā (the creator) and the reliance on the Brahmanic religious systems *in toto* to "the funny belief of a foolish man in the existence of some beautiful girl somewhere and his wish to enjoy her without knowing absolutely anything about her and her whereabouts."[6] Somewhere else we read that the first person the new Buddha meets upon his Enlightenment is a *brahman*, one "of a proud and contemptuous disposition." This person asks the Blessed One: ". . . what is it constitutes a *brahman*? and what are the *brahman* making qualities?" And the Buddha gives an unmistakable answer—one could say: exactly the answer the serpent prince had thought Yudhiṣṭhira should have given, a perfect spiritualization or allegorization of brahmanhood:

> The brahman who his evil traits has banished,
> Is free from pride, is self-restrained and spotless,
> Is learned, and the holy life has followed,
> 'T is he alone may claim the name of brahman;
> With things of earth he hath no point of contact.[7]

It is not necessary for our subject to discuss the cardinal issues of Buddhist doctrine. But it is of immediate relevance that the Buddha's message and technique of liberation concerned the human species and the human condition *as such*. They envisaged a total transcendance of all worldly bonds. The brahmanic tradition which held that the "ultimate" was already corporeally present in this world—the *brahmans* being gods on earth—made no sense to the Buddhist thinkers. For them, to recognize the unpleasantness, transitoriness, undependability of this world, not in the last place of all human divisions, was the first step toward *nirvāṇa*. If to be a *brahman* meant anything at all, it could have nothing to do with one's pedigree but could only mean realizing the implications of this fleeting world and experiencing a freedom beyond its bonds. In principle this realization and experience were open to all.

The Buddhist rejection of the Brahmanic order of the world had a profound influence on general ideas about mankind, but found no expression in any political reform. Why were no such attempts made?

The question might be answered simply by pointing to the notion of *karma* in all Buddhist thought. The law of *karma* determines all existence: our present existence is the result of acts we did in previous existences, and to reform social and economic conditions or to desire equality would be as nonsensical as fighting fate itself. Such an answer might be given; and yet the question itself is not fair. Somehow it seems to presuppose that equality is a sufficient and possible goal of religion, or at least of thought about mankind. But the Buddhist opposition to the Brahmanic heritage was more profound than that.

The Brahmanic class-system is discredited in many early Buddhist writings with the argument that it is not divine in origin but that it came about exactly as the diversity of the whole natural world came about—ultimately through craving, the cause of the round of births.[8] This means that the divisions of people too are seen in the light of Buddhism's central vision: the world is impermanent and liberation is possible in so far as this impermanence is grasped for what it is worth. That is very different from the ideal of a social reformation. The superficiality of many Westerners flirting with Buddhism often comes out when this point is touched. Advocating some form of Buddhism adapted to modern society, or brought in harmony with modern psychological insights or whatever else is done to it, they want to add a touch of social concern. This wish betrays a lack of understanding. The only thing really modern about it is the conceit or self-deception of the "modern" intellectual breeding on pocket books, suggesting that religions can be set side by side, adequately compared and examined on their usefulness, and that modifications can be manufactured on this basis. Should it be said? One cannot see the unity of Buddhism and its ideas about mankind by adding up the social, metaphysical and other aspects. From within, any religion has a total claim—whether it is missionary-minded or not—and it is from there that ideas about mankind receive their impulses. It is the discovery of the root of impermanence and suffering, the great Enlightenment, the type of the Buddha, which sets all other things in perspective. That is fundamental for the conception of mankind.

The unity Buddhism proposed did not destroy a social order, for it confronted the Brahmanic world not on the level of external symptoms but in the core of religious symbolism. And furthermore, as we shall see, because of its inner structure, Buddhism fostered a hierarchy of its own. Let me try to illustrate both these points.

"In three of the continents the Buddhas are never born; only in the continent of India are they born,"[9] says a birth story of the Buddha. This is of course not to be understood as an expression of national pride. Neither is it to be understood as a precise scientific geographical reference. It is a symbolic expression concerning the Buddha at the center of the world. He is at the center of a mythical geography. A text such as this one should be seen as a literary parallel to what we know from Buddhist architecture. Each sanctuary is somehow a summing-up of the world (well known in the maṇḍala symbolism in Indian culture). The most grandiose Buddhist sanctuary expressing this cosmic symbolism is the Borobudur in Java (8th century).[10] The sanctuary/cosmos has in itself the various levels of spiritual realization leading the devotee upward to the center of enlightenment. Generally in the architecture of later Buddhism four different Buddhas are represented as world protectors (lokapālas) at four points surrounding the center. A fifth Buddha is found at the center or zenith itself. The Borobudur shows a huge multiplication of the basic numerical structure. Each lokapāla is represented by ninety-two images, the fifth Buddha at the zenith by one hundred and eight (traditional auspicious number). It is clear that such symbolism has implications for an understanding of the world and involves a view of mankind as a whole.

As to the express symbolism of mankind's unity, an eloquent example is the conversion story of the four great, celestial kings, narrated with minor variations in several Buddhist traditions. The Buddha converted these kings to the "Good Law" by speaking to each in his own language. The first two kings (Dhṛtarāṣṭra and Virūdhaka) understood the ārya language (Sanskrit), the other two (Virūpakṣa and Vaiśravaṇa) did not. The texts state explicitly that the Buddha then addressed them in a dasyu language, a "barbaric" tongue. He spoke to Virūpakṣa in the drāviḍa language (one of the principal languages of South India) and to Vaiśravaṇa in one of the mleccha tongues. Thus the Buddha masters the world's languages and at the same time is shown to go beyond the traditional lines of division.[11] Most significantly however, the four "great celestial kings" (mahārājas) are none other than the mythical regents of the four points of the compass (another instance of the imagery of the four lokapālas) and thus together represent the whole world. It is these symbols of the whole world whose mission it is henceforth to protect the Good Law in their regions. The unity of mankind is not given in the equality of the four kings, but in the universal comprehensibility of the Buddha's words.

This type of symbolism has great consequences. Along with the tangible and ordinary class-system and its Brahmanic ideological basis (ultimately going back to the reality of the world itself) even the "practical" divisions lose their meaning in Buddhism. Brahmanism was opposed and seemingly even defeated on its own deepest level of symbolism.

But Buddhism, having developed a new sense of unity, also developed its own hierarchy, and it was not in the last place because of this that the Brahmanic-Hindu conception of mankind with its ancient roots came out victorious in the end.

The process leading Buddhism from a profound unity to a new hierarchy may seem mysterious, but there are helpful analogies. I would think of contemporary America. One of the most striking features of this country is the abandonment of the class structure of the "Old World." But equally striking is the fact that other things take over. It seems that if one's fixed place in society is no longer there, and a *general* sense of equality exists, people feel compelled to establish their individual level of achievement. The final goal of all individual activities is hard to pin down and the over-all image of one individual level with respect to another may be unclear. But this vagueness does not prevent a great many intellectuals from speaking about levels of realization or of individual "creativity." "Creativity" in particular becomes a sort of stock of which one can have "more" or "less."

Every analogy in history is at best an illustration and that is all this one is meant to be. Obviously Buddhist thinkers discussed the goal of the religious life under the Blessed One with great precision and at least in this respect the analogy goes lame. But the point of the analogy is a growing complexity in establishing levels and ways of realization. The way of the Buddha is a yoga process, a realization requiring several distinct steps. Also several procedures were distinguished, even in early Buddhism.

When the Buddha's teachings have been heard and recognized one becomes a *śrāvaka* (a "hearer"). However, it is also possible that a person finds out for himself and obtains Enlightenment without teaching others; such a one is a *pratyekabuddha*. When on the other hand he decides to teach others, he must be called a *samyaksambuddha*, for then he is a "completely enlightened one," like Śākyamuni himself. Further, it makes a difference whether one follows the Buddha's teachings because one has confidence in him and is devoted to him, or because one has gained a complete understanding of his teachings. Also, some may have conquered themselves completely and live their last life on earth now. Others may not have attained that level and may have to be reborn once more, or twice more. Nothing is left to chance in Buddhist theory, and each level, type and step has its own technical name.[12]

But—who is to tell the exact differences, their meaning and value, and determine the state one is in? Although the theory is perfect, the actual goings on in monastic discipline and selfdiscipline remain a matter of perfect analysis but also imperfect people. The differentation in levels of realization grew in complexity and number; for that very reason real vantage points seemed dimmer and less tangible.

In short, this was the situation: Buddhism did not concretely change the social stratification but in fact added an ideology of hierarchies. The later great developments of Buddhism (Mahāyāna and Vajrayāna) did not simplify matters in this respect. They were movements with a great popular impact. In addition to the already complex classification came the complex (and sometimes diffuse) ideologies of laymen and their levels of spiritual achievement and aspiration.

Professor Kern, the distinguished translator of *The Lotus of the True Law* (*Saddharmapuṇḍarīka*) gave a concise summary of the Mahāyāna teachings set forth in that text. This is what he said: "The teaching of the Lotus . . . comes to this, that every one should try to become a Buddha."[13] Indeed, ultimately Buddhahood is meant for all. The great compassion of the Lord in Mahāyāna Buddhism for every living creature is powerfully expressed in vertiginous numbers of stations and levels; thus there are not one or a few but innumerable Buddhas (perfectly enlightened ones) and likewise innumerable Boddhisattvas ("first-class Buddhists" as Edward Conze calls them somewhere; they are Buddhists who are ready to enter perfect enlightenment without having done so yet). The power and consistency of the arguments and parables in *The Lotus of the True Law* are much more appealing to most "modern" readers than the Brahmanic hierarchic view of the world. Yet it is not difficult to see how precisely this power and consistency could help to usher in a rejuvenated Brahmanic ideology.

Many pages of *The Lotus of the True Law* deal with the problem: when and how shall we finally reach enlightenment? In one moving scene we find the Lord and the famous disciple Ānanda in the company of more than two thousand monks, both fully initiated ones and such as are still under training. Ānanda submits a problem to the Lord and concludes with a clear request: ". . . it would seem meet, were the Lord ere long to predict our destiny to supreme and perfect enlightenment."[14] The many monks join in Ānanda's request. Indeed the question does not reflect merely an individual worry. It may be called one of the typical problems of Mahāyāna Buddhism. If one had expected the Lord to announce the precise date of the perfect enlightenment of everyone present, one is mistaken. After all, such an answer would have been too fragmentary and too mincing; it would have been in total disharmony with the universal relevance of the Buddhist teachings. The answer freeing the listeners from all doubts is one that underlines the universal significance of these teachings with dizzying numbers:

> Thou, Ānanda, shalt in future become a Tathāgata [a perfect Buddha] by the name of Sāgaravaradharabuddhivikrīḍitābhijña, an Arhat ["Saint"] &c., endowed with science and conduct, &c., After having honoured, respected, venerated, and worshipped sixty-two koṭis [1 koṭi = 10 millions] of Buddhas, kept in memory the true law of those Buddhas and received this command, thou shalt arrive at supreme and per-

fect enlightenment, and bring to full ripeness for supreme, perfect enlightenment twenty hundred thousand myriads of koṭis of Bodhisat-
tvas similar to the sands of twenty Ganges . . .[15]

To be sure, this text must not be seen as merely fantastic speculation.
The teachings of The Lotus have swept a good part of the earth. They
spoke of an "impossible possibility" and made a very subtle lore available
to many. As a result of the Lord's words, the text continues further on,
Ānanda actually "remembered the true law of many hundred thousand
myriads of koṭis of Buddhas . . ."[16]

Nevertheless, an inevitable by-product of such teachings as were set
forth so powerfully in The Lotus was a certain sense of "unreality" that
widened the gap between life-as-it-was and the spiritual goal envisaged
by monks and lay teachers. The subtle philosophy of earlier Buddhism
had a great anti-Brahmanic potential, but it is as if this subtle philosophy,
with its implications for a new unity and even an equality of men, was
approaching the end of its course. It began to impress on the mind of the
hearers not only the unreality of this chaotic world, but even the unreality
of the process of inner realization itself. The Lord is quoted as saying in
the Vajracchedikā (composed between 300 A.D. and 500 A.D.):

> As many beings as there are in the universe of beings, comprehended
> under the term "beings,"—either egg-born, or born from a womb, or
> moisture-born, or miraculously born; with or without form; with per-
> ception, without perception, or with neither perception nor no-percep-
> tion—as far as any conceivable universe of beings is conceived: all these
> should be by me led to Nirvāṇa, into that realm of Nirvāṇa which
> leaves nothing behind. And yet, although innumerable beings have
> thus been led to Nirvāṇa, no being at all has been led to Nirvāṇa.[17]

In the same period in which these words were written new and vehement religious movements developed, characterized by an urge for "instant realization." Although these movements occurred both in Hinduism
and Buddhism, the most influential stimuli and earliest forms were found
in Buddhist circles (in the "third vehicle," known as Vajrayāna). It is as
if attempts were made to bring about a new reality forcibly.

Historians give various reasons why Buddhism disappeared from India.
One fact is certain: a new theistic devotion arose. Yet to speak of this as
one of the reasons for the decline of Buddhism is not wholly correct. Also
Buddhism developed devotional forms. It also must be underlined that
the devotional movements are in many ways akin to and to quite an extent identical with the vehement movements aiming for "instant realiza-

tion" that originated in Buddhism. The point has also been made (by Louis de la Vallée Poussin) that on the popular level the line between Hinduism and Buddhism was by no means as precise as textbooks on Indian philosophy would make us believe.

It seems to me that our sketch of "mankind" as a problem in India may shed some light, not because it has uncovered new materials, but because it relates various points that have been made concerning the disappearance of Buddhism. The tendency toward devotion is naturally linked with a thirst for reality. The Brahmanic heritage provided a much better framework for this than the Buddhist heritage. The god of the *Bhagavadgītā*, which is based on the Vedic texts, is an unmistakable, real god. On the other hand, one would have great difficulty in answering the question who exactly the Lord is in a text like *The Lotus of the True Law*. Hindu statements concerning the reality of the world—and of God—could be supported by a long tradition and be made with much less ambiguity. But speaking about the reality of the world—the counterpart of the reality of God—means also speaking of social reality and its foundation. At this point the ways of Buddhism and Hinduism parted, no matter how much the two might have had in common and kept in common thereafter, culturally and philosophically.

Here we probably touch on one of the most powerful reasons why Buddhism disappeared from India. It was a slow and inevitable process. At the beginning Buddhism no doubt owed much of its success to its great intellectual clarity, versus a seemingly obscurantist attitude on the part of the learned *brahmans*. Later the world of the *brahmans* with all its conservatism, its holding on to an ideal-typical description of life seemed to conform to the normal, experienced reality more than the subtle Buddhist hierarchies of ideas and of people. To put it most simplistically: it is easier to maintain that only one class of people is divinely inspired to teach the rest of us the goal of life than to establish in each case the spiritual level of a person with respect to a metaphysical entity that seems forever out of reach. The *brahmans* were quite concrete, and it is not by chance that through them and their culture Hinduism has developed through the ages. In the end, Hinduism appeared clear and more down-to-earth, less obsessed with the unending dialectics typical of the Buddhist "way of life."

This is not to say that the Hindu culture did not inherit anything of the Buddhist complexity or had no complexities of its own. Nothing would be less true. But the eagerness for a divine reality that existed in the broad masses found no sturdier vantage point than in those who

represented the divine world on earth. The brahmanic (self-)conscious-
ness of Hinduism became, or rather became anew the cornerstone of all
thinking about "mankind."

It may perhaps be argued that the socio-ideological points I have discussed do not play a role of importance in the philosophical arguments of
Buddhist and Hindu thinkers in the final period of Indian Buddhism.
There are two points, however, which seem to me worthy of consideration and which at the same time may conclude our survey.

On the one hand, we may remind ourselves of it that our subject, "mankind," is not a thing that we can lay our hands on. "Mankind" is in the
first place our own concern. It is referred to only indirectly in the documents, often with turns we did not anticipate. In the Indian tradition—
as in our own—notions of "mankind" are impelled and preserved by
symbolism. That means almost always: by things that go without saying.

On the other hand, it would of course be an exaggeration to say that our
documents do not mirror changes at all. The positive acceptance of the
ancient socio-ideological system was too important for the thinkers who
opposed Buddhism to go unnoticed in their writings.

The most formidable opponent of Buddhism was the philosopher
Śaṃkara (8th century A.D.?). He does not fight Buddhism on the level
of social or political issues any more than Buddhism had conquered the
world on that level, but the validity of brahmanhood, the cornerstone of
the ancient class-system, is most certainly accepted or taken for granted
in various places of his oeuvre. It could hardly be expected otherwise in
a philosophy based on the Vedic (more precisely, the Upaniṣadic) texts.
Thus the world as it is "with its brahmans, and so on" can serve Śaṃkara
to illustrate the basic theme of his philosophy, the reality of the ātman,
the "Self."[18] He relies on the validity of brahmanhood without any
apology, and we may remember that not only he, but also the other great
Vedānta ācāryas ("spiritual preceptors," the most famous being Rāmā-
nuja and Madhva) were brahmans themselves. Śaṃkara wrote a concise
"textbook," presenting the basic tenets of his thought. It is meant for the
beginner and begins with a truly magnificent exposition of elementary
issues: what is the goal of the study, who qualifies as teacher, and who as
student. If anywhere, here we might have expected some justification for
the fact that the study of the highest knowledge (jñāna) is a brahmanic
pursuit. Instead, we are told without further ado: "Jñāna, that means to
final liberation, should be taught . . . to a pure brahman pupil . . ."
(Upadeśasāhasrī 1, 2)

No doubt, philosophical subtlety had grown for centuries during the
Buddhist supremacy. As of old, the liberating center and object of knowl-

edge would serve all men, but it would be guarded by the divine structure of society, which itself manifested its certainty.

v

The Bothersome and Instructive Problem

At the beginning of this chapter, I vented my feeling that the notion of "mankind" exists for us primarily as a problem, not as a polished tool. Our considerations about Indian views will have helped to realize what this restriction of our knowledge means. Some of the most articulate Indian traditions have shown us a constant change and renewal. It is true that our present concern about "mankind" appears greater than any earlier ones. However, this does not make it less necessary, but rather mandatory to see what other nations and great civilizations have arrived at. This intellectual duty becomes the more obvious as Indian thinkers have paid particular attention to questions that harass us most: how to preserve a unity of our understanding of man and yet do justice to individual people, nations and cultures. After all, to be able to do that would be the fulfillment of one of our deepest wishes in our worries about mankind. This ability would be no less than the ability to face the reality of the world with all its diversities. All Brahmanic reactions to Buddhism have this in common, that somehow they adhere to the reality of the world, including the structure of man's social organism. Perhaps some day the general Western distaste for the traditional Indian caste system will give way to an understanding of its intentions—to preserve the multicoloredness of life instead of painting it all with the same dull wash that is so often mistaken for progress. That will be a revolution, but it will be also a criterion by which we can measure our readiness to accept a workable notion of "mankind."

Of course, I am not saying that the Brahmanic ideology and Hindu society form a model that the modern world should copy. There are all sorts of reasons why their problems were not identical with ours; let me suggest merely the social setting of the discussions, which must have been unique: many of the Buddhist intellectual spokesmen were inhabitants of growing cities in the North in the ancient days; many were monks, merchants, urban people, not afraid of polluting themselves by associating with other nations; the Brahmanic tradition, seemingly submerged for centuries, remained strongest in the countryside, particularly in the South; there Hindu intellectual giants like Saṃkara arose. Such historical processes do not return. But we have much to learn from the nature of the ancient polemics. We are people who are very anxious to *realize* "mankind" as a true global empirical entity with all technical means available; we would do well to develop some attention and patience for the inner struggles "mankind" requires from us. Every man on the earth has some idea of the problem "mankind," and no peace can come from a technical assistance ignoring *his* idea of the problem. Buddhists approached the experts on Vedic learning and ritual on the only level worthy of the problem: the deepest level they themselves knew about. The Hindu thinkers in turn understood that Buddhism was an undermining not just of externals, but of their inner universe, and when the time was ripe they made their reply forcefully, yet without violence.

It must not be supposed that only intellectual giants like Śaṃkara turned the tide. There are in the same period popular stories mocking *yoga* practices, and in many quarters religious texts revealing doubt about the necessity for ascetic requirements, and some doing both. "Donkeys and other animals wander about naked too. Does that make them yogins?"[19] There was a general undercurrent of desire to turn from a chaos of possibilities to the certainty of the-world-as-it-is as the best medium to realize the highest goals. This world included the *brahmans*— as were Śaṃkara and all great *ācāryas* ("spiritual teachers")—whose word was trustworthy.

I believe that one point is more important than any other in the history of thoughts about mankind in India. It is that *some image beyond man* must have its part in order to allow us to think of mankind even in its most immediate physical aspects, and also those practical aspects we pay so much attention to: organization, equality, fulfillment of needs, economic opportunities, political rights. If we neglect such an image, we can only reap confusion in the small world we are in. Confusion of tongues can be a major obstacle in the most practical matters—like economic aid programs. It seems necessary to me to conclude that we need more than "mankind" (the organizable, equal ones) to penetrate what really makes the concept problematic; it is not just an imagery to please our sense of beauty—it is what I have referred to as symbolism. This more-than-mankind is the only bridge that has ever led to the notion "mankind."

Symbols are those underlying certainties that usually go without saying. Similarly, myths narrate those things that are mostly taken for granted and in normal life do not call for special justification. (The Indian class-system was "simply there.") Is not this how it is also with our ideas of "mankind"? It is not by chance or because of some unique secularization process that students of the unconscious have focused their attention on symbols and myths—so much so that it would seem that the very origin of the symbolic images is unconscious. In fact, things that are self-evident never occupy (or occupied in the past) the conscious mind of people very much. But we must not always, in this case can not afford to be silent about things that usually go without saying. When we look at an ancient period or a faraway culture, their self-evidences stand out. And a critical problem for ourselves forces us to look at our own self-evidences in their light.

The historian of religions cannot do much more than point to those crucial imageries elsewhere and hope that they will help us in our symbolic crises and renewals. The crisis of our understanding of mankind obviously has to take others and their views into consideration. Like all symbolisms about to be born, our notion of mankind can and must be thought about as consciously as possible, but only with one purpose (and in that too it is like all symbolism): to be alive and allow people to live. Somehow, in the clashes with other self-evidences, we shall have to revise our notions of equality and unity to live with others, which after all is what it means to live. How in the symbolisms of the future the basis of our customary notions of equality and unity can be maintained is a question that lies perhaps outside the academic scope. But there is no doubt that it can never be a matter of trading in our old notions for new ones, and also that the problem cannot be solved by dreaming of utopias. There will have to be constant re-examinations of our own traditional notions (such as caritas, agapē, dikaiosunē, zedaka, koinonia) and their basic imagery. Surely these notions do not imply the flat egalitarianism that poisons human relationships, not in the last place internationally. Now I ask that the Indian traditional ideas may stimulate our thoughts.

NOTES

1. mā́ṃ hi [Pārtha] vyapāśritya ye 'pi syuḥ pāpayonayaḥ striyo vaiśyās tathā śūdrās te 'pi yānti parāṃ gatim

2. H. Oldenberg, Die Religion des Veda (Berlin: Bessersche Buchhandlung, 1894), pp. 275, 276.

3. For a summary of the most important questions and bibliography concerning the Indo-European problem, see C. Scott Littleton, The New Comparative Mythology, an Anthropological Assessment of the Theories of Georges Dumézil (Berkeley: University of California Press, 1966). For the nature of the Indo-European tripartition, see especially Georges Dumézil, L'idéologie tripartie des Indo-Européens (Bruxelles: Latomus, 1958), pp. 17-18.

4. Jātaka 1, 74 ff. in Henry Warren, Buddhism in Translations (Cambridge: Harvard University Press, 1896), pp. 80-81.

5. As said by Aśvaghoṣa, Buddhacarita. See E. Conze, Buddhist Scriptures (Harmondworth: Penguin, 1959), p. 35.

6. Thus rendered by S. B. Dasgupta, *Obscure Religious Cults* (Calcutta: K. L. Mukhopadhyay, 1962), p. 72.

7. Mahā-Vagga, 1, 23, 1 ff. in Warren, p. 86.

8. See e.g. *Dīgha Nikāya*, 3, 80 ff. in Wm. Theodore de Bary, ed., *Sources in Indian Tradition* (New York: Columbia University Press, 1959), pp. 132-136.

9. Warren, *Buddhism in Translations*, p. 40.

10. Photograph in E. Zürcher, *Buddhism, Its Origin and Spread in Words, Maps and Pictures* (Amsterdam: Djambatan, 1962), p. 94.

11. The story is summarized in E. Lamotte, *Histoire du Bouddhisme indien*, Bibl. du Muséon, Vol. 43 (Louvain: Publications Universitaires, 1958) pp. 608, 609.

12. See summary in André Bareau, *Die Religionen Indiens* (Stuttgart: Kohlhammer, 1964), III, pp. 32-54.

13. H. Kern, trans., *Saddharmapuṇḍarīka or The Lotus of the True Law*, Sacred Books of the East, Vol. XXI (Oxford: Clarendon Press, 1884; reprinted, New York: Dover, 1963), p. xxxiv.

14. Ibid., p. 205.

15. Ibid., p. 206.

16. Ibid., p. 209.

17. Edward Conze, *Vajracchedikā Prajñāpāramitā*, edited and translated with introduction and glossary (Roma, Is. M.E.O., 1957), p. 66.

18. Śārīrakamīmāṃsābhāṣya, 1, 4, 19.

19. Kulārṇavatantra, 5, 48, quoted in M. Eliade, *Yoga, Immortality and Freedom* (New York: Pantheon, 1958), p. 204.

BIBLIOGRAPHY

A. Bareau. "*Der indische Buddhismus*" in *Die Religionen Indiens*, III (Volume XIII of the series *Die Religionen der Menschheit*; general ed. C. M. Schröder), Stuttgart: Kohlhammer, 1964.

Georg Bühler. *The Laws of Manu* (Sacred Books of the East. Vol. xxv), Oxford: Clarendon Press, 1886.

G. Coedès. *Les états hindouisés de l'Indochine et de l'Indonesie*, Paris: De Boccard, 1948.

J. H. Hutton. *Caste in India*, Cambridge: University Press, 1946.

P. V. Kane. *History of Dharmaśāstra*, 5 volumes, Poona: Bhandarkar Oriental Research Institute, 1930-1962.

R. C. Majumdar. *Hindu Colonies in the Far East*, 2d ed., Calcutta: Mukhopadhyay, 1963.

J. Muir. *Original Sanskrit Texts on the Origin and History of the People of India, their Religion and Institutions, collected translated and illustrated*, Volume I: *The Mythical and Legendary Accounts of the Origin of Caste, with an Enquiry into its Existence in the Vedic Age*, 3d ed., London: Trübner, 1890.

E. J. Thomas. *The History of Buddhist Thought*, New York: Barnes and Noble, 1953.

T W O

Mankind and World Order in Chinese History

HELMUT G. CALLIS
Departments of History and
Political Science
The University of Utah

Not Just Water Under the Bridge

"ALL CHINESE PHILOSOPHY," SAYS ARTHUR WALEY, "IS ESSEN-tially a study of how men can best be helped to live together in harmony and good order."

Confucius, China's "master teacher," lived in a convulsive time of transition when ancient Cathay was divided into several continuously warring states, each with its separate social, political, and economic systems and its separate literature, tradition, and beliefs. What characterizes our own time is a similar cultural and ideological conflict, but on a world-wide scale.

In place of the small feudal states of Confucian times, mankind's dominant races, cultures, and organized power blocs struggle today for supremacy in an emerging world civilization. The issue between communism and democratic capitalism is by no means the only example.

In a time like this, it is obviously vital that we ask ourselves what were the nature and inner essence of the Confucian principles for a harmonious social and inter-state order and what we may perhaps learn from them for our own age. Let us remember that it was on these principles that China, unique among innumerable cultures and empires now dead, survived as a state and civilization from pre-Christian centuries to the atomic age.

Confucius' "Great Principle" of World-Wide Harmony

Confucianism is based primarily on three great books, all written or edited by disciples of Confucius. The most profound of these books was the *Great Learning*, the work of Tsang Sin. It begins with the development of man's personality and virtues through the cultivation of humane and social relations and ends with the prerequisites for government leading to the final achievement of an ideal world commonwealth. When the right relation among men is established, it is easy, Confucius felt, to achieve a harmonious family, a peaceful state, and eventually a global commonwealth.

Mankind's ultimate aim is the achievement of *Ta T'ung*, the "Great Principle" of universal harmony. When the "Great Principle" prevails, the sage taught, the "world is like one home, common to all"; men of virtue and merit are to be elected rulers; sincerity and amity will pervade all dealings between man and man, and people will love not only their own parents and children, but also those of others. There will be care and charity for the poor, the downtrodden, the destitute. Good government will feel responsible not only to make those who live under it happy, but also to attract those who live far away. It will be a true commonwealth. Alas, concluded Confucius sadly, "We have not learned to serve men; how can we serve God?"

Ta T'ung, the "Great Principle" and its practical concomitant of a global commonwealth, was meant by the sage to be constructed in accordance with nature's order and, therefore, also with man's own true nature, which is fundamentally good and from which all his duties and rights are derived. What regulates nature, he said, is called "instructions." Man's duty, he held, was to discover the way of nature and thus avoid being swayed by doctrines and dogmas, which are always artificial, arbitrary, time-bound, and man-made. But if all follow *Ta T'ung*, all men within the four seas can become good brothers.

Confucius sought to create, by the unification of men's minds, a homogeneous community of all men in which there would be general and voluntary agreement regarding the objects worthy of desire and in which the careless, the selfish, and the antisocial would be subdued by the transforming influences of good example and exhortation.

Measured with the standard of perfection, of course, the sage's world commonwealth remained a happy, wishful dream. Even so, it had far-reaching beneficial consequences for his people who for two thousand years, until the ascendancy of communism in China, recognized him as their "master teacher."

Historical Consequences of Confucian Teachings

For two millennia the Chinese, following Confucian principles, presented the inspiring spectacle of a people gathered into one vast political body and united primarily not by regimentation from above but by a community of ideas, beliefs, and traditions. Although they always represented a very large fraction of the whole human race, all the Chinese wrote the same language, read the same literature, and enjoyed the same way and order of life.

Guided by the Confucian ideal, China, unlike Rome, did not succumb under the invasions of barbarians, but on the contrary, absorbed and civilized the invaders. Nor did she become the victim of dark ages and fratricidal wars as did Europe. More than any large, politically organized group, the Chinese excelled in peacefulness and civilized conduct, in self-sufficiency and self-reliance, thus writing for themselves an unprecedented historical record of unity, dignity and achievement. Rome, relying on the sword, fell by the sword; China, resting her faith on an ethical ideal which had appeal for all, survived the ages.

Most scholars have preferred to think of Confucianism as a social and ethical system and not as a religion because the sage based society on natural foundations common to all human beings anywhere on earth rather than on metaphysical speculations which have tended to divide men.

Indeed, the divorcing of ethics from metaphysics was perhaps one of Confucius' greatest achievements. It enabled his morals to live on while most other doctrines became antiquated or underwent drastic changes. It provided common ground on which men of diverse religions could live and work together (as they did in China in contrast to historical Europe or India).

The Cultural Concept of the Confucian State

In Confucian thinking, human society begins with the natural group of men of whatever race or faith they grow up in, namely, the family; and its natural principles of love and order retain validity as the family expands into the wider associations of clan, tribe, state and civilization.

Confucius taught that social instinct and the moral sense are the characteristic attributes of man and that every human heart has a natural inclination to perform the reciprocal obligations which alone make association with others fruitful and agreeable. Or, put differently, Confucius looked at rights as merely the other side of social obligations. What was a right for one man, was an obligation for another, and vice versa.

The sage admitted that man's nature may deteriorate, that man may try to dodge his natural obligations, thus infringing on the rights of others; yet he also saw that man-made laws cannot force him to be decent and reasonable, that law and force are only crutches for decadent and malfunctioning social systems.

Consequently, the function of the Confucian state was not to set up legal machinery as in the West to secure individual rights, but rather to foster the sense of responsibility by every means in its power—by education and exhortation, by leadership and example—to try to maintain a high standard of social conduct. Thus, rights could normally be maintained in Confucian China without the direct intervention of the state, although the social pressure on the individual was great.

In the Confucian world view, the state was not thought of as a piece of political machinery for enforcing the law, but primarily as a means to encourage, spread, and cultivate civilized behavior. Its ultimate aim was the realization of the Confucian maxim that "all under heaven constitute one family" and "within the four seas all men are brothers."[1]

In accordance with Confucian ideals, the Chinese thought that governments should rule by moral example and common views on justice and persuasion and not by crude force. Rightfully proud of the unifying force of their ideals, they regarded their culture as being so powerful that, in contrast to Europe and Japan, military methods were held in contempt in traditional China.

Because the Chinese could not conceive of civilized mankind except as one and undivided, they admitted only one legitimate ruler. "As there was only one sun in heaven, there could be only one Emperor on earth." It is, therefore, no exaggeration to say that the idea of world government was taken for granted by the Confucian Chinese.

But Chinese traditions recognized as civilized only those who conformed to Confucian ethics and the Chinese way of life. All others were "barbarians." In the Chinese view of society, Confucian morality was the only standard of human morality everywhere, regardless of place or race, and they were convinced that there could be only one moral standard on earth.

Hence, the Chinese state and empire, held together by cultural rather than political or legal ties, was regarded geographically as unlimited and as including all civilized mankind. This was the Chinese theory of "cosmopolitan, ethical dominion." Their theory of the "Middle Kingdom," called upon to civilize the rest of the world, focused on the ideal of a universal state which was coextensive with a world-wide community of civilized peoples. In Confucian political thought, the state was conceived as having an essentially civilized, moral, and peace-preserving function, not only within its realm, but also in its relations with other states. The superiority of wang-tao, "rule by virtue and good sense," over pao-tao, "rule by force," was never questioned.

All individuals as well as all states could become accepted members of China's universal commonwealth on the condition that they adopted the moral principles inherent in Chinese civilization. It was a barbarian's disgrace not to be admitted into the selected circle of China's "tributary" states or dependencies. For the individual, too, in Chinese Confucian views, the mark of distinction was culture and morality rather than race and nationality. Consequently, the Chinese were remarkably tolerant of the religions, customs, even laws of foreigners, as long as they did not encroach upon their own; after all, every man was expected to venerate his own ancestors and to be loyal to his native family traditions. No wonder China, in her long history, accepted alien religions and races from nearly all parts of the world, yet never lost her identity.

The Principles Underlying Traditional China's International Relations

At the same time, the Chinese theory of a universal state centered in China, the "Middle Kingdom," precluded China's recognition of another nation's equality with herself. This is understandable because Chinese international theories, like most theories, had grown out of China's experience and were an adaptation to the environment in which she lived: a huge nation surrounded by many small ones. China looked at this cluster of East Asian states, some of which she had actually helped to create, as a family, with China as the world-mother.

This family concept of international relations led by its very nature to a set of principles of conduct between states in the Chinese realm which can only strike the impartial observer as much more natural and humane than the basic rules underlying the national state system in the West, with its insistence on the legal equality and sovereignty of nations. The morality and timeless importance of traditional China's principles of international behavior can be gauged even by mere enumeration:

1. Wars, especially wars of annexation, are senseless on both moral and utilitarian grounds.
2. The attack on small states by larger ones must be adjudged a crucial abuse of power.
3. War criminals should suffer the penalty of death.

4. Rights and obligations between states should be reciprocal; if imposed by unlawful governments, they need not be regarded as binding.

5. Intervention in the internal affairs of a state and punitive sanctions against a government inconsiderate of the commonweal and unyielding to moral persuasion is permissible only as an act of justice and solely to the central authority speaking in the name and acting in the interest of the community of civilized states.

6. National security can best be attained by voluntary agreements between governments and not by reliance on defense with arms and fortifications. To cultivate a spirit of international good will and reciprocity, governments are enjoined to follow the same golden rule, which assures peace and cooperation between individuals: "Do not unto others. . . ."[2]

Leibniz, the great German philosopher, was so impressed by this display of high-principled Chinese wisdom that he wrote in the preface of his *Novissima Sinica* (1697) that "judged by the principles of civilized life, there exists in the world a people who excel ourselves."

It is noteworthy that the principles and rules governing the life of China's family of nations were not the inventions of theorists, but the hard-won fruits of painful political experience gained during a period of ancient Chinese history known as the "era of the warring states" (late Chou Dynasty 480-221 B.C.). In that tumultuous age, the states of a then still divided China varied greatly in size, wealth, and development; but like the states in our contemporary world, all regarded themselves as sovereign equals, recognizing no authority other than their own. Conscious of their importance, the governments of those states, suspicious and jealous, constantly made wars against each other and, in the interludes between wars, formed alliances, made treaties, and engaged in trade to be prepared for future armed conflicts. In brief, their relations followed the well-known patterns of sovereign states in seeking "security." But that frantic search led only to more wars, and, in turn, led to social chaos, while the common people suffered, starved and died. Finally, in 545 B.C., fourteen states entered into a "League to Preserve Peace," which survived a few years but perished when the powerful states began to ignore the rights of the League's smaller and weaker members.

This episode preceded China's unification by Emperor Shih Huang Ti in 221 B.C., ending the "era of the states at war."

Thus, through long historical experience—theirs is the longest continuous history of any politically organized nation—the Chinese learned important lessons for the ordering of international relations:

They accepted the Confucian axiom that any nation consists basically of families, and if it wishes to be civilized, it ought to behave like a decent family among good neighboring families: peacefully, considerately, and helpfully, and in a friendly manner.

On the other hand, to think of all states as equals seemed utterly unrealistic to the Chinese. After all, states differ drastically in size, age, culture, resources, and population, and, therefore, differ from other states in importance and power.

Furthermore, smaller states do need protection and the most natural place to find it, the Chinese felt, was in reliance on a benevolent, powerful, big state, which is in geographical proximity and culturally related.

Finally and correspondingly, the big state must assume its social responsibilities by guaranteeing the maintenance of peace and other basic prerequisites of the international order within the orbit of its power and accepted influence.

China's Tributary System as a Model for World Order

China's tributary state system translated the basic Chinese principles of international order into practical policies. It is worth our while to study these; for in our world vainly in search for international order, the politics not less than the underlying principles appear extraordinarily timely and important for the age in which we live.

International order in the Chinese version postulated the national inequality of states and by the same token excluded any notion of "sovereignty." It ordered international relations along the lines of a natural family through personal and social interaction, sharing of goods and ideas, and reciprocal bonds of rights and obligations which were traditional and culturally accepted. In the contest of such human and cultural relationships, the legal concept of sovereignty was so utterly senseless that it did not even occur to the traditional, Confucian-oriented Chinese. Since the emphasis was on ideas and mutual cooperation between states within one civilization, the question of boundaries between them was irrelevant. They were not competitors, neither politically, economically, nor culturally; they formed one harmonious family. As in the natural family, inequality of status was the natural a priori basis of order in the Chinese family of nations.

The younger and "lesser" members of the family were dependent on dominant senior members and had obligations toward them; on the other hand, the latter were, in turn, expected to be kind, benevolent, and interested in the welfare of the junior members, at least while their conduct was proper according to Confucian ethical rules and rites. If the junior members violated these rules, however, the elders had the right to "correct" and punish.

In the international sphere, this meant that all peoples and nations were members of the human family, but that they were unequal in status, age, size, power, and levels of culture. Or, as applied more specifically to the Far Eastern area to which the Chinese outlook and influence were traditionally confined, it meant that China, the "Middle Kingdom," was the senior member *par excellence* in a Confucian family of lesser states which were all dependent on China, the "father" state, and related to it by clearly defined rights and obligations. To hold the status of a tributary state was not regarded as a disgrace but, on the contrary, as a great honor which "barbarians" could not attain. The boundary states viewed themselves as "younger brothers," as happy "children" of one international family.

As usual in a family, the "father" or "elder brother" was not supposed to exercise his utmost authority except in emergencies. In other words, the control of domestic as well as foreign affairs was ordinarily left to the individual rulers of "boundary states." Force between Confucian states was used only to secure recognition by tributaries of a new Chinese dynasty as truly holding the "mandate of heaven" or to chastize a dependent ruler who had strayed from the proper rules, thus causing disorders in his country. War, in the Western sense of the word, was incompatible with the Confucian theory which required that an unsubmissive people should be conquered by persuasion and an appeal to reason, by an exemplary display of civil culture and virtue; for the Confucian government was one of instruction, not of force; it was the indoctrination of inferiors by superiors with the rules of proper conduct.

Dependence of the lesser states found its expression not in intervention of the parent state in their domestic affairs but in the mutual observance of traditionally accepted ways of regulated intercourse.

For example, the dependent status of a tributary king expressed itself ceremonially in his acceptance of the investiture from the Chinese emperor in the form of a seal to be used as a badge of office. This, in modern language, meant diplomatic recognition. Of equal significance for the maintenance of close relations were the periodic visits by plenipotentiaries of either state, the acceptance on the part of the father state of an unwritten obligation to give economic aid to the lesser state in case of natural calamities, and the regular "tribute missions" sent to Peking by dependent rulers. These missions, far from being merely ceremonial, were designed for the specific economic purpose of furthering the international exchanges of goods within the vast reaches of the Empire and to diversify production.

As a rule, China returned "presents" of greater value than the so-called "tribute" she had received from a dependent state. Thus, the exchange had the effect of a subsidy to a lesser kingdom, intended to maintain its loyalty and indirectly to encourage yet unaffiliated areas to come into the Chinese orbit. Cultural attachment of the suzerain peoples to the Middle Kingdom was promoted, moreover, by the age-old custom of educating princes of tributary kingdoms at the Chinese court and by marrying high-born Chinese women to suzerain rulers.

Also part of this Confucian system of interstate relations were the rights to mutual military assistance. For instance, had the paramount nation decided on a military expedition, possibly for the "correction" of an obnoxious ruler, the lesser nation could be required to furnish men and military supplies. The father state, in turn, would assist the smaller states with fighting forces, if their established government were threatened by internal revolt or attacked by an outside enemy.

The states regularly listed as junior or boundary nations (shu-pang) by the Chinese were Burma, Laos, Siam, Vietnam, the Liu Chiu Islands, and Korea. Japan was only at times part of the system. During the T'ang period, Japan sent tributary missions continuously, but Japan's allegiance was broken during the Sung and Mongol dynasties. In the 15th and 16th centuries, Japan's military dictators, the Shoguns, again accepted investiture by the Chinese emperor and acknowledged their tributary status under the Ming dynasty. After 1549, however, Japan seceded for good and was afterward a passive, though very interested observer of happenings on the Chinese mainland. It is noteworthy that, in Korean records, relations with China were described as sadae, or serving the elder brother, while those with Japan were known as kyorin, or relations with a neighbor. China, on the other hand, until modern times, continued to view Japan as a recalcitrant member of her Asiatic order.

It is apparent even to a superficial observer that the international relations which assured the peace and welfare of China's tributary states for many centuries foreshadowed policies now frequently thought of as innovations of our 20th century. Among the most constructive of those practiced for ages by China in her family of nations were the following:

1. The utilization of geopolitical proximity and cultural kinship to coordinate states for maintaining the peace and assuring international co-operation.

2. The recognition of the need of small or under-developed countries

for military, economic, and educational aid from the more powerful, wealthier, and more advanced members of the international community.

3. The creation of a common market binding together states having similar economic interests to avoid economic wastage and cut-throat competition. In China's tributary system, the merchants who accompanied the tributary mission to Peking were allowed to import their goods duty free.

4. The use of border states as buffers for defending the realm against invaders. Highly informative regarding this security function of border states was the statement made by China's foreign minister Li Hung-chang in 1883:

> . . . the limits of the empire were well defined. Here was China and there were the tributaries of China. These tributaries were self-governing except in the fact that they owed the Emperor an allegiance which was satisfied by acts of tribute and ceremony. These offices done, the Emperor never interfered in their internal affairs. At the same time their independence concerned China and she could not be insensible to any attack upon it.[3]

Pointing in the same direction was the practice, customary upon the death of the monarch of a lesser kingdom, of his successor's sending a petition to the Chinese emperor asking him for confirmation of his succession to the throne as a guard on the frontier of the empire. The emperor know the value of small states as "fences" against foreign invaders. He knew also that only if the lesser governments were genuinely loyal would the "fence" be sturdy and protective. There is, therefore, no need to doubt the sincerity of the assurance of a high Chinese official made, in this instance, to Korea:

> Korea is a state tributary of our Empire . . . the throne has always looked upon her happiness and her sorrow with the same interest as upon those of our own family.

Even if we take for granted the political interest of the "Son of Heaven" in treating the lesser states with consideration, the question still remains open whether or not the latter found the relationship with the "father" state not also advantageous for themselves. Were they really happy, did they not find the burden of their tributary obligations onerous, did they not feel their unequal dependent status grossly humiliating and a good reason for seeking complete independence?

Surprisingly, the historical record testifies that the boundary states were not only satisfied but also proud of the tributary relationship and had no intention to cut the ties which bound them to the Celestial Empire.

For example, in 1591, Hideyoshi, the Japanese military dictator, tried to persuade the Korean king to ally himself with Japan against China; the request was rejected by the Korean monarch with passionate indignation:

> You stated in your letter that you were planning to invade the paramount nation (China) and requested that our Kingdom (Korea) join in your military undertaking. . . . We cannot even understand how you have dared to plan such an undertaking and make such a request of us. For thousands of years from the time of yore when Chi-tzu, the founder of the Kingdom of Korea, received the investiture from the Chou dynasty, up to our own time our Kingdom has always been known as a nation of righteousness. . . . The relation of ruler and subject has been strictly observed between the paramount nation and our own Kingdom . . . generation after generation we have reverently adhered and attended to all duties and obligations due from a tributary state of Chung Chao (China). . . . Our two nations have acted as a single family maintaining the relationship of father and son as well as that of ruler and subject. . . . We shall certainly not desert "our lord and father" nation. Moreover to invade another nation is an act of which men of culture and intellectual attainment should feel ashamed. . . . We would conclude this letter by saying that your proposed undertaking is the most reckless, imprudent, and daring of any of which we have ever heard.[4]

The same profound respect for the father nation and his genuine pride in being a member of China's civilized family of nations is expressed by a Korean author:

> Our ceremonies, our enjoyments, our laws, our usages, our dress, our literature, our foods have all followed after the models of China. The (five) great relationships shine forth from those above and the teachings pass down to those below making the force of our customs like to that of the Flowery Lord; so that the Chinese themselves praise us saying "Korea is little China."[5]

History would scarcely support the argument that other tributary states were unwilling members of the system. True, the Vietnamese bolted the Empire in 939 A.D. when the Chinese tried to destroy Vietnam's autonomy and national identity by governing the country directly as one of their provinces. But by so doing they caused a violent patriotic rebellion which soon persuaded the Chinese emperor to grant Vietnam "independence" within the Chinese tributary system. Interestingly, the small country then continued peaceably in this state for 1,000 years until the French set out to impose their sovereignty on the Vietnamese colony-to-be. The result of French actions was an undeclared war lasting four years (1882-1885), in which the Vietnamese, together with the Chinese, fought fiercely but unsuccessfully against the modern weaponry of the French invaders.

Burma, to give another example, continued to send tributary missions to Peking even after Britain had forced recognition of British sovereignty there through the Anglo-Chinese convention of 1886. Such sentimental gestures could not change history. European power was the decisive factor and destroyed the ancient form of the Chinese Empire.

Disintegration of the Tributary System

The question is natural: If the tributary system worked so well, why did it disintegrate? The answer may be given with a quote from the Book of Common Prayer of 1549:

> There was never anything by the wit of man so well devised or so sure established which in the continuance of time hath not been corrupted.

Chinese civilization became infected with one of the deadliest cultural illnesses known to history: orthodoxy and formalism. True to St. Paul's saying that "the letter killeth while the spirit giveth life," the Chinese believed so rigidly and self-righteously in the unsurpassable excellence of their ways that they forgot that life is, first of all, adaptation to change and that its problems had to be mastered in every age anew through new learning and fresh thinking.

As it were, the hidebound conservatism of the 19th century Chinese could not master even China's domestic problems: over-population, corruption, exploitation, mass ignorance, and starvation, as well as the formidable and simultaneous challenges they were faced with from without. Perhaps the outward challenge was the more dangerous to China's traditional structure of society and state, because it could not be met with the traditional means of rebellion and change of dynasty. These European "foreign devils" and "sea barbarians," as the Chinese called them, were, indeed, agents of revolutionary changes unprecedented in history. Equipped with the tremendous power their advance in science and technology had given them, the Westerners began to overrun the earth searching for markets and sources of supply. Spreading from Europe, the industrial revolution swept over all continents. Soon, conservative, stagnant China was beleaguered and challenged to compete on equal terms. She was not prepared to do so, nor could she even had she wanted to. Her leadership was much too proud to remake China's society by taking the cue from "barbarians."

The inability to resist successfully the ideas, the institutions, and the armies of the foreigners glaringly showed up the inadequacies of China's once great but now sterile society. In sharp contrast to Western culture, Chinese culture had not developed any ideal of technical or social "progress." The merchant class had been held in low esteem by Chinese officialdom and profitmaking was actually discouraged by bureaucratic interference and exactions. In no respect was there fertile soil in China for free enterprise and capitalist development.

Consequently, China showed herself incapable of transplanting industry as Japan was doing and of developing military power to match that of the foreigners. Step by step, China's great society was broken up, her economy reduced to a semicolonial condition, and her empire, after losing several wars, destroyed.

In the historic clash of cultures, no compromise seemed possible. Like wood and fire, they were too different. In the centuries preceding the meeting of East and West, Western society had developed in nearly opposite directions from that of the Chinese. The West had become less orthodox, less set in its ways, but China more so. Western culture had become an open society which favored socially aggressive individuals and nations, whereas Chinese culture had closed itself up, was wary of initiative, and stressed virtues of contentment and social discipline.

In China the emperor's supremacy over all mankind was the foundation of state power, and the Confucian doctrine of government by personal example, virtue, and wisdom was the only accepted one. But these theories were clearly opposed to Western concepts of supremacy of law, individual rights, and the self-determination of nations, all of which were unrecognized in China where, by contrast, all those who accepted Confucian civilization were to be embraced by a single state. Every one of these cultural differences had deep historical roots.

In Europe the rise of absolute monarchies and the more or less frank acceptance of a Machiavellian ideology of the relations between sovereignties made force the final arbiter in the dealings of states with states. Machiavelli's idea that politics is an end in itself and ought to be divorced from religious, moral, and social considerations, or Hegel's opinion that war rather than peace shows the health of a state, was the mere intellectual mirror of politics as it was actually practiced; but both Western political theory and practice were manifestly anathema to the Confucian way of thinking.

It is evident that the Confucian ideology was incompatible with the concepts on which the Western national system was built with its emphasis on state boundaries, language, race, competitive economic interests, sovereign equality, national self-determination, and armed security.

Furthermore, and rather surprisingly, political philosophy in traditional China had no place for nationalism. If there had been one, the Confucian Chinese would surely have scorned it as a dividing, asocial element, a vicious virus dangerous to all cultures, not merely their own.

Ironically, this was precisely what nationalism became in Western civilization where, in the Middle Ages, nationalistically inspired religious dogmatism first brought about the ominous schism between Catholic Western Europe and Orthodox Russia, forerunner of our "cold war." Later on, during and after the Reformation, this nationalism divided Christian civilization under the absolutism of power-greedy princes still further into hostile sovereign states and, at last, under the cloak of democratic sovereignty and national socialism, it drove the Western nations to mass murder and destruction in two world wars.

But long before that happened European nationalism had destroyed the Chinese Empire. Insisting on their sovereign rights to equality, diplomatic intercourse, missionary activities, international trade, and the right to make war if vital interests were threatened, the Western states demanded that China drop its claim to cultural superiority, join the international trading world, and give up its tributary system.

The Chinese thought the Westerners had no rights for their demands. They regarded foreign trade which included the wholesale importation of opium[6] and traffic in human beings as a "source of social demoralization." They thought of the Christian cross, which followed flag and trade as a "pioneer of the sword," as undermining the whole fabric of habitual belief on which the stability of their society depended. They regarded the presence of embassies, after several defeats by foreign powers, as a "sign of national humiliation."[7]

And why attack and destroy their proud and ancient empire, once so well integrated that, unique among empires, it survived two millennia? Commenting on the remark of a 19th-century Western official that "in modern times . . . under the rule of civilized nation," there were "no such institutions as tributary states" and that a colony was as much a part of the empire as the capital, China's foreign minister, Li Hung-chang, asked

> whether or not the Western States could rightly assume that their international law was the only system to be recognized and applied in a part of the world whose divergent system antedated that of the West by thousands of years and whose record of maintaining international peace among the nations in its sphere surpassed that of the West. Because there existed in Western practice no relation such as that which China claimed for herself and Korea. . . . (he could see) no reason why the outside nations should destroy relations that had existed between China

and their outlying nations for ages. They had gone on well together, doing each other good. . . .[8]

For Western diplomats this was an alien point of view. For them a territory was either a colony over which one power or another had sovereign sway, or it was independent and a possible target for future colonization, if its independence could not be successfully defended. Hence, a nation's "dependence without control," as China claimed for her younger brother states, made no sense in Western diplomacy. On the other hand, the marking off of a certain territory within which the will of another nation was the highest law was not contemplated in Chinese theory. To the West it appeared that China was the suzerain over various "vassal" states, although this term was never clarified. The average European diplomat could simply not discover any merit in these Chinese concepts although some Westerners rather exceptionally did understand the implications of the Confucian system. For example, William H. Seward, U. S. Minister and one-time Secretary of State of President Lincoln, wrote in 1870:

> It is not too much to say that it has been within the power of China for a very long period to overrun and subdue these petty states. . . . A great people filling all their territory to the brink of its sustaining power but remaining for centuries self-constrained, regardful of their own dignity and place but regardful also of the right of the petty powers about them is a spectacle not very common in the history of the world. It is one upon which we may pause to raise the question whether a state capable of such conduct has not for some reason a poise and balance of judgment and temper greater than we have been in the habit of attributing to her, and which entitled her to a large measure of respect and esteem.[9]

Pointing to a historical precedent and to the morality of her case did not help China. The powers, each ruthlessly seeking its own political advantage, had no use for Seward's broadly liberal, mankind-oriented point of view. Echoing him from the other side of the river, a Chinese official at the turn of the century wrote in bitterness:

> We submitted because we had to. . . . We were not a military power. But do you suppose our sense of justice was not outraged? Or later, when every power in Europe on some protest or other has seized and retained some part of our territory, do you suppose because we cannot resist, we do not feel? . . . It is the nations of Christendom who have come to us to teach by sword and fire that Right in this world is powerless unless it is supported by Might. O, do not doubt that we shall learn the lesson! And woe to Europe when we have acquired it![10]

Chinese Nationalism: Sun Yat-sen and Mao T'se-tung

The Chinese did "learn the lesson"—too well. Western gunboats proved to them that they had to acquire modern arms and technology, take an interest in Western science, and the art of Western politics. As the prestige of the Confucian classics evaporated and the Chinese family system weakened, aggressive nationalism, unknown to the Chinese until then, took over as a sort of counter-poison against the encroachments of the foreigners on China's body politic and society.

At the turn of the century and fifty years before China's takeover by the communists, the Chinese mob, already determined to "cast the foreigners into the sea," went on a rampage known as the "Boxer Rebellion," which resulted in large-scale massacres of Chinese and Western Christians. This action was followed by the imposition on China by the powers of even greater humiliations. The fiery proclamation of rebel leader Yu Tung-chen left no doubt about the nationalist motives of the Boxers:

> These foreigners, under the pretext of trading and teaching Christianity, are in reality taking away the land, food and clothing of the people; besides over-turning the teaching of the sages, they are poisoning us with opium and ruining us with debauchery. Since the time of Tao Kuang[11] they seized our territory and cheated us out of our money; they have eaten our children as food and piled up the public debt as high as the hills; they have burnt our places and overthrown our tributary states, occupied Shanghai, devastated Formosa, forcibly opened Kiachow and now wish to divide China like a melon.[12]

Aside from a single, obvious exaggeration, the assertions of the proclamation were true.

A few years later, during World War I, Chinese nationalism reached its second stage of development under the influence of the ideas and revolutionary activities of Sun Yat-sen, who is famed among Chinese of all walks of life and persuasions as the father and founder of the Chinese Republic. In his speeches and writings, Sun made no attempt to conceal his aroused nationalist feelings. Proud of China's dedication to world civilization, he berated the imperialist powers which, he felt, pursued nothing but political self-interest while making cosmopolitan pretensions:

> Our civilization has already advanced two thousand years beyond yours. . . . Two thousand years ago we discarded imperialism and advocated a policy of peace . . . (p. 94) Many of our race have thought of a political world civilization . . . but . . . the cosmopolitanism which Europeans are telling about today is really a principle supported by force without justice . . . (p. 99) Hongkong can exert a strangle-

hold on all the southern provinces of China. Soldiers drill there and marines stay there. . . . In two months at the most England could wipe out China. The French also have a base very close to China—Vietnam—. . . . So France like England, could destroy China within two months. (pp. 106-107)[13]

Sun's "nationalism," as his writings show, was still quite close to traditional Confucianism inasmuch as it transcended the ethnic boundaries of a nation in the Western sense. His concept of a nation comprised, in addition to Chinese, all the other races historically bound to China, such as the Manchus, Mongols, Tibetans, and the Moslems of Turkestan in the Chinese northwest. When Sun spoke of China, he really thought of a Greater China, one that included all the territories of the historical Chinese Empire. No doubt he also looked forward to the return into the Chinese orbit of all colonial peoples in Asia who, like the Vietnamese, Burmese, and Koreans, had once been China's tributaries; thus he saw the one-time empire reborn in modern form as a federal union with China as the center and its member races enjoying a measured degree of autonomy.

This Chinese federation would leave small states their independence. For Sun the term "independence" did not, however, denote national self-determination in the Wilsonian sense, but rather the elimination of imperialist, i.e., non-Chinese, influences from these countries so as to make them secure under Chinese protection and to keep them receptive to the "light of Chinese civilization." In other words, Sun returned, so to say, through the back door to the old Confucian ideal of tying small states to a senior state in a regional family of nations.

We may conclude from the foregoing that Sun regarded the success of Chinese nationalism as a necessary first step toward a viable world order which, however, for him was conditional upon the return of China to her traditional central position in eastern Asia. In this region a modernized China would have predominant influence, but elsewhere she would recognize her equal partnership with other cultures of the world. Thus breaking with China's traditional claim to superiority over all other cultures, Sun no longer insisted that Chinese civilization and morality were the only ones possible on earth and, as such, were to be accepted by civilized men everywhere. Sun now unashamedly admitted that the Chinese people had much to learn and therefore recommended the amalgamation of the best traditions of China's civilization with the best contributions of all other cultures. In this way, Sun gave China's ethnocentric system a modern twist which allowed the inclusion, not only in theory but also in fact, of the whole of mankind.

Similarly, in the economic field, Sun Yat-sen definitely thought in global terms when he unfolded a grandiose international plan for China's modernization in his book on *The International Development of China*. In that volume he pointed out that the industrialization of China's untouched hinterland could become a main, stabilizing factor for the economy of the whole world and appealed to the producers of industrial equipment in the capitalist West to participate profitably in the modernization of China.

Unfortunately, Sun's dreams of a China which would find her place as a happy member of a global community of nations soon collapsed in the diplomatic aftermath of the First World War, when the statesmen of Europe at the peace conference of Versailles rewarded Japan's aggression against her Chinese neighbor by transferring to Japan Germany's ill-gotten "rights" in Shantung, China's sacred province and birthplace of Confucius. Under the circumstances, the walkout under protest of the Chinese delegates from the Peace Conference became the signal for even greater turmoil in the Far East. It was in those days of bitter disappointment that China's Communist Party was founded. The foundation year was 1921.

The rise of the Chinese Communists within and Japan's aggression from without made the era of Generalissimo Chiang Kai-shek's rule on the Chinese mainland hardly more than an episode. Its main significance was China's nominal reunification under his "Nationalist" Party, the Kuomintang, and the substitution of its party dictatorship for China's traditional dynastic rule. This dictatorship, in spite of its right-wing orientation, was faithfully modeled after Soviet Russian lines which the Generalissimo had diligently studied during his stay in the Soviet Union. Representing a small propertied minority of landlords, bureaucrats, businessmen and generals, Chiang's regime had no place and little love for China's peasant masses, who were left to their fate and became easy victims of Communist propaganda. Nor can we safely assume that democracy, with scarcely any roots in the Chinese tradition, could have solved the combined pressures of China's vast domestic and international problems. Under the weight of these problems, the additional plagues of corruption, inflation and large-scale war were bound to lead to national catastrophe and, following catastrophe, to communism, which, in turn, may not be the end of the road.

The Communist regime draws heavily upon the bitter lessons of China's past experience with Western imperialism; its resentment of the West runs so deep that it no longer recognizes a need for Confucian cosmopolitanism. If any trace of cosmopolitanism remains, it can be seen only in the perverted, negative form of yearning for world revolution and a paranoiac determination to liberate the world from the monster of imperialism. Confucianism is now being denounced in China as a feudal doctrine, incorrigibly hostile to social change and scientific progress. The sage's ideals of respecting the golden rule, of cultivating social service, of showing tolerance for other people's viewpoints, and of enjoining nations to live together like friendly families, have been abandoned by the regime. That Confucian humanism survives as a thorn in its flesh, however, is amply demonstrated by the many attacks launched against Confucian teachings by the political leadership and by the frequent purges of humanist writers, of Chinese "Pasternaks" such as Wu Han and Ten To.

But the present intransigent posture of China's Communist government toward the West enjoys a considerable measure of popular support. The outside world will have to learn to understand the exasperating attitudes of China's new leaders against the backdrop of Chinese history and recognize that we are dealing here not only with a small clique of power-hungry zealots but also with 750 million people strongly conscious of their historic greatness, their rich culture, their traditional leading role in Asia, and their potentialities for future progress. Whatever the feeling of the Chinese about Maoist Communism, we can safely assume that they all share an ambition to see China restored to prominence in the world, if not as the "Middle Kingdom" of the civilized world, at least as a respected equal in the community of nations.

NOTES

1. In "The Evolution of Li," Book of Rites (Li Chi).

2. Abstracted from the works of Confucius, Motzu, and Mencius; see also Hsiao Kung-chuan, China's Contribution to World Peace, pp. 18 ff. It is instructive to compare the above principles with the stipulations contained in articles 10 and 16 of the League of Nations and article 2, sections 4 and 7, as well as Chapter VII of the Charter of the United Nations.

3. To J. R. Young, U.S. Minister in China.

4. Quoted in Y. S. Kuno, Japanese Expansion on the Asiatic Continent (Berkeley: 1937-40), Vol. I. App. 32, pp. 303-304.

5. Quoted in M. I. Nelson, Korea and the Old Order in Eastern Asia (Baton Rouge, La.: 1945), p. 85.

6. Reference here is to the Opium War (1839-1842) and the coolie trade, which began in the late 1840's and continued for more than thiry years.

7. Quotes are taken from Letters of a Chinese Official (New York: Doubleday, Page and Co., 1909), p. 12, and passim.

8. J. R. Young, U.S. Minister to China, February 2, also March 24, 1883; *China Dispatches*, Vol. XLIV, No. 230, Washington, D.C.

9. U.S. *Foreign Relations*, Washington, D.C., 1880, p. 179.

10. *Letters of a Chinese Official*, op. cit., pp. 64, 69.

11. The emperor who ruled at the time of the Opium War.

12. J. M. D. Pringle, *China Struggles for Unity*, Harmondsworth, England, 1939, pp. 24-28.

13. Sun Yat-sen, *San Min Chu I* (The Three Principles of the People), excerpts from his fourth and fifth lectures on nationalism, first delivered in March, 1924, translated by F. W. Price, new edition published in Chungking, 1943, passim, pages as marked in the quotation.

THREE

Jewish Universalism

ELIEZER BERKOVITS
Chairman, Department of Jewish
  Philosophy
The Hebrew Theological College

I. THE BIBLICAL TRADITION

Cosmic Universalism

WHEN THE GREEK MIND CONCEIVED THE IDEA OF THE COSMOS, it performed a great feat of the intellect. It was not easy to discover unity in the manifoldness of the phenomena; a great deal of imagination was required to behold permanence in the midst of change. Intellectual courage was demanded in order to recognize oneness in a world whose various domains were neatly apportioned between the many ruling deities in accordance with the prevailing polytheistic world view. The Jew, however, stumbled upon the idea almost inadvertently. He took possession of it effortlessly. The One God is the creator of the one world. Because God is one, his world too is one. The world of monotheism is a universe. God's oneness posits his creation as a cosmos; the unity of the cosmos reflects the unity of its maker. "The heavens declare the glory of God and the firmament showeth His handiwork."[1] But not only the heavens, all creation reveals its creator. "All the earth"[2] sings to the Lord and "every soul"[3] praises him. God's contact with the world is not to be severed. He is not only the creator, but also the sustainer. He maintains his creation by his rule. "His kingdom ruleth over all"[4]; over all Nature and all men. His kingdom and his rule is the universal law of the cosmos. Judaism rests firmly on the foundations of a God-anchored cosmic universalism.

Cosmic universalism expresses the nature of God's relatedness to the world. This is how Isaiah puts it:

> "Lift up your eyes on high,
> And see: who hath created these?
> He that bringeth out their host by number,
> He calleth them all by name;
> By the greatness of His might, and for that He is
>   strong in power,
> No one is missing."[5]

To number and to call by name is to enter into relation. One numbers in order to preserve; one calls by name in order to make sure of a presence. The care for those called brings it about that "no one is missing." Divine omnipotence not only creates, but also protects. Cosmic universalism is a combination of creative power and caring might. The psalmist said it with less sophistication and greater immediacy: "The Lord is good to all; and his tender mercies are over all his works."[6] God's concern for all his works is a recurring theme in the Bible. It is hardly ever realized that God's justice originates in God's concern for all his creatures. It is probably correct to say that whenever God exercises justice, he does it out of mercy for someone oppressed and persecuted. The great and mighty God, who considers no person and is not to be bribed, "does justice" for the orphan and the widow. In the same context it is also said of him that he "loveth the stranger, in giving him food and raiment."[7] When he considers the plight of the orphan, the widow, and the stranger, he "considers no person." He has no tolerance with those responsible for the plight of the poor. As he loves and supports the helpless stranger, he also "does justice" for the orphan and the widow. God does justice in order to save; he saves because his concern is over all his works. This too is a theme that permeates the entire Biblical tradition. When God judges the world in righteousness and the nations with equity, he is a "high tower for the oppressed, a high tower in times of trouble."[8] God judges because of his protecting care for all his creatures. Even when he is called "the judge of all the earth," it is because of the cry of Sodom and Gomorrah that God judges.[9] The cosmic universalism of the Bible envisages God the creator of the universe in protective relation with his creation. Thus Isaiah could say of him:

> "The humble shall increase their joy in the Lord,
> And the neediest among men shall exult in the Holy
>   One of Israel."[10]

The God worshipped by Israel is the source of joy for all the sons of men in need.

Universality of Mankind

What is man and his function within the framework of cosmic universalism? In the words of Zechariah, the God who stretched forth the heavens and laid the foundation of the earth also "formed the spirit of man within him."[11] Man takes his place in the universal scheme, he is part of the cosmic unity. The same act of creation that established the heavens and the earth also formed the spirit of man. Man stands in community with the rest of creation. This has its specific relevance for man's relation to his fellow. This may be expressed in quasi-biological terms, as was done by Job:

> "If I did despise the cause of my man-servant,
> Or of my maid-servant, when they contended with me—
> What then shall I do when God riseth up?
> And when He remembereth, what shall I answer Him?
> Did not He that made me in the womb make him?
> And did He not fashion us in a like womb?"[12]

All men's existential condition is alike. Their origin is the same. In keeping with the literally, perhaps not altogether unintended, meaning of the Hebrew original, one is even tempted to say that what Job has in mind is the one cosmic womb from which all issues. The passage speaks of the creaturely equality of all, of a communality of being, an ontic universalism. This is a mere statement of fact. As such, it may describe a form of existential relatedness between man and man. It is, however, by itself not sufficient to create a consciously realized relation of responsibility toward others. Yet, Job does speak of such a relation. It is not based on the biological equality alone, but on the fact that the sameness of origin is God-fashioned. Thus existential equality does not stare into one's face as a brute fact, but as the God-intended human condition. It has meaning and value. It makes one responsible, it obligates to justice and fairness toward all. Ontic universalism, because it is God-given, confronts man with the idea of the universality of mankind as an ethical demand.

When Zechariah spoke of God who "formed the spirit of man within him," he formulated in metaphysical terms the same idea of ontic universalism as existential equality grounded in the spirit. Thus he was interpreting the phrase in Genesis that God created man in "his likeness" or in "his image." The same womb and the same image establish the universality of mankind, the brotherhood of men. This finds its clear formulation in the early chapters of Genesis. The essence of man is defined by the image of God; but the image of God is an obligation to brotherhood. Thus, the Bible says: "and at the hand of man, even at the hand of every man's brother, will I require the life of man. Whoso sheddeth man's blood, by man shall his blood be shed; for in the image of God made He man."[13] The image of God makes all men brothers of each other and responsible for each other. Ontic universalism, whether based on creaturely equality or the metaphysical community of the spirit, is ethical. It has to be since both have their root in God's creative act. One might also say that the cosmic universalism with which God confronts his creation becomes ethical universalism with which man ought to confront his fellow man. Not to acknowledge this and act accordingly is an insult to the creator. "He that oppresseth the poor blasphemeth his Maker; but he that is gracious unto the needy honoreth Him."[14] In acknowledging our neighbor we acknowledge God.

Universality of the Law

One of the major consequences that follow from ethical universalism is the principle that there is to be one law for all people living in a given society. There shall be one manner of law for the stranger and the home-born is the biblical command.[15] And as the chief concern of divine justice is the protection of the poor and the easily-oppressed, so the equality before the law demands that the mighty not be revered against the weak, nor the indigenous citizen preferred to against the stranger. According to Deuteronomy, Moses' charge to the judges was:

> "Hear the causes between your brethren, and judge righteously between a man and his brother, and the stranger that is with him. Ye shall not respect persons in judgment; ye shall hear the small and the great alike; ye shall not be afraid of the face of any man. . ."[16]

The obligation toward the stranger is not different from that toward the brother. For even the one who is by the accident of history or society a stranger, as a bearer of the divine image he is yet like unto a brother. Indeed, he is occasionally referred to as such. Thus we read in Leviticus:

> "And if thy brother be waxen poor, and his means fail with thee; then thou shalt uphold him, be he even a stranger or a settler, that he may live with thee."[17]

The stranger and the settler are here actually referred to as "thy brother," whom one should support when he falls on evil days, that he may not just live, but live with thee. The stranger is "the poor" and is to be treated like your own poor. Countless are the biblical warnings against the oppression or the wronging of the stranger in any manner. He is in the same category as orphans and widows of one's own people. Every effort is made in the Bible to remove the stigma of the alien from him. The Israelite ought to know the soul of the stranger, ought to understand his feelings, for he too was a stranger in the land of Egypt. The often recurring reminder that "ye too were strangers" was to impress upon the children of Israel that to be a stranger is a mere accident of history that must not erect barriers between man and man. By mere chance one may be a stranger, but by essential nature a stranger too is like you.

There is no distinction made in the Bible between the legal rights of the stranger and his claim to sympathy and charity. The demand for charity is not much different from that for justice. Both flow from the fundamental equality of all men. Thus in one and the same passage we read of equal justice and equal charity.

"Thou shalt not pervert the justice due to the stranger, or to the fatherless; nor take the widow's raiment to pledge. But thou shalt remember that thou wast a bondman in Egypt, and the Lord thy God redeemed thee thence; therefore I command thee to do this thing.
When thou reapest in the harvest in thy field, and hast forgot a sheaf in the field, thou shalt not go back to fetch it; it shall be for the stranger, for the fatherless, and for the widow; that the Lord thy God may bless thee in all the work of thy hands.
When thou beatest thine olive tree, thou shalt not go over the boughs again; it shall be for the stranger, for the fatherless, and for the widow. When thou gatherest the grapes of thy vineyard thou shalt not glean it after thee; it shall be for the stranger, for the fatherless, and for the widow. And thou shalt remember that thou wast a bondman in the land of Egypt; therefore I command thee to do this thing."[18]

Not only equality before the law is commanded, but equality of treatment in every area of the social and personal realm. This should be no surprise. The equality before the law does not derive from the abstract idea of justice. It is the ontic equality of existence that calls for equality of treatment, be it before the law or in the other fields of inter-human relations. One is familiar with the biblical command that one should love one's neighbor as oneself. However, hardly ever is reference made to the fact that the same command is explicitly repeated for one's relation to the stranger, whom, too, one should love as oneself; for "the stranger that sojourneth with you shall be unto you as the home-born among you."[19]

As often emphasized in the Bible, all this is demanded in the name of God. What one's attitude is to be to a neighbor, how one should treat a stranger, in what manner should justice be administered and charity practiced, it is all determined by faith in God. "For judgment is the Lord's" or "For I am the Lord thy God" are the reasons given for the practice of equality. It is not so much the word of God as the reality of God from which these determinations follow. It is God's creative act and his consequent relation to his creation that conditions the quality of all existence. Because of what God is in the universe, these things ought to prevail among men. From the cosmic universalism of divine creation follows the ethical universalism for the human creature.

Universalism in History and the Chosen People

It is often assumed that the idea of the Chosen People militates against the concept of universalism. It is at times maintained that there are two contradictory tendencies in Judaism: the one prophetic and universalistic; the other, Mosaic and separatist. We have seen that such an assumption is inadmissible. Jewish universalism is inseparable from the Jewish idea of God the Creator and Sustainer and it is found in the Mosaic books no less than in the prophets. On the other hand, the concept of the chosen people is at least as conspicuously present in the prophetic books as in the Mosaic record. Universalism and the idea of the chosenness of Israel permeate the entire biblical tradition. He who does not see both as parts of a consistent whole misses the Judaic position completely.

Before analyzing the meaning of chosenness, let us recall some points which are relevant for our discussion. There is nothing in any of the biblical passages dealing with the chosen people that in any way infringes either on cosmic universalism or on the ontic equality of all men, or on the resulting principle of ethical universalism. There is nothing in the idea of chosenness that would permit any kind of human behavior that violated the universalistic responsibility of the human being. As we have seen, any such behavior would be an insult to the Creator. Even prior to the covenant with Israel, God had made a covenant with Noah and his children, a covenant to endure for their seeds after them.[20] The covenant of a protective providence with the children of men precedes the covenant with the children of Israel and remains in effect for all times. The God who brought the children of Israel out of Egypt has also liberated the Philistines from Caphtor and Aram from Kir.[21] The prophets of Israel are also concerned with the destinies of other nations and prophecy concerning them. Jeremiah is called to be "a prophet for the nations." Isaiah and Ezekiel raise their lamentations for the disasters that befall the mighty nations around them, for Moab and Damascus, for Assyria and Babylon, for Tyre and Egypt. Most impressive is Amos' castigations of Damascus and Gaza, of Tyre and Edom, of Ammon and Moab for their violations of the principles of a universal morality. He does it in the same breath in which he also remonstrates with Judah for its transgressions.[22] Yet, he is the prophet whose message concludes with the prophecy:

> "And I will turn the captivity of My people Israel,
> And they shall build the waste cities and inhabit them;
> And they shall plant vineyards, and drink the wine
>   thereof;
> They shall also make gardens, and eat the fruit of them.
> And I will plant them upon their land,
> And they shall no more be plucked up
> Out of their land which I have given them,
> Saith the Lord thy God."

Such are, too, the words of a great prophet of universalism. Ethical universalism and the election of Israel were no conflicting elements in his world view. Quite clearly, when God chose Israel, he did not abdicate his universal authority or his concern for the rest of mankind. God never ceases addressing himself to all men: "Look unto Me and be ye saved, all the ends of the earth; for I am God, and there is none else."[23]

Why then a chosen people? In our opinion, it is the necessary corollary to universalism. While cosmic universalism indicates the reality of God's relation to the world, while ontic universalism bespeaks the reality of the creaturely condition of man, there is no universalism in the history of man. The only form of universalism that matters in human history is the ethical one. But ethical universalism has no reality. Mankind does not exist as a historic reality, but is an ideal yet to be realized. Indeed, one might say that ethical universalism is the basis of all history. Without it, history can only be the story of the past, the future, only the vain repetition of the heathens. Ethical universalism, because it is an ideal, sets a goal; it creates time as the true future. It creates history as events and things yet to come. But what kind of a strategy is ethical universalism to pursue in its unrealized condition in history? In its biblical form it chooses for itself a people to make the direction manifest toward the envisaged goal. A people it has to be and not individuals. Individuals come and go; a people that endures may consistently crystallize the main features of a direction in history. In this sense, only a people is a historic entity, not an individual. God and Israel entered into the partnership of a covenant. That Israel is to be God's people and God, Israel's God means that a special relation is to be established between God and Israel. The significance of the relation consists in bringing a people into existence whose calling as a people is to know God, to listen to his voice, to keep his commandments and, ultimately, to absorb his Torah into their innermost parts.[24] But since the voice of God is that of cosmic universalism and since the Torah of God is the teaching of ethical universalism, Israel was called by God to live its own life in awareness of the cosmic universalism of the Torah. Israel was chosen by God to be burdened with the universalism of the Torah in the midst of universalism's uncertain destiny in history. This has made Israel a distinct people, a people whose uniqueness consists in anticipating the ultimate goal of ethical universalism as a national responsibility.

That the election of Israel does not imply God's rejection of other nations is born out by the fact that Israel is referred to as God's "first-born" or "the first-fruits of the increase."[25] The "first-born" is never the only son and "the first-fruits" are never all the fruits. We have to bear in mind that Judaism is not only a system of teaching, but a striving for realization. It lives in history. And in history there are always firsts. There is, of course, also rejection in the Bible, but it is completely unrelated to the election of Israel. Not because Israel is chosen is it allowed to inherit the promised land. It is because of "these abominations that God is driving them out from before thee."[26] The root of rejection is to be found in ethical universalism. The unredeemed condition of history, at times, necessitates rejection. That such rejection of others does not—in itself—imply approval of Israel is often emphasized in the Bible. To assume such approval is a form of conceit against which the children of Israel are warned again and again. How independent the chosenness of Israel is from the rejection of other nations is impressively expressed in another passage in Deuteronomy:

> "Speak not thou in thy heart, after that the Lord thy God hath thrust them out from before thee, saying: 'For my righteousness the Lord hath brought me to possess this land'; whereas for the wickedness of these nations the Lord doth drive them out from before thee. Not for thy righteousness, or for thy uprightness of thy heart, dost thou go in to possess their land; But for the wickedness of these nations the Lord thy God doth drive them out from before thee. . . . Know therefore that it is not for thy righteousness that the Lord thy God giveth thee this good land to possess it; for thou art a stiffnecked people."[27]

This text is most revealing. It speaks of "the Lord thy God"; but he must be also the God of other nations for he judges them. If he judges them, he expects them to adhere to a universal code. He must be watching them and is waiting for them. On the other hand, even though he is "the Lord thy God," he indulges in no partiality toward Israel, "for thou art a stiffnecked people." We know what this means in the Bible. "The Lord thy God" judges his chosen people no less than he judges the other peoples. As other nations were driven out of their land because of their wickedness, so may God's chosen people lose the promised land for the same reason. Ethical universalism "considers no person." It is, indeed, universal in its critical application. It is even more critical of the chosen one than of others, for the chosen one should have known better. As Amos puts it:

"You only have I known of all the families of the earth; therefore I will visit upon you all your iniquities."[28]

The English rendering is somewhat misleading. God has, of course, known all the families of the earth. The Hebrew meaning of "to know" is to love, to be close, to be associated. Because of the covenant with Israel, God is more demanding of Israel.

The election of Israel is a tactical move in the time-bound strategy of cosmic universalism. Israel is God's instrument in the strategy, by which God's theme is introduced, not into synagogues or churches, but into history. Israel is chosen for the sake of a mankind yet to come into being. But this is a process that develops in historic time. The messianic goal, toward which history is moving according to the Bible, is the emergence of mankind as a fact. The messianic goal, which is envisaged at "the end of days," is described in many different ways, yet all the descriptions have one common theme, i.e., the transformation of the ideal of ethical universalism into reality. It is the goal that, for the first time in human history, held up before the eyes of man the vision of eternal peace as expressed in Isaiah's inspired words:

"And He shall judge between the nations,
And shall decide for many peoples;
And they shall beat their swords into plowshares,
And their spears into pruning hooks;
Nation shall not lift up sword against nation,
Neither shall they learn war any more."[29]

In the light of the messianic process, the chosenness of Israel seems to be a temporary affair. Not that Israel is to be replaced by another chosen one. If exile, which is visited upon Israel, is rejection, all the prophets are one in their affirmation that God will return to Israel and Israel to God; the end of the days will also see the comforting of Israel. The chosenness of Israel is temporary because the goal of history is to choose all nations. "And many nations shall join themselves to the Lord in that day and shall be My people," says God.[30] God means to choose his priests from among all the nations.[31] Within this frame of reference history is moving toward the time when "Israel will be the third with Egypt and Assyria, a blessing in the midst of the earth; for that the Lord of hosts hath blessed him saying: 'Blessed be Egypt My people and Assyria the work of My hands, and Israel mine inheritance.' "[32] Messianic universalism is the fulfillment of ethical universalism in history, the establishment of this earth as the Kingdom of God, when God will be king over all the earth.[33] We have commenced our discussion with cosmic universalism, which is founded in God's relation to the universe, in his creative act and his sustaining concern. We conclude with the insight that in messianic fulfillment, cosmic universalism becomes the order of history, relating man to man, nation to nation, and mankind to the rest of creation. The thought found its expression in the words of Isaiah:

> "And the wolf shall dwell with the lamb,
> And the leopard shall lie down with the kid;
> And the calf and the young lion and the fatling together;
> And a little child shall lead them.
> And the cow and the bear shall feed;
> Their young ones shall lie down together;
> And the lion shall eat straw like the ox.
> And the sucking child shall play on the hole of the asp,
> And the weaned child shall put his hand on the basilisk's
>   den.
> They shall not hurt nor destroy
> In all my holy mountain;
> For the earth shall be full of the knowledge of the Lord,
> As the waters cover the sea."[34]

Messianic universalism is cosmic universalism turned history in its final realization of its God-implanted theme.

It is a point still to be noted that messianic universalism does not require a uniform mankind in which all nations lose their identity. Israel remains Israel as Egypt and Assyria retain their identity. Only because of that does the unity among them represent "a blessing in the earth." The texts speak of the *nations* that shall go up to the mountain of the Lord. The *nations* shall seek the Lord and follow him.[35] The very essence of the messianic age is that universalism is realized without the surrendering of identity. Does it mean that all mankind will ultimately accept Judaism? The question is not a biblical one. It cannot be asked within the frame of reference of biblical ideas. Judaism is not a religion, but the way of life of the Jew. Judaism made Israel what it is. It is not possible for the nations to accept Judaism and yet retain their respective individualities. An acceptance of Judaism would make all mankind Israel. This is not anticipated. What is hoped for is that the nations will acknowledge God and walk in his ways. In the same context in which the prophets speak of "the end of days," when the peoples shall "flow to the mountain of the Lord, to the house of the God of Jacob," they also say:

> "For let all the peoples walk each one in the name of
>   its God,
> But we will walk in the name of the Lord our God for
>   ever and ever."[36]

"Its God" is the God of the universe, just as "the Lord our God" is the God of all creation. For it is the God of Jacob of whose ways the nations will desire to learn. "Its God" is each nation's specific way, its specific relation to the God of All.

II. THE TALMUDIC TRADITION

God and Israel

The Talmudic tradition is based on the biblical one. It is its interpretation and application to a given situation. The outstanding feature of this tradition with regard to our present discussion is the consciousness of the uniqueness of Israel. Israel is a people unlike other peoples. During the biblical period this uniqueness was emerging gradually into historic reality. In talmudical times it is the established fact of Jewish existence. However, as in the Bible so in the Talmud, the uniqueness of Israel does not involve the rejection of the rest of mankind. In a striking passage the great talmudic teacher Rabbi Akiba affirms at the same time the existential dignity of every human being as well as the specific status of Israel. This is how he puts it:

> "Beloved is man, for he was created in the image of God: it is by special divine love that he is informed that he was created in the image of God, as it is said: 'For God made him in his own image.' Beloved are Israel, for they were called the children of God; it is by special divine love that they are informed that they were called the children of God, as it is said: You are the children of the Lord your God. Beloved are Israel, for to them was given a precious instrument (the Torah); it is by special divine love that they are informed that to them was given the precious instrument through which the world was created, as it is said: 'For I give you good doctrine; forsake not my Torah.' "[37]

The added dignity of Israel is due to the fact that the Jews are the recipients of the Torah. The basic dignity of man, however, is unconditional; it is the image of God in which all men are created. The image of God, bestowed upon man, is here seen as an expression of divine love for all men. This love is irrevocable as is the image of God itself. It is rather interesting to note that whereas it is normal biblical usage to call God "the

Lord your God" or "the Lord our God," at least in one significant passage the teachers of the Talmud seem to take a critical look at the phraseology. In the famous passage of "Hear, O Israel" it is said, "the Lord our God, the Lord is One." It is asked, why should God be referred to as "our God." That he is one should be an adequate statement concerning him. A number of other passages are quoted in the same context which make reference to God as "your God" or the "God of Israel." The same question is asked: the designation "the Lord" alone says it all, why should one refer to him as "yours"? Two answers are offered. One explanation is that his association with Israel is closer than with other nations; the other is that he is our God now, but he will be the one God of all mankind in times to come.[38] The monotheistic association with God gives distinction to Israel; it does not, however, devaluate the intrinsic dignity of all other men. This distinction of Israel beside the universal dignity of the human being seems to have occupied a great deal the minds of the rabbis. They are not satisfied to see the chosenness of Israel as a one-sided affair. Basing themselves on biblical interpretation, they maintain that it was not only God who chose Jacob, but Jacob, too, chose the Holy One, blessed be He.[39] To be chosen and to choose are complementary to each other. He who chooses is chosen and he who is chosen also chooses. Thus they could also say that "the Holy One blessed be He does not disqualify any one of his creatures. The gates are always open; every one who wishes to enter may do so."[40]

The Unity of Mankind

Notwithstanding the specific relation in which Israel stands to God, the unity of the human race is strongly affirmed. It is said of Abraham that he made all men into a brotherhood.[41] This does not mean that as the result of Abraham's life work the brotherhood of men became a reality. The meaning is that Abraham laid the ideological foundation for universal brotherhood. In a polytheistic society men derive their origin from various deities; they know not of a common origin. But when Abraham introduced the One God of monotheism into history, the families of men became one in their common origin and their common dignity as God's creatures. On several occasions the rabbis discussed the question why man was created "alone," why the history of the human race was started with a single human being. One of the answers they gave was: so that he may not be misled into thinking that there was more than one creator. The single creature requires a single creator and, vice versa, the One Creator guarantees the oneness of creation and, thus, the unity of the race of men. And so it is also said that man was created one that no one should be able to say to his neighbor, my father is greater than your father, I am of nobler descent.[42] Nowhere in the Talmud is the fundamental unity of mankind in doubt. It could not be since, as in the biblical tradition, it follows from the basic faith in the One God. The idea of unity is affirmed even when it requires application to the enemies of Israel. In one passage it is couched in the following language: "At the time when the children of Israel were crossing the Red Sea (and the Egyptians were perishing), the angels of the Lord—as is their daily wont—were preparing to sing hymns unto God. The Holy One, blessed be He interrupted them saying: 'The works of My hand are drowning in the sea and you desire to sing my praise?' "[43] In this manner the rabbis gave expression to their idea that one should not rejoice at the defeat of even one's deadliest enemy for he, too, is "the work of God's hands." At one time of very severe persecution by the Romans, the Jewish representatives pleaded with the authorities saying: "Are we not all brothers! Are we not all the children of the same father and mother!"[44] This was not only a politically opportune way of pleading one's cause. The idea of the brotherhood of all men is too deeply embedded in the Judaic tradition of Bible and Talmud.

The Value of Man

The starting of the human race by the creation of one man by the One Creator also determines the value of every individual life. The question we have mentioned earlier is also answered in this fashion: "Man was created alone to teach you that he who preserves the life of a single person is like one who preserves a whole world and he who destroys a single life is as if he had destroyed a whole world."[45] The entire human race derives from one couple; thus every human being may be the progenitor of an entire race. It is, of course, assumed that existence itself is a good; and so it must be, since it is God's creation. However, the value of man is not only based on his biological potential, but also on his capacity for a meaningful life. If, as we saw, the Bible anticipates the time when God will choose his priests from among all nations, the Talmudic tradition seems to assume that those days are already with us. Thus, on the verse in the Psalms, "Let Thy priests be clothed with righteousness"[46] the rabbis make the comment: "These are the righteous of the nations of the world. For they are priests unto the Holy One, blessed be He, already in this world."[47] The emphasis here on "already in this world" is noteworthy. That this will be the case in a future time, in the end of days, it was never doubted by Judaism, but it was a bold statement to make that it was happening at a contemporary moment. Actual references are made to historic personalities as examples of God's priests of righteousness among the gentiles.

The distinguished Mishnaic teacher, Rabbi Meir, makes the statement that even a gentile who occupies himself with the Torah is like the High Priest. For of the Torah it is said: "which if a man do, he shall live by them."[48] It is not said, "which an Israelite do," but "a man," any human being.[49] This text is, of course, rather restrictive as compared with the previous one. The recognition of the gentile is made dependent on the Torah. It should however be noted that one cannot be righteous without "Torah." We place the word between quotes because we do not mean the Torah of Israel. Judaism knows of a Torah of the gentiles, the seven commandments of the son of Noah. One cannot be a righteous man without it. Everyone must have a "Torah." Indeed, in one Talmudic passage the statement of Rabbi Meir is explained as referring to "the seven commandments."[50]

What seems to be decisive for the teachers of the Talmud is not so much the religious belief as the actions of a person. A statement put into the mouth of the prophet Elijah declares: "I call to witness heaven and earth that be one a Jew or a gentile, man or woman, male or female slave, the holy spirit rests upon a person in accordance with one's deeds."[51] A characteristic midrashic passage takes the form of interpreting the verse in Psalms: "No good thing will He withhold from them that walk uprightly (literally: in wholeheartedness)."[52] This is the comment of the rabbis:

> He that walks "in wholeheartedness" is Abraham. To him were the words addressed: "Walk before Me and be wholehearted." But if the verse meant only Abraham, why the plural form, "them that walk in wholeheartedness"? This teaches us that as in the case of Abraham, who because he walked in wholeheartedness before the Holy One blessed be He, God became his shield, so it happens to everyone who walks before Him in wholeheartedness, God becomes his shield. And how does the text continue? "O Lord of hosts, happy is the man that trusteth in Thee." Abraham is not mentioned here, but "man"; it applies to any man.[53]

Quite clearly it is assumed that one need not be a Jew in order to walk before God "in wholeheartedness." Any man is capable of it. But one can hardly imagine a nobler Jewish confirmation of the potential for the godly life present in all men than the comparison to the patriarch Abraham.

A Universal Law

The Torah, even though it was given to Israel, has universal validity. In fact, according to talmudic teaching, originally it was not intended for

Israel alone, but for all mankind. According to a midrashic passage, God first went with the Torah from nation to nation, offering it to each one of them. It happened, however, that its contents was not in keeping with their natural inclination and desires and they rejected God's gift to them.[54] In this manner the teachers of the Talmud expressed the idea that the Torah has universal significance and is waiting to this day to be acknowledged by all men. The idea is also connected with the manner of the revelation at Sinai. The Torah was given in the desert and not in the promised land. Had it been given in the land of Israel, the nations might have said: this does not concern us; we have no share in it. Instead the Torah was given in a public assembly in the no-man's land of a desert, thus indicating that anyone who so desires may approach and receive it.[55] But more significant is the fact that the rabbis assumed that certain basic ethical principles were dictated by universal reason and should have been obligatory upon all men independently of any divine revelation. It is said of them, "even if they had not been written down (in the Torah), it would have been proper for them to be accepted." There are unwritten principles of human conduct which ought to be considered a universal law. Forbidden to men are: idolatry (which in biblical times especially was associated with perverse sexual and sacrificial practices, the "abominations" referred to in the Bible), blasphemy, adultery and incest, murder, and robbery.[56] Indeed, these are the core of a "Torah" of the gentiles. Two more principles are added to them to form the "Seven Commandments of the Son of Noah." The two are the establishment of a just judiciary and the prohibition to partake of the limb of a living animal.[57] One might see in these principles the talmudic requirement of a universally binding natural law. According to some opinion in the Talmud certain aspects of such a minimal natural law one may find manifested even in the behavior of some animals, so that even without the Torah one might learn from the animal world.[58] There is therefore a universal "Torah" of reason and nature in existence for all mankind. He who adheres to it is deserving of salvation. Thus it is stated that the pious of all the nations have a share in the world to come.[59]

However, more than on reason and nature, the universality of a fundamental ethical code is based on divine example and the *imitatio dei*, following from it. Commenting on the words of *Ecclesiastes*, "God seeketh that which is pursued," the masters elaborate: "The wicked pursues the righteous—God seeketh the pursued; the righteous pursues the righteous—God seeketh the pursued; the wicked pursues the wicked— God seeketh the pursued; and even when the righteous pursues the wicked—God seeketh the pursued. Always God seeketh the pursued."[60]

But God, of course, represents the universal principle that is to be followed by all men toward all men. "As He is gracious so shalt thou be gracious; as He is merciful so shalt thou be merciful; as He is holy, so shalt thou be holy."[61] This is a general principle of human behavior which is incumbent upon all in all their dealings, not only with their fellow men, but with every creature on earth. When Job wonders how he could answer God, should he despise the cause of his servants, the rabbis placed his words in the mouth of the world's universal spirit (Sar Ha'Olam), addressing it to all men: "when God arises to judge the world, who can stand! And why does God arise to judge?—'For the oppression of the poor, for the sighing of the needy, now will I arise,' saith the Lord."[62] The importance of the observance of the universal law of ethics is illustrated by the comparison of two biblical stories: the one, the story of the flood; the other, the story of the tower of Babel. Both were rebellious and wicked people, yet their punishment was very different. The generation of the flood perished altogether, wheras that of the tower of Babel were only scattered over the face of the earth. The explanation is given that the people of the flood sinned against each other. They were steeped in robbery and violent crimes against each other, therefore they were completely annihilated. At the tower of Babel men rebelled against God, but lived in harmony with each other, therefore they were, though punished, yet permitted to survive.[63] This too is a thought deeply rooted in talmudic teaching. It has been formulated as a general principle by Rabbi Gamaliel, the son of Rabbi Yehuda Ha'Nassi, who said: "From the Heavens mercy is shown to one who has mercy on his fellow men (lit., creatures); but no mercy is shown to one who does not act mercifully toward his fellows."[64]

It may be advisable to list here some of the rules meant to guide human behavior toward all, as an illustration of the universality of ethical obligations toward one's fellow. These are sayings by various teachers which have been embodied in a tractate of the Mishnah which to this day is read and studied by Jews regularly as a volume of ethics. We select some of the many relevant ones almost at random.

> "Judge all men favorably.
> Be of the disciples of Aaron, loving peace and pursuing peace; be one who loves his fellow men (lit., all creatures) and draws them near to the Torah.
> The evil eye (envy), the evil impulse, and hatred of mankind shorten a man's life.
> Receive all men cheerfully.
> Do not despise any man, and do not consider anything as impossible;

for there is not a man who has not his hour, and there is not a thing that
has not its place.
Meet every man with a friendly greeting.
Who is wise? He who learns from every man.
Who is honored? He who honors his fellow men."[65]

We find most revealing the last statement because of the reason given
for asserting it. Why is the one honored who honors his fellow men? For
it is written:[66] "Those who honor me I will honor, and those who despise
me shall be lightly esteemed." Now this verse is not about honoring man,
but about honoring God. Obviously, the rabbis understood the honoring
of man to be the equivalent of honoring God. This is a familiar talmudical
concept. It derives from the fact that every human being is a bearer of
the divine image in which he was created. Some of the sages of the Talmud
would rise before any old man out of respect for the many vicissitudes
that might have passed over him. Others would give their hands to help
an old man along his way; others again would send their servants to assist
him. The biblical command, "Thou shall rise before a hoary head," was
understood to include any old man, without discrimination of race, religion, or social status.[67] The most venerable among the rabbis would go
out of his way to show respect to the lowliest among the aged. Finally, let
us recall a saying by one of the later talmudic teachers who was wont to
enjoin it on his disciples: "Be soft in answering; assuage anger; talk peace
to your brothers and relatives, and to every human being, even to a
gentile in the market place; that you be beloved on high and desired
below, and accepted by the people."[68]

Discrimination and Ethical Universalism

There are, however, a number of discriminatory laws in the Talmud
directed against the Akum.[69] One must not steal from him or cheat him,
but neither should one return a find to him as is obligatory in the case of a
Jew. If the animal of a Kanaanite, i.e., Akum, damages the animal of an
Israelite, the Kanaanite—as is the Jewish law—pays for the damage; but
in the reverse case, when the animal of the Israelite damages that of a
Kanaanite, the Israelite does not pay, as is the Kanaanite law.[70] There
are a few more laws of a similar nature. One might say that the general
principle is that one must not harm an Akum, but neither is one permitted to do anything from which any advantage may accrue to the
Akum. Who are the Akum? They are gentiles. But not all gentiles are
Akum. Quite clearly these discriminatory regulations do not apply to a
gentile who observes the code of natural law, the Seven Commandments, which we have discussed earlier. Are they idolators? They are, but

not all idol worshippers are subject to these laws. One must examine these rules against the *Akum* in the light of other rules whose purpose is to eliminate all discrimination. There is, for instance, an entire group of regulations whose purpose is to foster peaceful relations between Jew and *Akum*. One should support the poor of the *Akum* together with the Jewish poor. One should visit their sick as one visits the Jewish sick. One should bury their dead as one is obligated to do with the Jewish dead.[71] Even more impressive is the rule that obligates the guardians of a city in which Jews and *Akum* live together not only to support all poor indiscriminately, but also to tax Jew and *Akum* alike for their support. One should also eulogize the dead of the *Akum* as one eulogizes Jewish dead and comfort their mourners as one comforts Jewish mourners. All this is to be done "for the sake of the ways of peace." The significance of this reason is all the more important, since in the same context, it is also asserted that the whole of the *Torah* exists "for the sake of the ways of peace."[72]

How then are these two groups of regulations to be reconciled, the one discriminatory, the other universal? We have seen that *Akum* are gentiles, but not all gentiles are *Akum*. Now we must conclude that these discriminatory regulations did not apply to all *Akum*, only to some of them, to a certain group among them. According to one talmudic opinion the concept *Akum* applies only to the Kanaanites and their descendants in the land of Israel. Rabbi Hiyya the son of Rabbi Abba said in the name of Rabbi Yohanan (approx. end of second century of the Christian era): Gentiles outside the land of Israel are not to be considered *Akum*. Their practices are only "the customs of their fathers in their hands."[73] In other words, they do not represent a consciously realized faith. We must also add that those customs as such were not ethically objectionable, otherwise they could not have been dismissed so lightly. The discriminatory regulations would then represent a very old tradition, applicable to a certain type of *Akum*, one moreover which did not exist outside the land of Israel during the later phase of the talmudic period. On the other hand, to all the other *Akum*, even if they did not observe all the Seven Commandments, applied the non-discriminatory rules of "the ways of peace."

A number of other regulations bear out this distinction. Thus it was forbidden to sell an *Akum* wild animals or any kind of object that was capable of causing damage to the public. This was done in order to protect the public. The *Akum* was not trusted to be conscientiously concerned about the public welfare and would not take adequate care of the dangerous animals or other objects in his possession. The *Akum* was also suspect of easily resorting to murder. Therefore a Jew was advised to take adequate precaution when walking on the road with an *Akum*. A number of other precautionary measures were recommended in all kinds of situations in order to be on one's guard against the *Akum*.[74] An *Akum* was a dangerous person. Since, as we saw, it was clearly stated that the gentiles outside of the land of Israel were not to be considered *Akum*, the *Akum* that was meant was a historically known group of anti-social and barbarous people. But apart from that historically definable group, the universally valid ethical code was to be applied to all gentiles and to all other *Akum*. The "discrimination" was ethical condemnation of a group of outcasts. That this is so is shown by the fact that occasionally even Jews were considered *Akum*. It is stated that one must not push an *Akum* into a pit where he may perish. But if an *Akum* has fallen into a pit, one should not make the effort to save him. Needless to say that this cannot mean the *Akum* whose poor one must support as one supports the Jewish poor and whose sick one should visit and whose mourners one must comfort. Meant are obviously the other type of anti-social *Akum*. Significant, however, is the addition that this rule also applies to the Jewish sheep-herders. Neither should they be helped.[75] Now this did not mean that all shepherds were condemned at all times. Obviously, the rule referred to a definite time and a definite place when and where sheep-herders—Jews or gentile—were anti-social dangerous outcasts. Such a Jew was treated like an *Akum*.

This leads us to a passage in the Talmud which actually gives us a definition of the *Akum* against whom discrimination was practiced. In a remarkable passage we are told that the rabbis taught that one must not sell the *Akum* any lethal weapons. This was an old tradition to which a later teacher added: As it is forbidden to sell to an *Akum*, so it is also forbidden to sell weapons to Jewish brigands. But now the question is asked: "What kind of brigand is he? Is he capable of murder, then it is obvious that it is so. Such a Jew is an *Akum*!"[76] The question is, what need is there to state explicitly that the rule applies to the Jewish brigands as well. It was implicit in the original statement. Noteworthy is not only the statement that such a Jew was an *Akum*, but the surprise that it had to be explicitly so maintained. It was taken for granted that a Jewish brigand, likely to commit murder, was an *Akum*. This was assumed to be so well known that it required no specific affirmation. We conclude that the *Akum* of the discriminatory legislation is neither a racial concept— it does not mean the gentile—nor is it a religious one—it does not mean the follower of another religion; it is an ethical concept—an anti-social, dangerous gentile or Jew, against whom society has to be protected. One might say that it was the acknowledgment of ethical universalism, the acceptance of a universally binding code of natural law that brought about the singling out of a distinctive group—in a certain limited sense—as having placed themselves outside the equality demanded by that law. Ideologically there is no conflict between a universal law and the discriminatory regulations for an ethically defined group of Akum. On the contrary, it is the rigorous application of the universal law that is responsible for the exception.

The term Akum also has a purely religious connotation, meaning the follower of an idolatrous religion. There are rules which prescribe certain forms of conduct toward him. However, those rules have an exclusively religious significance. In general, their purpose is to enjoin the Jew to refrain from any activity that may permit the Akum to increase his respect for his god.[77] Not even indirectly must the Jew be responsible for the enhancement of the hold that the false gods may have upon their followers. As to the treatment of the Akum, however, the universality of the ethical law must not be impaired.

Common Destiny

The rabbis were willing to acknowledge the value of a social order that was not based either on Judaism or even on a non-Jewish faith in God. Gentile societies were esteemed for their humane and civilized qualities. It is well-known that, according to the Bible, at the end of the six days of creation God looked upon the world and beheld that it was very good. Said one of the rabbis: "Behold it was good," that is, the kingdom of heaven (i.e., a world order ruled by God); but "very good" is the earthly kingdom (i.e., the one ruled by man). But is it really so? Is the earthly kingdom indeed very good? The answer is: "Yes! For it espouses the cause of the oppressed." One must of course qualify the statement by saying: When it espouses the cause of the oppressed. Interesting, however, is the biblical "proof" which is adduced in support of the idea. It is the rather innocuous verse from Isaiah, "I, even I, have made the earth, and created man upon it."[78] The rabbi's interpretation is: I have made the earth, says God; what counts, however, is the man whom I placed upon it. The value of the man-made order in society recalls the Hobbesian saying of the Mishnah: "Pray for the welfare of the government, since were it not for the fear of it men would swallow each other alive."[79] According to one interpretation of certain passages in Ezekiel, the prophet was remonstrating with Israel for having forsaken the laws of the Torah for those of the nations. They are most severely criticized for having followed the laws of the uncivilized among the nations. If only they had adopted the ways of some other civilized order of society![80] Numerous other passages show that the teachers of the Talmud had a fair appreciation of the values of a secular society based on universal humane principles. Such an order was not the ideal for Jews, but it had its place of respect within the universal scheme of things.

Such appreciation must have derived from their insight into the interconnectedness of all human destinies. On the New Year, which is the Day of Judgment in the Jewish calendar, preceding the Day of Atonement, not only Israel is being judged, but all the world. Individuals and cities, provinces and entire countries, nations and the entire world are judged. In the final balance, all destinies are inter-dependent, all share in the judgment of all.[81] This realization of the inter-dependence of human destinies goes so far that one of the rabbis expressed the opinion that any misfortune that befalls the Jews alone is not a real misfortune. Only one which is shared by the Jews and the nations of the earth is a true misfortune.[82] The meaning is that problems which may afflict the Jews alone are easily soluble; the real problem arises when the Jewish tribulation is part of an affliction from which other nations suffer too. One might see in this statement the seed of a philosophy of Jewish history which interprets the Jewish experience in the context of a wider universal experience. It may well be applied to the latest world misfortune that overtook the Jewish people on the nazified European continent. Notwithstanding their insight into a common world destiny, the rabbis nevertheless recognized that Israel holds a unique position in the universal context. For they also said: When evil times befall the world, the first to feel it is Israel; when the good is near Israel again is the first to sense it.[83] Universal destiny is reflected in the national destiny of the Jew.

Summary

Notwithstanding the God-anchored cosmic universalism, which man is to translate into the ethical universalism realized in history, Judaism is seen as the superior religion. It is, however, considered superior not because it is the faith of the Jew, but because it is faith in the One God, the Creator and sustainer of the universe. Because of Judaism Israel is a unique people, but this uniqueness is not due to any racial characteristics, but depends on the acceptance of the Torah and the special relation between Israel and God. Israel is a nation formed by the Torah. However, its uniqueness is not one of achievement, but one of responsibility. This is what is meant by the election of Israel.

The election does not represent the rejection of other nations. God remains the Creator and the father of all even after the election of Israel. Israel was elected by God and it elected God. The same road is open to all men. The gates are forever open and all who wish to enter may do so and will be received. This does not require of the nations to accept Judaism, but it does require the acceptance of a universal natural law which is formulated in the Seven Commandments of the Sons of Noah. Israel is not the only son, but only the first-born. Others are to follow. Ultimately all will be chosen.

If any one is rejected, it is not because of the election of Israel, but because he has been judged by the standards of a universal code. But so is Israel judged by the standards of the *Torah*. Not the gentile is rejected but the ethically objectionable, and Israel, too, is often judged and found wanting. Can Israel be rejected? Yes: it has ofen been rejected temporarily. But the covenant with God is not to be severed. The people that is rejected in the light of the *Torah* still stands in that light. Being found wanting by the measuring rod of the *Torah*, it remains the people of the *Torah* in its very failure.

Cosmic universalism is a divine reality, but a human ideal; thus the election of Israel is maintained in history in the context of the ideal. If there is a goal in history, in the light of cosmic universalism it can only be the broadening of the base of election until it becomes all-comprehensive. Uniqueness thus affirms the universality of the ethical principle, binding upon all in their dealings with all. Will cosmic universalism ever become the reality of the human condition in history? Will it ever be accomplished? And how will it be accomplished: by human effort, by miraculous divine intervention, by cooperation between God and Man? Jewish tradition is open to interpretation on this point. According to one opinion in the *Talmud* the Messiah will come when all deserve it or when all will be guilty. But come he will; God is the guarantor.

One more point should be recalled. Jewish universalism is not cosmopolitan. God may deal with individuals in the privacy of their personal lives, but world history is enacted by nations and through nations. Israel too is a nation and not a church. It is a nation formed by the word of God; the only nation on earth that came into being in this manner. This is why it is called Am Adonai, the people of God. A church signifies the personal relation between God and the individual. God's people make manifest the relation between God and the history of mankind. The nations are not to disappear but are to be reconciled to each other; the history making forces are not to be eliminated, but are to be harmonized with each other.

Jewish universalism found its most solemn expression in the ancient liturgy of the High Holy Days, which to this day is recited by every believing Jew on those days of awe. In conclusion we let a passage from that liturgy convey its own message:

"Now, Lord our God, put thy awe upon all whom thou hast made, thy dread upon all whom thou hast created; let thy works revere thee, let all thy creatures worship thee; may they all blend into one brotherhood to do thy will with a perfect heart. For we know, Lord our God, that thine is dominion, power and might; thou art revered above all that thou hast created.

Now, O Lord, grant honor to thy people, glory to those who revere thee, hope to those who seek thee, free speech to those who yearn for thee, joy to thy land and gladness to thy city, rising strength to David, thy servant, a shining light to the son of Jesse, thy chosen one, speedily in our days.

May now the righteous see this and rejoice, the upright exult, and the godly thrill with delight. Iniquity shall shut its mouth, wickedness shall vanish like smoke, when thou wilt abolish the rule of tyranny on earth.

Thou shalt reign over all whom thou hast made, thou alone, O Lord, on Mount Zion the abode of thy majesty, in Jerusalem thy holy city, as it is written in thy holy Scriptures: 'The Lord shall reign forever, your God, O Zion, for all generations.' "

NOTES

1. Psalms, 19,2.
2. Ibid., 96, 1.
3. Ibid., 150, 6.
4. Ibid., 103, 19.
5. Isaiah, 40, 26. While we normally use the translation of the J. P. S., the line "No one is missing" is our own rendering, intended to bring out our interpretation more clearly.
6. Psalms, 145, 9.
7. Deuteronomy, 10, 17-19.
8. Psalms, 9, 9.
9. Genesis, 18, 25, 20-21.
10. Isaiah, 29, 19.
11. Zechariah, 12, 1.
12. Job, 31, 13-15. We depart here from the usual rendering, "And did not One fashion us in the womb." We feel that our translation does more justice to the Hebrew syntax.
13. Genesis, 9, 5-6.
14. Proverbs, 14, 31.

15. Leviticus, 24, 22.

16. Deuteronomy, 1, 17-18.

17. Leviticus, 25, 36. While we normally use the J. P. S. translation, our deviation in this text brings our rendering closer to the AV. We believe that our rendering is the correct one. It is also in keeping with the way the text was understood by Judaism. See *Torat Kohanim*, loc. cit.; Talmud Babli, Pesahim, 21/6, and numerous other Talmudical passages.

18. Deuteronomy, 24, 17-22.

19. Leviticus, 20, 34.

20. Genesis, 9, 9.

21. Amos, 9, 7.

22. Ibid., chapters 1 and 2.

23. Isaiah, 45, 22.

24. Cf. Deuteronomy, 26, 18; 27, 9; 28, 9; 29, 12; Jeremiah, 7, 23; 24, 7; 31, 32; Ezekiel, 11, 20; etc.

25. Exodus, 4, 22; Jeremiah, 2, 3.

26. Deuteronomy, 18, 12.

27. Ibid., 9, 4-6.

28. Amos, 3, 2.

29. Isaiah, 2, 4.

30. Zechariah, 2, 14.

31. Isaiah, 66, 21.

32. Ibid., 19, 24-25.

33. Zechariah, 14, 9.

34. Isaiah, 11, 6-9.

35. Cf., Isaiah, 2, 2; Zechariah, 8, 20; 2, 14; etc.

36. Micah, 4, 5.

37. Aboth, 3, 18.

38. Sifrei, 6, 31.

39. Ibid., 312.

40. Sm'moth Rabba, 19, 4.

41. B'reshith Rabba, 39, 1.

42. Talmud Babli, Sanhedrin, 38/b, 37/a.

43. Ibid., 39/b and Sh'moth Rabba, 20.

44. Talmud Babli, Ta'anith, 18/a.

45. Ibid., Sanhedrin, 37/a. The version in the Mishnah is: "He who preserves the life of a Jew," etc. The context, however, shows clearly that not a Jew is meant, but any human being. The idea derives from the fact that the human race developed from a single person and that when Cain killed his brother "the bloods of all the generations that might have descended from Abel cried to heaven." Indeed, Maimonides quotes the text as follows: "Man was created alone to teach you that he who destroys a single life is as if he had destroyed a whole world; and he who preserves a single life is as if he had preserved a whole world" (Sanhedrin, ch. 12, 3).

46. Psalms, 132, 9.

47. Tanna debe' Eliyahu Zuta, 20.

48. Leviticus, 18, 5.

49. Talmud Babli, Baba Kama, 38/a; Abodah Zarah, 3/a; Sanhedrin, 59/a.

50. Ibid., Sanhedrin, loc. cit.

51. Tanna debe' Eliyahu Rabba, 10.

52. Psalms, 84, 12.

53. Midrash T'hillim, 1, 1.

54. Sifrei, Deuteronomy, 343.

55. M'chilta, Exodus, 19, 2.

56. Talmud Babli, Yoma, 67/b.

57. Ibid., Sanhedrin, 56/a and Shir Ha-Shirim Rabba, 1,16.

58. Ibid., Erubin, 100/b.

59. Ibid., Sanhedrin, 105/a.

60. Vayikra Rabba, 27, 5; Tanhuma, Emor, 9.

61. Talmud Babli, Soteh, 14/a; Sifrei, 49.

62. Shmot Rabba, 17, 4.

63. B'reshith Rabba, 38, 6.

64. Talmud Babli, Shabbath, 151/b.

65. Talmud, Aboth, the chapters 1, 6; 1, 12; 2, 16; 3, 16; 4, 3; 4, 20; 4, 1.

66. I Samuel, 2, 30.

67. Leviticus 19, 32 and Talmud Babli, Kiddushin, 33/a.

68. Talmud Babli, B'rahoth, 17/a.

69. Akum is the acrostic of the words, Obdei Kocharim Umazaloth, worshippers of the stars and the planets.

70. Talmud Babli, Baba Kama, 114/b and 37/b.

71. Talmud Babli, Gittin, 59/a. In this passage not Akum is mentioned, but a stranger, a gentile. Since, however, in the same context in the preceding Mishnah—ibid., 58/b—Akum occurs and so also in the Tosefta that we quote in the text, we conclude that Akum is included there in the concept of the gentile.

72. Ibid., 58/b.

73. Ibid., Hulin, 13/b.

74. Ibid., Abodah Zara, 16/a and b; 22/a; 25/b; etc.

75. Ibid., 26/b.

76. Ibid., 15/b.

77. Cf., for instance, the first Mishnah in Talmud, Abodah Zarah.

78. Isaiah, 45, 12.

79. Talmud, Aboth, 3, 2.

80. Talmud Babli, Sanhedrin, 39/b.

81. Maimonides, based on the Talmud, Hilchot T'shubah, 3, 1.

82. Debarim Rabba, 2, 14.

83. Eicha Rabbathi, 2.

FOUR

The Concept of
Mankind in Islam

S. D. GOITEIN

Emeritus Professor, Department
of Oriental Studies
University of Pennsylvania

"WHAT SHALL I DO, OH MUSLIMS?! FOR I DO NOT RECOGNIZE myself."

"I am neither a Christian, nor a Jew, nor a Gabr, nor a Muslim."

"I am not of the East, nor of the West, nor of the land, nor of the sea."

"I am not of India, nor of China, nor of the city of Bulghar, nor of that of Saqsin."

"I am not of the kingdom of the two Iraqs, nor of the country of Khorasan."

"My place is the Placeless, my trace is the Traceless;"

"It is neither body nor soul, for I belong to the soul of souls."

These famous lines of the Persian mystic Jalal al-Din Rumi (1207-1273) emphasize that with the attainment of union with God all differences of religion, race or domicile are dissolved into insignificance. When man fully becomes man, a true image of God, mankind becomes one, like God himself.

Islamic religion had to traverse many stages of transformation until it reached the degree of sophistication revealed in the verses of Jalal al-Din Rumi quoted above. The concept of mankind, however, was inherent in it from its very beginnings. The vision of the totality of human beings assembled before the throne of the heavenly judge on the Day of Resurrection dominated the imagination of the founder of Islam from the very outset of his prophetical mission. It has left an indelible imprint on the whole development of Islam.

The later prophets of Israel used the Hebrew word *basar*, translated in the authorized version as "all flesh" to denote the idea of mankind. "He (God) is entering into judgment with all flesh," prophesies Jeremiah (25:3). Isaiah II, the prophet of the exiled, says: "All flesh shall come to worship Me" (66:23). And Zechariah, one of the latest of the biblical prophets, says: "Be silent, all flesh, before the Lord" (2:13). Precisely the same word, in its Arabic version of course, (*bashar*), appears in the same meaning in the earliest utterings of the prophet of Islam. "This"—Muhammad's message—"is but a reminder to all flesh." (Qur'an, Sura, i.e. chapter, 74:31). "This"—again God's word as transmitted by Muhammad —"is the greatest thing coming as a warning to all flesh" (74:36).

The term *basar-bashar* designates the human race as mere mortals, as mere flesh and blood, in contrast to God and the heavenly hosts. The word commonly expressing the notion of mankind in Muhammad's early proclamations was *nas* or *unas*, men.

"Do those think they will not be raised up on a great day, a day when men will stand before the Lord of the worlds?" (83:4-6).

"On the day when men will be like scattered moths" (101:4).

"The reckoning draws near to men, but they turn aside in heedlessness" (21:1).

This is a complete example of one of the early visions in which mankind is described as facing the Last Judgment:

"When the earth quivers from its quakes,
and the earth brings forth her burdens,
    and man cries out: 'What ails her?'
On that day she will tell her story,
    for the Lord has revealed it to her.
On that day men will come forward in groups to be shown their works.
And whoever has done good of the weight of an ant will see it;
and whoever has done bad of the weight of an ant will see it." (99:1-8).

Instead of the plural, *nas*, or together with it (as in the Sura just quoted), the singular, *insan*, man, is used, which emphasizes the individual responsibility of each human being before God, but also demonstrates Muhammad's universalistic approach: he addresses man, not persons of a particular people. In his very first revelation (according to Islamic tradition, Sura 96:1-5), God is praised as the creator and teacher of man, a twin subject, often repeated in the Qur'an (e.g. 55:3-4). The following passage, in which the term "man" recurs five times is typical for Muhammad's early preaching:

"Does man think We will not join his bones together?!
Yea! We are able to put together the smallest bones of his fingers.
But man prefers to sin at liberty.
asking (mockingly): 'When will be the Day of Resurrection?'
But when the sight is dazed,
and the moon eclipsed,
and the sun and moon are joined—
on that day man will say: 'Where is the refuge?'
No, there is no escape;
the recourse on that day is to your Lord.
Man will be told on that day all his deeds from beginning to end.
Yea, man will be evidence against himself" (75:3-14).

Another favorite expression for mankind used by Muhammad is *al-alamin*, literally "the worlds," originally a Jewish and Christian term, which had penetrated into the Arabic language prior to the rise of Islam. This word is of particular importance since it occurs in the opening phrase of the "Lord's Prayer" of Islam, the Fatiha, or first chapter of the Qur'an, which is repeated by the faithful Muslim fifteen to twenty times a day during the five obligatory prayers. In Hebrew, "the worlds" was understood literally, in the sense of this world and the world to come, or all the worlds, namely those created before ours and those that will be created after ours is destroyed, and this is the meaning of the word in the phrase "Lord of the Worlds," a common appellative of God in rabbinical literature. In Arabic, *al-alamin* means mankind. This is evident from its usage in the earliest chapters of the Qur'an, where it appears in contexts in which we have found *bashar*, all flesh, or *nas*, mankind. E.g., "This"— Muhammad's message—"is a reminder for the worlds" (81:27; 68:52. Repeated in 6:90); Blessed be He who has sent down the Furqan (another term for "Qur'an") upon his servant so that he should become a warner for the worlds" (25:1). That "the worlds" equals "mankind" is even more evident in a context such as this: "God knows best what is in the hearts of the worlds" (29:10/9). In later Suras, the prophets—fourteen are mentioned by name—are described as "chosen out of the worlds" (6:86). The same is said of the Children of Israel (45:16/15); repeated twice in Medina, (2:47/44; 2:122/116); and in Medina Muhammad has God say to Mary, the mother of Jesus: "I have chosen you out of all women of the worlds" (3:42/37).

The Fatiha, the opening chapter of the Qur'an, was not selected as a text for the daily prayer after the death of Muhammad. It was created by Muhammad deliberately as a liturgical composition at a very early stage of his prophetical career. It does not contain a single word referring expressly to the Muslim community or even to the message of Muhammad. The Fatiha is a prayer of universal character, and, as has often been remarked, could be said by any Jew or Christian believing in God and the Last Judgment. It reflects the period of Muhammad's primitive universalism (see below).

I am aware, of course, of the traditional explanation of the concluding passage of the Fatiha, an explanation attributed to Muhammad himself. It is as follows:

"Guide us in the right Path (literally: Street),
The Path of those to whom you showed grace"—i.e., the Muslims,
"Not those on whom is wrath"—i.e., the Jews,
"Nor those who have gone astray"—i.e., the Christians.

It is definitely possible that Muhammad in his later days, when his prophetical message had turned into a militant church, occasionally gave himself such an interpretation, but, as a purely philological analysis of the language of the Qur'an proves above doubt, at the time when the Fatiha was composed, the phrase "on whom is wrath" designated the sinners and "those who have gone astray" the idolators; Muhammad describes himself with this phrase with regard to his pre-Muslim period of life (93:7).

The idea of the unity of the human race is underlined in the Qur'an by the acceptance of the biblical notion of one father of all men—Adam. While, however, in Hebrew *adam* is a common noun, meaning "man," and consequently *bene* (the sons of) *adam* means "men," in Arabic Adam is solely a proper name, taken over together with the biblical story, and, therefore, *bani Adam* denotes the descendants of Adam, the human race as the offspring of the one man called by that name. This usage is particularly noticeable in Sura Seven, where the term occurs five times and is directly connected with the story of the Paradise and the Fall (see 7:26-27/25-26), and likewise in Sura Seventeen, which is full of biblical reminiscences:

"We (God is speaking) have honored the Children of Adam, We carried them on land and sea, provided them with good food and granted them great prerogatives over many of those We created" (17:70/72). The concluding phrase echoes Genesis 1:28, where God gives man domination over fish, birds and other living things. The story of the Creation is followed in the Qur'an immediately by the vision of the Last Judgment, where the expression "Children of Adam" is replaced by "mankind" (here in the form *unas*). "On the day when We shall call all mankind with their leader(s)—Whoever is given his book in his right hand will

read their book and they shall not be wronged a thread" (17:71/73).
This Sura is from a later Meccan period, when Muhammad had already
become aware of the unbridgeable gulf which divided the various monotheistic denominations of his time. Therefore here—as in other Suras contemporary with this—he lets mankind appear, not, as he had done at first,
in two sections of righteous men and evildoers, but in several groups, each
headed by the founder of its religious system.

Of particular significance is the occurrence of the expression "Children
of Adam" in the following verse: "O Children of Adam, when there will
come to you messengers from your midst recounting to you My signs,
then whoever is pious and acts righteously—no fear shall be upon them
neither shall they be grieved" (7:35/33). The concluding phrase of this
Meccan verse is repeated verbally in two almost identical verses, promulgated in Medina at a time when Muhammad was at the height of heated
polemics with Christians and Jews: "Those who believe (i.e., the Muslims), and those who are Jewish, and the Christians and the Sabians, whoever believes in God and the Last Day and does righteous works— no
fear shall be upon them neither shall they be grieved" (2:62/59; 5:69/73,
where the Sabians are mentioned before the Christians). These verses
sound universalistic and magnanimous when read together with the
surrounding sections, which contain vehement attacks on Christians and
Jews, but seem to be particularistic and exclusive if compared with the
verse from Sura Seventeen, quoted above, where good hope for salvation
is held out for the Children of Adam, i.e., for the totality of mankind.
However, a closer examination of the Qur'anic text dissolves this apparent
contradiction. Adam was not only the father of mankind, but also a
prophet with whom God had concluded a covenant binding on him and
all his posterity (20:115/114; 36:60). This concept, which goes back to
a biblical passage ("And they, like Adam, broke the covenant," Hosea 6:7)
according to both rabbinical and Christian interpretation, has the corollary that those who do not belong to a religious community based on
revelation put themselves outside the ideal community of mankind. It is
not so much the physical descent from Adam, as the spiritual belonging to
"humanity" which counts.

With this we have arrived at the central issue of Muhammad's concept
of mankind, of what we have called above the Prophet's primitive
universalism. There has been much scientific discussion as to whether he
intended his message to be one directed solely or primarily to his Arab
countrymen, even only to his Meccan compatriots, or to a wider audience,
or to humanity at large. Even some Muslim commentators occasionally
explain various of the verses quoted above, in which the words "men,"

"mankind," occur, as referring to the Quraysh, the inhabitants of Mecca. (To be sure, official Islamic opinion has it that the Prophet was sent to "the Red and the Black," i.e., to peoples of all colors and races). Frants Buhl, the author of a deep-searching critical biography of Muhammad, wrote a paper specifically devoted to this problem, where he arrived at the conclusion that Muhammad's vision could not have reached much beyond the borders of the Arab peninsula, a view which he defended also in his book. His opinion was shared by many, such as Sir William Muir, and the prolific students of early Islamic history, Prince Leone Caetani, and Henry Lammans. The opposite view was expressed by that ardent defender of Islam, I. Goldziher, and, with similar fervor, but somehow less critical acumen, Sir Thomas Arnold.

Those who oppose Muhammad's claim on universality point to such verses as 26:214 "Warn the nearest to you of your clan," or 42:7/5 "We have revealed to you a Qur'an in Arabic so that you should warn (the people of) the metropolis and those (who dwell) around her" (repeated in 6:92). These verses refer, however, to specific circumstances, as their contexts clearly indicate. Muhammad had incurred difficulties and even dangers in his endeavor to convert quickly wide circles; here, he encourages himself by the consolation that his immediate task was to address only those people who were near to him and would understand him. On the other hand, not too much should be made of single Meccan verses seemingly stressing that Muhammad's message was addressed to the totality of mankind, such as 34:28/27: "We have not sent you otherwise than unto mankind in general"; for, again, an attentive reading of the context shows that Muhammad was not concerned here to prove that his message was universal and not parochial, but was trying hard to convince his hearers that his Qur'an contained the truth. The entire question must be taken up at a higher, or we should rather say deeper, level, the question of the basic, elementary concepts of Muhammad's prophecy which had an enduring impact on Islam.

Buhl and others who insisted that Muhammad could never have conceived his message as one destined for humanity at large based their contention mainly on the Prophet's assertion, repeated about twenty times, that he was sent to promulgate a Qur'an in "clear Arabic language" (26:195), so that his countrymen could understand it (43:3/2): if the novelty of Muhammad's contribution consisted in its linguistic aspect, how could it be destined for the totality of mankind, the majority of whom were not familiar with Arabic? Now there can be no doubt that the linguistic garb was an extremely important ingredient in the religious creation represented by the Qur'an. The Muslim scholars who taught that the knowledge of the Arabic language was a religious requirement, knew what they were talking about. We certainly must understand the appearance of Muhammad as part and parcel of Arabic history, of that miraculous process by which an Arab nation was formed through the rise of a literary language common to all the different tribes and regions of Arabia. Islam—there can be no doubt about this—was the most perfect and powerful expression of the self-assertion of a new people in the process of formation. Still, it is precisely the passages emphasizing the Arabic character of the Qur'an which, by implication, bear witness to its universalistic character. All we have to do is to read them as they stand, that is, linked to their context.

"We (God) have made it a Qur'an (i.e., a book for recitation) in Arabic so that you might understand it. Lo, it (namely, this Arabic version) is in the mother-book (the archetype) with Us, sublime and full of wisdom. . . . How many a prophet have We sent among the ancient!" (43: 3-6/2-5)

". . . A warner in clear Arabic speech. It is contained in the scriptures of those who were before you. Is it not a sign (i.e., a proof) to them that the learned of the Children of Israel know it? Had We sent it down through one of the foreigners and had he recited it to them, they (the Arabs) would not have believed in it" (26:192-199).

Thus, Muhammad's preaching, far from being intended to become a new divider of mankind, derived its justification from its attempt to introduce the Arabs into the spiritual community of the Children of Adam. The Qur'an was but a version of the archetype of a book preserved with God of which other versions had "come down" previously. The proof for the truth of its content was its identity with that found in the scriptures of the religious communities preceding Islam. The pagans are challenged to check the validity of this assertion by asking the People of the Book, i.e., those who were already in possession of a version of the heavenly Book, identified in 26:197 with "the learned among the children of Israel."

The idea of one heavenly book which was promulgated in different versions at different times is matched by the concept that mankind originally formed one umma, or religious community, but later split into rivalling, and sometimes hostile, denominations. If God wished, he could restore that unity. But just as it was God's arbitrary "word" which divided mankind, thus he will keep it in this state of division until the day of resurrection (which Muhammad expected to occur during his lifetime or shortly afterwards).

"Mankind were only one religious community. Then they disagreed with each other. Had it not been for a word emanating from your Lord, their disagreements would have been resolved" (19:19/20).

"Had God wished, he would have made mankind one umma, but they continue with their disagreements" (11:118/120; 42:8/6).

Much has been written about the origin of this "theory of revelation" of Muhammad, which seems so unexpected in a man growing up in an unsophisticated society in a barbarian age. One looks for a Judaeo-Christian gnostic sect or the remnants of other syncretistic or inter-religious traditions. However, a close study of the whole body of Muhammad's Meccan pronouncements reveals a natural and self-contained development which makes the assumption of such influences redundant. Muhammad's concept of the one heavenly book carrying the same message for all peoples was originally extremely elementary. At the beginning his knowledge of the older religions was slight. He had heard of Abraham and Moses as the propagators of faith and also of scriptures. Therefore, at first, he made Abraham, like Moses, author, or rather, transmitter, of a book (87:19; 53:37/38). Soon, the unique role of Moses as bearer of a written revelation became known to him. Hence the oaths by Mount Sinai, paired with the "Book written on parchment" and the Ka'ba of Mecca, opening the ancient Suras 95 and 52, as well as the repeated announcement: "Before it (the Qur'an), there was the book of Moses . . . and this is a book confirming it in Arabic language" (46:12/11 and 30/29; 28:48), verses that read as if there had been no other book before or after Moses.

"They (the unbelievers) have not measured God with his true measure when they say: 'God has never sent anything down on any mortal.' Say: 'Who has sent down the book that Moses brought as a light and a guidance to mankind?' " (6:91). Moses' message, like that of Muhammad, was destined for "men" in general, although he acted among the Children of Israel, just as Muhammad was sent to the Arabs.

In the course of the years, as the Qur'an clearly evidences, Muhammad made a more extensive study of the earlier prophets. This occupation brought him into closer contact with adherents of different monotheistic denominations and he discovered to his dismay the deep antagonisms prevailing between them. The Children of Israel became divided after having received the book of Moses (32:23-25; 45:16-17; 10:93), a tragedy understandable only as brought about by a decree of God, just as the division of mankind about which we had read before (41:45; 11:110/112).

It goes without saying that Muhammad, as the inhabitant of a flourishing caravan city, whose merchants commuted to Byzantine Palestine and

Egypt, as well as to Yemen, Iraq and Abyssinia, knew from his youth about
the existence of Jews and Christians and probably also about the contrast
between Oriental (Syriac and Coptic) Christians and their Greek overlords, although he was naturally unaware of the theological issues dividing
them. The words "Christian" and "Jew" are well documented in pre-
Islamic Arabic poetry (unlike the expression "Children of Israel," which
Muhammad learned when he studied the history of Moses). However,
precisely because Muhammad knew of the existence of various monotheistic denominations he was impressed so much by the uniformity of
the teachings contained in the sermons and other utterings of those Jews
and Christians to whom he had opportunity to listen during his earlier
years. Those non-professional missionaries stressed only a very few essential points, leaving aside the specific doctrines of their denomination
which were irrelevant to their crude listeners. They taught man's responsibility before God, the punishment which was awaiting him in the world
to come, partly also in this world, as well as a few concrete moral teachings, such as honesty in dealings, restraint in sexual matters and mercy
with fellow men (particularly impressive for Muhammad, who remembered his childhood, when he was a poor orphan, 93:6-8). The haughty
disbelievers of old, such as the people of the Flood, who did not listen to
the admonitions of Noah, or those who built the Tower of Babylon, or
Pharaoh of Egypt, were presented as deterrent examples, and a similar
religious moral was drawn from the fate of some ancient peoples of
Arabia, which, according to local legends, had perished in catastrophes of
various kinds. Several of these self-appointed preachers held in their hands
"parchments" of which they said that they were copies of a book brought
down from heaven, containing the knowledge by which man was saved.
Passages were read out by them and translated verse by verse into Arabic,
which was far from perfect and an offense to the Arab ear which had
become so receptive to beautiful literary expression. Here Muhammad became electrified. Why should the word of God, on which man's salvation
depended, be brought to him in such an imperfect form? Who could
fulfill this task better than an Arab endowed with "clear Arabic speech"?
The legends told by the preachers proved that "warners" had been sent
to many peoples, even in Arabia itself. Why should Muhammad not become like one of them? What those warners had to say was always the
same. Consequently, there could be no doubt about the content of the
message which Muhammad had to convey. We find, indeed, that despite
their seemingly disconnected, erratic form, even Muhammad's earliest
utterings combine into a well ordered, coherent system of a few basic
ideas.

The point we have tried to bring home in this reconstruction of Muhammad's beginnings is the understanding that Muhammad's concept of the human race as forming originally one religious community united through one heavenly book, was not a foreign idea, borrowed by him, lock, stock, and barrel, from some obscure sect, but grew in him organically during his period of incubation and preparation. It was indeed the background for his adoption of the role of prophet. Because of this origin as an innermost and decisive personal experience this "primitive universalism" remained a strong force in Islam despite later developments which run counter to it.

These developments took place in Muhammad's lifetime, and not, as commonly assumed, at first in Medina, when the Prophet became head of a state, but far earlier. The change took place in Mecca, after he had made a more thorough study of the older religions and also experienced the first unfavorable reactions of members of those religions to his own creation. There is little doubt that Muhammad's beginnings were met with approval by at least some of his monotheistic acquaintances: "Those to whom We (God) have given the book are happy about what has been sent down to you" (13:36). "Those to whom We have given the book before it (the Qur'an) believe in it. And when it is recited to them they say: 'We believe in it, it is the truth from our Lord, we have been Muslims (i.e., dedicated to God) even before it" (28:52-53). The more tightly, however, Muhammad's flock of followers organized into a well-knit religious fellowship, the stronger grew the opposition to him not only on the side of the pagans, but on that of the monotheists as well. This discovery was a great shock to him. He was of course familiar with the phenomenon of various religions existing side by side. But he had not assumed that the People of the Book were so sharply divided and consequently could not expect so much opposition to himself from these quarters. This state of affairs caused him great anguish, as is shown in the moving prayer 39:46/47:

"Oh God, Creator of heaven and earth, who knows the hidden and the manifest, you will judge between your servants on their dissensions."

From the middle of the Meccan period of his prophetical career to his very end Muhammad was painfully aware of this mysterious tragedy of one truth causing the rise of different and antagonistic religious communities. He never made his mind up definitely how this stumbling block to human progress could be removed. At first, he meekly resigns himself to the situation, accepting it as an inscrutable decree of God, preaching coexistence with the other monotheistic religions, but demanding recognition from them.

"He (God) has laid down for you as religion that which He has commanded Noah and that which We (God) have revealed to you (Muhammad) and that which We have commanded Abraham, Moses and Jesus, namely: 'keep the religion and do not become disunited.' That to which you call the idolaters is hard for them, but God will select whomsoever He will and guide to Himself whomsoever is penitent.

"They became disunited only after Knowledge had come to them, oppressing one another . . .

"Therefore, you (Muhammad) call (to your religion) and be steadfast, as you have been commanded and do not follow their partisanships. And say: 'I believe in whatever book God has sent down. I was ordered to keep the middle between you. God is our Lord and your Lord. We have our works and you have your works. There is no argument between us and you. God will bring us together (on the Day of Judgment) and to him we finally go' " (42:13-15/12-14).

Thus God had originally commanded that there should be unity among the followers of the true religion, i.e., mankind, for in principle there exists only one religion. But God's command was not obeyed, and (as Muhammad's travelling compatriots, or he himself had opportunity to observe), there was even oppression occurring among the followers of Moses, i.e., Christians and Jews, and also among those of Jesus, such as the oriental Christians and their Greek overlords. As in many other passages of the Qur'an, Muhammad alludes here to the fact that he was urged by Jews and Christians to embrace their religion and claims that his teaching followed a middle, i.e., right, path, but concludes in a reconciliatory tone: there was no reason to quarrel since every partaker in the heavenly book had prospect of salvation if he did the right works; the ultimate decision rested with God.

In the same spirit Muhammad instructs his followers:

"Do not dispute with the People of the Book save in the fairest manner—except for those who do wrong—and say: 'we believe in what has been sent down to us and what has been sent down to you. Our God and your God is one' " (29:45-46/44-45).

This "ecumenical" idea that it was not membership in any particular group, but the individual piety of a person which counted, is fittingly compressed in a famous verse of the Qur'an which became a rallying cry of a great movement in classical Islam and is frequently quoted by Muslims of all shades of opinion in our own time:

"O mankind, We have created you from one male and one female and made you into peoples and tribes that you might know one another.

Verily, the noblest among you in the sight of God is the most Godfearing of you" (49:13).

The context of this verse, which forms part of the latest Medinese Suras, clearly indicates that Muhammad refers here to the rivalries between the Arab tribes within the Islamic community. It is in this sense that the verse became the key text for a great movement which fought against the prerogatives of the Arab race in Islam and for the recognition of equal rights for other peoples. On the other hand, the allusion to Adam and Eve and the address to "men" at large shows that Muhammad intended to proclaim here a general truth. Therefore, modern Muslims are justified in adducing this verse as a shining example of Qur'anic universalism.

There is no need to describe here the long route traversed by the Arab prophet, beginning with what we have called his "primitive universalism," leading to his "ecumenical" attitude towards the other monotheistic religions, and ending in the establishment of an exclusive and militant church. The system finally arrived at was strongly nationalistic, incorporating, with slight alterations, the pagan cults of the Ka'ba and of the sanctuaries in the neighborhood of Mecca with their strange rites; Christians and Jews alike were now denounced in the harshest terms as polytheists and unbelievers and their subjugation made obligatory:

"Fight those who do not believe in God and the Last Day and do not forbid what God and his messenger have forbidden and do not follow the true religion—of those who have been given the Book—until they pay the tribute. . . while they are in a state of submission.

"The Jews say: 'Uzayr is the son of God,' and the Christians say: 'Christ is the son of God.' This is what they say with their mouth, thus being like the unbelievers before them." (9:29-39).

No Jewish sect is known to have worshipped a son of God, nor is the Christian concept of the Trinity polytheism, but this is beside the point. In this, Muhammad's definitive pronouncement on the relationship of Islam with other religions, Christians and Jews had to receive the status of unbelievers and therefore they had to be charged with the deadliest of sins: polytheism. This verse forms the basis of the position of non-Muslims in Islamic law, and kafir, Infidel, is the usual designation for a Christian or a Jew in Islamic popular literature.

But this is not the whole story. Pointing to Suras 2:62/59 and 5:69/73, we have had opportunity to remark that even at the time of grave disputes with Christians and Jews Muhammad still takes the ecumenical view that believing monotheists who also act according to the commandments of their religion, are like Muslims: they have nothing to fear on the

Day of Judgment. Sura Two, which is loaded with polemics, concludes
with the following declaration of faith:

"The Messenger (Muhammad) believes in what was sent down to him
from his Lord, and so do the believers. Each ones believes in God, His
angels, His books and His messengers. We make no distinction between
any of His messengers" (2:285).

Even the prominence given to the Ka'ba as a specifically Arabic and
Islamic sanctuary did not rob Islam of its universalistic character. For
Abraham was made founder of that holy place, and Abraham was
"neither Jew nor Christian" (3:67/60), but the father of religion, the
first who dedicated himself entirely to God (2:128, 131/122, 125). The
very term *Islam*, which means submission and self-dedication to God, and
which has Hebrew precedents, came into being in connection with the
figure of the patriarch, as is evidenced by an analysis of the Qur'anic
Abraham stories. Thus, Abraham's role as founder of the Ka'ba and first
promulgator of Islam was not a side issue, but a central credo of the
new religion.

These two faces of Islam, its deeply anchored belief in the unity of
mankind through the service of God on the one hand and its character of
a militant church on the other—both of which were innate in the work
of its founder—remained with it throughout the generations. There is
nothing wrong with a man's conviction that his religion is the best (at
least for himself), as long as this belief does not make him blind to the
virtues of others and as long as the supreme values of morality and mercy
are not sacrificed to confessional fanaticism. With this qualification in
mind, we shall now shortly survey how the idea of mankind fared in Islam
after its prophet had passed away.

During the period of conquest and colonization (622—ca. 850) there
prevailed a curious antagonism as well as a blend of the two ideas of
universalism and confessionalism; both gained in strength and depth, in
practice as well as in theory. On the one hand, it goes without saying that
those gigantic wars of conquest could not have been fought except by
warriors convinced of their right to smash everything in their way. The
sweeping victories could not but strengthen the conviction that Islam
was the only true religion, and the vast extent of the countries conquered
suggested the idea that the subjugation of the entire inhabited earth was
not out of reach. Surprisingly early, the Muslim lawyers developed the
theory that the world was divided into an area of Islam and one of war,
the supposition being that the Muslims as a whole had not fulfilled their
destiny as long as they had not conquered the latter. According to this
theory (which has remained binding in Islamic law), the Muslims are not

permitted to conclude a permanent peace treaty with a non-Muslim state; the most which is allowed is an armistice for the duration of a maximum of ten years (the scholars of the various schools disagree about the length of the armistice period; some put it at two years). Christianity made of course the same claim to world dominion. But according to Majid Khadduri, who has made a special study of this subject, the difference was this: while Christianity was at the outset a non-state religion which, even when it was connected with politics, kept Church and State apart, "Islam combined the dualism of a universal religion and a universal state." Be this as it may, this concept of the dichotomy of the world into an area of Islam and another with which eternal war was obligatory contains in itself both a strong particularistic and an equally strong universalistic outlook. While regarding Islam as the superior religion which has not only the right, but the duty to subjugate all others, it is also concerned with mankind at large which should be united—or, according to the Qur'an, we should say: reunited, in the proper service of God.

A fresco painted at the end of the first century of Islam gives pictorial expression to this idea. I am referring, of course, to the famous (now destroyed) painting in the Umayyad desert castle of Qusayr 'Amrah (Jordan), which depicts the caliph as seated, while the six other rulers of the earth stand at an appropriate distance paying homage to him. They are shown not as vanquished enemies, but with a gesture of acclamation comparable to that with which, in approximately contemporary Christian mosaics, the apostles meet Christ. Richard Ettinghausen, while summarizing previous results of research on the much discussed painting, properly remarks that the idea of world domination is accentuated here not only in "the Cosmokrator-like representation of the enthroned figure," but also by sea monsters symbolizing the ocean which surrounds the earth, and by birds representing the all-covering sky. Thus, according to its latest interpreters, the painting expresses acceptance of the superiority of Islam by the nations of the earth rather than subjugation.

Domination—combined with the striving for endless expansion—constituted only one aspect of the contacts made by Islam during the fateful period of conquest and colonization. There were the equally significant processes of social, economic and cultural adjustment. As is natural, we see this process not such much in making as in its results. It is the literature and arts of the third and fourth centuries of Islam (approximately 830-1030) which reveal to us how the national religion of the Arabs had become the frame and base of a worldwide civilization of a definitely specific character and, at the same time, of general human appeal. The formation of this new culture thus had taken an amazingly short stretch of time. Compare this with the slow development of Western European civilization rising out of the ashes of the Roman empire and the devastation of the Germanic invasions. The difference was this: the Islamic conquest was not a *Völkerwanderung* stretching over many centuries, but a systematic military operation, guided by a central authority and resulting in the acquisition of the core of the future Islamic territory in a matter of two decades. And perhaps even more important: the conquering Muslims were no barbarians, but had two great cultural assets: their poetry, including the genealogical and historical traditions connected with it, and their Qur'an, which represented a completely satisfactory guidance for life. Both Arabic poetry and the Qur'an are extremely repetitive, a form of expression which easily leaves its mark on simple minds. Thus, in addition to military, administrative, social and economic domination there was this element of a most impressive cultural force which made the Muslims capable of exercising a unifying influence over a vast area, in which, though, for a considerable period, they formed a minority.

Finally, there was at work another most important character trait of the conquering Muslims, which was perhaps related to the fact that both their leaders, the Quraysh of Mecca and the bedouins of the desert, had been connected with the great transcontinental trade for centuries. The exchange of goods draws man's attention to the valuable things in the hands of others, and since the Arabs, as we have seen, were not unconcerned with spiritual matters, they proved to be most receptive to the values of culture possessed by the peoples conquered by them.

Naturally, the first to be closely contacted by the Muslims were the People of the Book, so often mentioned in the Qur'an, Christians and Jews, who formed also the bulk of the population in the central countries of the newly formed empire of Islam. Without recourse to the Bible and other writings in the hands of the Jews and the Christians many passages of the Qur'an remained simply unintelligible. It is, however, also natural that, after the initial thirst for knowledge has been quenched, Muslims recoiled from exposing what could be interpreted as ignorance. Therefore, in contradistinction to the saying: "Ask the People of the Book without hesitation," and similar teachings attributed to the Prophet, there were others disapproving of close contacts. In this, as in all other respects, universalism and confessionalism existed side by side. The contents and look of Islamic civilization prove, however, that lively exchanges must have occurred over prolonged periods. The leading specifically Islamic science, the Hadith, or Traditions of the Prophet, which include also the early exegesis of the Qur'an, and Islamic law which is connected with it, in spirit, form and content, closely resemble Jewish "oral law" and its literature. Remarks on relevant literary connections are found in the writings of I. Goldziher, Joseph Horovitz and other scholars. A comprehensive study of this intriguing subject is still to be made. The impact on Islam of Christian theology and of the elaborate cult of the Oriental Church has been noted long ago, and the pietists of Islam acknowledged their indebtedness to the Christian monks in their writings. "When our students of law exaggerate, they become Jews; when our pious exaggerate, they become Christians." This remark of censure, attributed to an authority of the second Islamic century, patently betrays the affinities sensed by the Muslims.

Another heritage to which Islam acceded early and intensively was the ancient culture of Iran. Iran was incorporated in its totality in the caliphal empire immediately after its foundation, and during the first four or five hundred years of Islam many, if not most, of the Muslim writers were of Iranian descent. Persian civilization itself had been of an extremely composite character and had absorbed also much of the culture of India, over parts of which Iranians had ruled intermittently for over a thousand years. The very first classic of Arabic prose in Islam is the *Kalila wa-Dimna*, a book of Indian wisdom in the form of animal stories which had been translated into Middle-Persian about a century prior to the Islamic conquest. The Arabic version was translated not only into all the languages of Islamic civilization, and of course into Hebrew (from which, during the Middle Ages, it was translated into Latin), but into those of Europe as well. Thus Kalila wa-Dimna, like The Arabian Nights, whose original core also goes back to a Persian translation of Indian stories, constitutes a real piece of world literature.

Indian spirituality entered Islam also through another channel. As is well known, Buddhism was driven out of its country of origin, India, but flourished in many other countries of Asia. Islam came into contact with Buddhism through the conquest of Central Asia, where this religion was particularly strong. In that north eastern corner of the Islamic world a most intensive variety of culture developed. The Muslim *madrasa* (a college with a dormitory) appears first in those regions and was perhaps modeled on the example of the Buddhist convents. Islamic mysticism developed first and strongest in that region and absorbed Indian elements both in its practices and its theory. The Indian rosary, adopted first by the Muslim mystics, soon became popular in most Islamic countries and came into use in the Catholic church as well. Thus, this little utensil of piety is a symbol of the middle-man role of Islam in world culture.

The strangest, and in certain respects, one of the most fruitful results of the conquest of Islam was its encounter with the heritage of Hellas.

Greek sciences were still known well by Syriac clerics and secular scholars, also by some Persians and Jews, at the time of the advent of Islam. The Arabs never cared to learn Greek, but translation into Arabic started early, and, at the beginning of the third Islamic century, such a feverish activity of translation set in that soon the whole corpus of Greek science and literature, as far as it was still available at that time (ninth Christian century) was turned into Arabic. The effect of this activity was tremendous. The world-wide horizon and secular character of the Greek sciences imbued the new Islamic civilization, which then was in its formative stage and continued to flourish for about four hundred years (850-1250). These two aspects of the Greek heritage were so effective in Islam because the latter itself had contacted geographically the whole known world—from Christian Europe to India and Malaya, from pagan Africa to China and Japan—and because the Muslims, unlike Christians and Jews, were endowed through the study of pre-Islamic poetry (which was regarded as an indispensable equipment for any educated man) with a strong secular disposition in their mental make-up.

All these cultural contacts—the Judaeo-Christian, the Indo-Iranian, the Greek, in combination with the fact that Islam strove after world domination and actually ruled over a large section of the globe—strengthened the pristine universalism contained in Muhammad's message and kept the idea of mankind alive in the mind of the Muslims. The Muslims were extremely history-conscious, and history began for them with Adam and Eve, with the Dispersion of Mankind after the Flood and continued with the biblical account as outlined already in the Qur'an. This was complemented by the pre-Islamic history not only of the Arabs and Persians, but soon also of the Rum, a common designation for Greeks and Romans. The political history of the latter with their strange institutions of republics and democracies had little interest for the Muslims. The history of the Rum, as far as included in Muslim books, was therefore mainly that of their cultural achievements. The same applied to the Indians, albeit for different reasons: there was no proper book on Indian political history in existence. The earliest creations of Islamic historiography were monographs of limited size, some of which bear titles such as Tabulbal al-Alsina, The Confusion of Languages, i.e., the story of how God confounded the speech of the human race which originally was one (using the same Semitic root as that occurring in the relevant story in Genesis 11:7). The interest in such topics was aroused by the widening of the geographical horizon of the Muslims and their becoming acquainted with new peoples and tongues the very existence of which had been unknown to them before.

Soon the favorite form of Muslim historiography was to be world history, each author devoting longer or shorter sections to the pre-Islamic period. The titles of their books are indicative of their attitude: *The Book of the Prophets and the Kings* by Tabari (d. 923), *The History of the Princes of the Earth and the Prophets* by Hamza al-Isfahani (d. ca. 965) or *The Experiences of the Nations* by Miskawayh (d. 1030)—all this shows that the authors intended to write the history of mankind, as imperfect as the realization of the idea may seem to us. The Spaniard Ibn Sa'id (d. 1070) made in his *Classes of Nations* a deliberate attempt to provide a comparative appraisal of the achievements of the peoples of the earth. He was preceded by that great traveller and humanist al-Mas'udi (d. 956 or 957) in various of his still extant works. Ibn Khaldun (d. 1406), the unique philosopher of history, tried to lay down laws for the political, social and economic history of mankind, although we know—and he himself conceded—that his material was derived from the study of the Islamic area alone, including of course pre-Islamic history, as it was presented by al-Mas'udi and other classical Muslim historians.

A particular title of honor of Islamic civilization is the creation of the science of comparative religion. We have in mind a book such as Shahrastani's (d. 1153) *Book of Religions and Sects*, in which he describes the Islamic, Christian, Jewish, Zoroastrian, Manichaean and other denominations in considerable detail, followed by shorter expositions of the opinions of the Greek philosophers and their Muslim disciples and concluding with an account of the tenets held by the pre-Islamic Arabs, and finally, the religion of the people of India. This objective and valuable survey of human belief and thought is one of the finest expressions of the concept of mankind in Islam.

Such comparative study, which was initiated in Islam at a rather early period, revealed how much human beings had in common despite their different allegiances. Miskawayh, whom we have already met as the author of the precious *Experiences of the Nations*, made a vast collection of Arabic, Persian, Indian and Greek sayings of wisdom which he called *Eternal Wisdom*, defining his aim as follows: "The title *Eternal Wisdom* has been chosen in order to inform the reader that the intellectual make-up of all nations is the same. It does not differ according to countries. It does not change according to periods. It never becomes superannuated."

Because of the vast extent of the realm of Islam and the great variety of peoples and languages found in it the Muslim experienced the concept of mankind while moving within the Islamic world. To quote a third book of Miskawayh: after explaining that the word *insan*, 'human being,' was derived from *uns*, 'sociability, human intercourse,' he demonstrated that religion itself promotes human contacts, the daily prayers bringing together the people of a neighborhood, the Friday service uniting the inhabitants of a town, the Holiday prayers—those of a district, and the Pilgrimage to Mecca—those of the whole world. In the entire and very lengthy passage the words Islam or Muslim are never used. The institutions of the Islamic religion are conceived as furthering the unity of mankind in general.

This attitude, which is natural, remained characteristic even for the finest minds of Islam. The philosophers, building on the foundations laid by the Greek philosophers, speak everywhere about man in general. But the idea of the unity of the human race seems not to have occupied their thinking very much. In his famous treatise on the good state al-Farabi (d. 950) mentions the possibility of a state comprising the entire inhabited world, but he does not elaborate this point. The idea of eternal peace between the nations is found in an Arabic letter ascribed to Aristotle, which, until recently, was known only through a Hebrew translation. I quote from the latter: "I have found an important statement by Rabbi Moses Ibn Ezra, of blessed memory, which he attributes to Aristotle and maintains that he took it from a letter sent to his student Alexander. In the letter, though not in these precise words, the philosopher foresees a great new world composed of one society, with one king and one (social) contract. 'In this world (he says) men will gather in one accord, war and destruction will cease, and all will agree on pursuing that which is useful for their state and land. Peace and security will encompass mankind.' . . . This is the essence of the letter. Would that I knew how some spirit of God passed from us to speak to him." Naturally, the Jewish authors, familiar with Isaiah 2:1-4, and similar biblical passages, were intrigued to find similar ideas in an Arabic letter attributed to Aristotle.

In later Islam, the confessional aspect became more and more dominant. This is already clearly discernible in the writings of al-Ghazali (d. 1111), who was a mystic and certainly the most humane and most original of the great Muslim theologians. We are impressed when we read in his classic *The Revival of the Sciences of Religion* that the love of God inevitably induces us to love all of his creatures; for we are prone to love everything related to our beloved—even the dogs roaming in the neighborhood where our beloved lives. This remarkable statement, however, is for him only a premise to the postulate that we are bound above all to love the Prophet, the choicest of all of God's creations.

In modern Islam, the problem is compounded by the delicate theological situation. The belief in God and his direct and constant interference in all our affairs has been weakened—to say the least. Instead, spiritual refuge is sought in the attachment to the inherited religion, a situation which is detrimental to a truly ecumenical attitude transcending the established religions. The modern Muslim, as far as he is modern, belongs to the contemporary scientific-technological world civilization rather than to the traditional Islam with which we are concerned here.

In this essay an attempt has been made to study the concept of mankind in Islam at the time of the foundation of this religion and to trace its development during the period of the formation and the heyday of Islamic civilization. I wish to conclude with a quotation referring to the time of the Prophet, but found in a classic of Arabic literature compiled about three hundred years after him. The verses are put into the mouth of a Jewish poet of Medina, whose wife had embraced Islam:

> "She called me to Islam, when I met her,
>   but I said to her: 'no, come back to me and become a Jewess.
> We live according to the Torah of Moses and his religion,
>   but—by my faith—the religion of Muhammad is also good.
> Each of us believes that his religion is the right way,
>   but he is on the right way who is guided to the
>   gates of righteousness.'"

Whether these verses are genuine or not is irrelevant. What counts is the spectacle of a Muslim writer of the fourth Islamic century who lets a Jewish poet of the Prophet's time express the idea that it was not belonging to a particular confession, but man's personal piety which counted. This is the concept of mankind in Islam at its best.

FIVE

The Western Tradition

W. WARREN WAGAR
Department of History
State University of New York
at Binghamton

STUDENTS OF UNIVERSAL HISTORY, INCLUDING OSWALD SPENGLER and Arnold J. Toynbee, distinguish two major "Western" civilizations, the Helleno-Roman ecumenical society that flourished from the middle of the first millennium B.C. until the fifth century A.D., and the modern West, which grew from the ruins of the Latin half of the Roman empire and now occupies most of Europe, the Americas, and Australasia. One could also classify as Western the pre-classical empires of Egypt and Mesopotamia, the medieval Greek Christian civilization centered in Constantinople (together with its Russian offshoot), and even the Islamic world. But in the pages that follow, we shall confine our attention to classical Greece and Rome and Latin Christendom, down to the beginnings of the Scientific Revolution of the seventeenth century. More than two thousand years of Western history must be explored.

Yet, as in China and India, so in the West: the conceptions of world and man dominant in the great traditional civilizations have been drawn from a relatively small number of sources, and descend from generation to generation with relatively little change, until one reaches quite recent times. The chief sources of Western thought, clearly, are the Greek schools of philosophy of the sixth to third centuries B.C. and the teachings of the early Christian church. At various points Greek philosophy reveals pre-classical influences, and Christian doctrine bears the same filial relationship to Biblical Judaism that Buddhism bears to Hinduism, but it is from Greek philosophy and primitive Christianity that the Western tradition has directly sprung, and it is here that we must seek the immediate origins of the Western idea of human unity.

In some ways the West has found it more difficult than the Asian civilizations to embrace an explicitly cosmopolitan world-view. Neither the classical Greeks nor the Jews of the Old or the New Testament were an imperial people. The peculiarities of Western geography and ethnography in any event rendered the task of empire-building more hazardous than in China or India. Europe is not so much a continent as a remarkably irregular peninsula; along its southern shores, the inhabitable areas are small and cut off from one another by seas and mountains. In early antiquity, the natural form of polity in southern Europe was the city-state; the word polity itself comes from the Greek *polis*, a term properly applied only to city-states of the Greek type. Even long after commerce, military exploits, and the general diffusion and intermingling of cultures in the Mediterranean world had made the sovereign *polis* obsolete, the idea of civic loyalty continued to exert a powerful influence upon political thought.[1]

Like most ancient peoples, the Greeks were also inclined to ethnocentrist attitudes that raised unconscionably high barriers between themselves and all other peoples not of the same blood and tongue. Jewish thought even at its most exalted could not entirely overcome the tribalism of its historical origins. In the traditional Greek view, held by such transcendent intellects as Plato and Aristotle, the world was naturally divided into Greeks, who lived in *poleis*, and "barbarians," who did not. Barbarians could not expect to achieve full humanity, nor could Greeks and barbarians ever live in true peace.

But ethnocentrism was logically inconsistent with the theological and metaphysical underpinnings of Greek thought, and in due course it came to be strongly challenged. From the first, Greek philosophy displayed the salient characteristics of what Karl Jaspers terms the "axial period" in human thought, the period in which, quite independently throughout the ancient world, the conventional wisdom was exposed to sceptical and self-aware re-thinking. Axial thought produced in its highest thrusts a spiritualized, universalized conception of reality that bears the stamp of powerful individual minds. Confucianism, Buddhism, and the Judaism of the Prophets were fruits of the axial period in Asia.[2]

In Greece, the axial revolution expressed itself very differently, and yet to the same ultimate effect. The speculations of the pre-Socratic cosmologists, from Thales of Miletus to Parmenides of Elea, pictured the universe as a rational and ordered unity: as a *kosmos*, sustained by a rational supreme being or principle. Monotheism can be traced as far back as Xenophanes in the sixth century, who held that "there is one god, supreme among gods and men; resembling mortals neither in form nor in mind. The whole of him sees, the whole of him thinks, the whole of him hears. Without toil he rules all things by the power of his mind."[3] Elaborate theories of the hierarchical unity of being were constructed by Plato and Aristotle, who borrowed from the full range of pre-Socratic thought and arrived each at his own definition of God, Plato's "idea of the good" and Aristotle's "unmoved first mover." Both saw man as a rational creature, disposed by his very form or nature to strive for the good life prescribed by reason.

A doctrine of human unity is thus implicit in Greek philosophy. But the implicit is not always explicit; timeless truths may lose their force when translated into the circumstances of the historical world. Conflict between Greek and barbarian, and the stratification of society into higher and lower classes, free men and slaves, were facts of life. So also was the sovereign *polis*. Only when some of these facts began to change did the universalism of Greek philosophy assert itself vigorously against traditional Greek xenophobia and racial pride. The crucial moment came in 431 B.C. Certain wealthy and ambitious *poleis*—most notably Athens—in the terms of classical Greek tragedy "overreached" themselves, precipitating a century of civil war among the Hellenic peoples at the end of which the Balkan kingdom of Macedonia brought not only the Greeks but most of the ancient world under its sway. Although the empire of Alexander the Great was short-lived, it signaled the end of the era of the self-determined *polis* and presaged the more durable empire of Rome.

But political events—conquests, war-time coalitions, the formation of empires and new monarchical states—should not be made to bear the whole responsibility for the decline of the *polis*. Despite the barriers of custom and geography, men moved with increasing freedom from one part of the Mediterranean world to the other on every sort of errand in the fifth century. Among them were the peripatetic professional teachers known as the Sophists. Some of these Sophists outraged the more conservative sensibilities of Socrates and Plato, not only because they taught for pay, but also because they professed a "sophisticated" relativism with respect to laws, morals, and truth that seemed to make the search for wisdom a hopeless enterprise. But the Sophists, their ill usage in the writings of Plato notwithstanding, were at times more faithful to the fundamental impulses of Greek philosophy than the Attic school of Socrates. For some of them reached the conclusion that underlying all the differences of class, blood, culture, and law that appeared to divide the peoples of the Mediterranean world, there existed a common *physis* or nature transcending all differences, which reduced to insignificance the claims of rival moralities and rival states, and transformed all men into brothers.

One Sophist, Antiphon of Athens, a contemporary of Socrates, deplored both the class and the racial snobbery of the Hellenes. "By nature," he wrote, "we all equally...have an entirely similar origin: for it is fitting to fulfill the natural satisfactions which are necessary to all men: all have the ability to fulfill these in the same way, and in all this none of us is different either as barbarian or as Greek." The supreme rule of life was *homonoia*, or concord, "the harmony which through [justice] is called forth in individuals and in states and in humanity as a whole; it embraces everything and all men; from the union of many states it descends to the most circumscribed but all-important internal harmony of the individual." One of Antiphon's followers, Hippias of Elis, enlarged his conception of a common mankind by stressing the universality of human sympathy. As Mario Untersteiner points out, Hippias's teachings, "to which was opposed the inhuman nationalism of Plato," led him "to recognize as friends and kinsmen the men of all cities and all nations." The cosmopolitanism of Hippias surpassed that of Antiphon, since Antiphon "had laid his emphasis on identity of physical needs among men of different social classes, and among Greeks and barbarians, whereas Hippias seems to have omitted any reference to this preeminently materialistic and egotistic natural motive in order to insist on the ties of sentiment which are their nobler consequences."[4]

But the Socratics were perhaps justified in their fears that the cultural relativism and cosmopolitanism of the Sophists would help dissolve the loyalties that, for better or worse, had bound the Greek peoples to their *poleis* for centuries. The negative and almost other-worldly qualities of the thought of Antiphon and Hippias recur in exaggerated form in the so-called Cynic school of the fourth century B.C., which apparently derived its name from its doctrine that a man should live like a stray dog (*kyon*), without homeland or possessions. The Cynic teaching of Diogenes of Sinope and Crates of Thebes proclaimed the vanity of all pursuits but that of natural virtue. Service to the state and the quest for riches and pleasure alike were reviled as artificial. The Cynics affected a disdain for earthly goods that recalls the mendicant holy men of India or even Jesus of Nazareth; they also taught that the enlightened man was a citizen of the world, rather than of any particular city or country. It is the Cynics who first spoke of the *kosmopolis* or world-city, by which they meant not any real or possible empire, but the invisible community of the wise and the good —a concept not far removed from St. Augustine's *civitas Dei*.

Although Cynicism persisted into the Roman era, it never attracted a large following. Its chief importance historically is rather the influence that it exerted on the dominant philosophical school of the next five hundred years, Stoicism. No less a scholar than W. W. Tarn insists, without contemporary evidence, that Alexander the Great originated the doctrines of human brotherhood and concord put forward by the Stoics after his death, but it seems much more plausible that Stoicism took the better part of its inspiration from the Cynics.⁵ Quite apart from similarities of doctrine, Zeno of Citium, the founder of Stoicism, was a pupil of the Cynic philosopher Crates.⁶

In any event, through Stoicism the universalism deeply embedded in the Greek philosophical mind at last reached full fruition and penetrated the thought and lives of the educated classes everywhere in the Mediterranean world. This singular school of later classical thought was founded in Athens early in the third century by a gaunt, abstemious Phoenician from Cyprus. Zeno of Citium (not to be confused with Zeno the Eleatic, the author of the famous paradoxes) gave his discourses at a decorated colonnade or *stoa* in Athens, from which his followers took the name of "Stoics." His biographer Diogenes Laertius says of Zeno's first book, *The Republic*, that according to a contemporary joke "he had written it upon the tail of the dog"—an obvious reference to his studies with the Cynic Crates.⁷

The full text of this first Stoic classic is now lost to us, but we know enough of its argument to be sure that it differed fundamentally from Plato's dialogue of the same title. Although both books depicted utopias, Zeno's concept of the ideal republic was that of a world-city, the city of Zeus, where all men and all women were citizens and members of one another in true equality, a commonwealth without slavery, family life, coinage, courts, schools, temples, or national distinctions. Such a world-city, it is clear, derived its authority from the cosmic order itself, which Zeno represented in various works as both divine and rational. God, the ground of being, arranged all things according to reason; by virtue of his rationality, man enjoyed a unique kinship with the deity, which placed him above the other animals, transforming him into a social animal bound to his fellows by ties of sympathy and mutual need. Man's reason also enabled him to obey freely the will of providence and to understand that all things worked to good ends, no matter how much suffering might be required along life's path.⁸

The essential piety, as well as cosmopolitanism, of the early Stoa is also clearly evident in the only Stoic writing that survives in its entirety from the third century, the "Hymn to Zeus," by Cleanthes of Assos. Formerly a manual laborer who worked at night so that he could hear Zeno's lectures during the day, Cleanthes replaced him as head of the school after his death in 263 B.C., and was in turn succeeded by Chrysippus of Soloi. "We are thy children," Cleanthes sang to Zeus, "we alone, of all/ On earth's broad ways that wander to and fro,/ Bearing thine image wheresoe'er we go." Zeus knew how to make the crooked straight, and harmonized "Things evil with things good, that there should be/ One Word through all things everlastingly." Those wayward souls who deserted their duty to pursue fame, riches, and sensuous pleasures, "wander, fruitless still,/ For ever seeking good and finding ill," but with the help of Zeus his children could be saved by wisdom "from error's deadly sway."[9]

Although the first Stoics like the first Christians preached a rarefied doctrine that could not readily become the basis of a practical political philosophy, it had its political applications even in the days of Zeno. Diogenes Laertius reports that King Antigonus Gonatas of Macedonia "used to attend his lectures whenever he came to Athens and was constantly inviting Zeno to visit him." Zeno refused, citing age and ill health, but sent two of his pupils in his place.[10] The King apparently filled his court with poets and philosophers of the Stoic persuasion; Mason Hammond finds no reason to doubt that "Antigonus consciously conformed to the Stoic concept of the ruler"—as a just and virtuous man who sought to bring his laws and policies into harmony with cosmic reason.[11]

But the monarchies of the Hellenistic period did not give the Stoic vision of the city of Zeus the full scope that it logically demanded. After the accession of Rome in the second century B.C. to the imperial power first won by Alexander, the Roman republic in effect became a world-city, with some of the outward characteristics of the republic described by Zeno, and responsibility for the peace of most of the known world. The old provincial town on the western coast of Italy was now a metropolis and a cultural center irresistibly attractive to men of all nations. The native Romans developed a taste for foreign fashions, including an amateur interest in philosophy, which was brought to them by a variety of Greek and Hellenized teachers, including numerous Stoics. The first Stoic to visit Rome was Panaetius of Rhodes, who headed the Stoic school in Athens toward the end of the second century B.C. Panaetius taught that all mankind comprised a single universal society, but that service to one's own state did not demean the wise man. On the contrary, withdrawal from civic duties and refusal to cooperate loyally with one's fellow citizens smacked of inhumanity. The state, on its side, was obliged to promote justice and protect the rights of all its subjects in a spirit of benevolence and charity. His successor, Posidonius of Apamea, who numbered Cicero among his students, went still further to equate Roman imperialism with the Stoic mission. As Moses Hadas points out, Posidonius argued that all the world "must welcome the rule of the empire, and the empire, for its part, must discharge its high obligation as the vicar of the divine."[12] Confronted with the vigor of young Rome and the rapid growth of the *Pax Romana*, Stoic-

ism climbed down somewhat from its unearthly counsels of perfection and
sought to adapt itself to the needs of statesmen in the real world.

Little survives of the writings of these philosophers of the so-called
Middle Stoa, but the gist of their philosophy can be judged from the reports of later writers and from its influence on Roman politics and jurisprudence. Two concepts in particular that enjoyed wide currency in
Roman thought reflect their teaching: the idea of the *jus naturale* and the
idea of *humanitas*.

Even before the arrival of Stoicism, the republic had been compelled to
take account of the differences in positive law between Rome herself and
the countries of the innumerable foreigners who lived under Roman juris-
diction. The solution of Roman jurists was to create a body of special law,
known as the *jus gentium*, grounded in reason and equity, which could
be applied to foreigners and also had the effect of gradually enlightening
the traditional civil code of Rome. When the Stoics spoke of an overrid-
ing law of nature (in Latin, the *jus naturale*), which transcended all customary law and took its authority from reason, the universal moving principle of the cosmos, their Roman pupils were easily persuaded that the
jus gentium was in fact a translation of the *jus naturale* into positive law,
and that in the final analysis all positive law should be conformable to the
jus naturale. Long before the establishment of the Augustan principate,
therefore, the Romans had accustomed themselves to the idea of a world
rule of law. "Compared with Athens in 322," George H. Sabine suggests,
"the Mediterranean world of two centuries later was almost modern....
Accepting as accomplished fact the wreckage of the city-state and the impossibility of its self-centered provincialism, of its rigid distinction between citizens and foreigners...Stoicism had boldly undertaken to rein-
terpret political ideals to fit the Great State." In place of the idea of blind
loyalty to the city, the Stoics had proposed the conception of a world-wide
brotherhood of men equal by nature "united in the bonds of a justice
broad enough to include them all."[13] Little by little, Roman jurisprudence
clothed the Stoic vision with firm legal flesh; the final step was perhaps the
granting of universal Roman citizenship by the Emperor Caracalla in
212 A.D.

Also significant, on a different plane, was the Ciceronian idea of *humanitas*. As Hans Kohn writes, *humanitas* combined and Latinized the
Greek concepts of humane culture (*paideia*) and the love of mankind
(*philanthropeia*). "Under Stoic influences it became both an individual
norm that man might become a real man, might cultivate the human in
himself; and, at the same time, a universal norm, the consciousness of the
human quality common to all human beings, the oneness of humanity."[14]

In theory if not always in practice, *humanitas* replaced the conventional warrior virtues as the guide to right conduct and the spirit of the laws. It helped to inspire the evolution of Roman law and public administration in the centuries thereafter, down to the *Pandects* of Justinian.

But the Roman *imperium* even at its most resplendent was still only a pale copy of Zeno's ideal republic. Its citizens were not equal in all respects, its emperors not always wise or just, its subject nations not always contented. Even as Stoic cosmopolitanism continued to humanize and rationalize the law in the first centuries of the Christian era, the last representatives of Stoicism as a school of philosophy, from Seneca and Epictetus to the philosopher-emperor Marcus Aurelius, gave voice to a growing disenchantment with the world that recalls the austere perfectionism of the earliest Stoics. Men were still regarded as brothers, children of one God and citizens of one great world-city; but as time passed it became increasingly difficult to identify that sublime society in any way with the often sordid realities of Roman world politics. "My city and country," wrote Marcus Aurelius, "so far as I am Antoninus, is Rome, but so far as I am a man, it is the world."[15] Clearly he owed his higher loyalty to "the world." For Marcus Aurelius as for Seneca before him, Rome was nothing more than a *polis*, of rather extraordinary proportions perhaps, yet not comparable with the *kosmopolis* of the wise and the good proclaimed by Crates the Cynic and by Zeno and Chrysippus half a millennium before.[16] In any case, by the third century A.D. the surviving professional philosophers of the ancient world had abandoned Stoicism. Even Seneca, Epictetus, and Marcus Aurelius themselves cannot be described as first-rate philosophical minds.

At the same time, it must be remembered that the decay of Stoicism was scarcely an isolated phenomenon in late antiquity. Except for the neo-Platonism of Plotinus, late pagan thought produced little of interest to historians of philosophy. Nor did the decline of Stoicism as a formal school entail the immediate decline of the influence of Stoic concepts in Roman law and life. Long after its own internal development had come to an end, Stoicism continued to flourish, a philosophy without philosophers, drawing on the intellectual and spiritual capital of the past.

Stoicism also survived through its links with early Christian thought. The first Christian theologian, Paul of Tarsus, was almost certainly influenced by the universalism of the Stoics. He could have been exposed to it in his native city, the seat of a well-known university where Stoicism was taught. Stoic terms for God's creative power—word (*logos*) and breath (*pneuma*)—appear in the Gospel of St. John, who may have taken them from the teachings of Philo, a Hellenized Jewish philosopher of Alexandria of the early first century A.D. In good time, nearly the whole range of Stoic concepts was incorporated in one way or another into Christian philosophy by the fathers and doctors of the Church. No Eastern religion shared more common ground with any Greek school of philosophy than Christianity shared with Stoicism.

But there were also differences. As Ernst Troeltsch argues, the Stoics tended to represent the outlook of the upper classes. Stoicism "fostered the aristocratic self-sufficient spirit of a ruling class which has been recently enlightened and ethically deepened." It hoped for reform, through the teaching of wisdom, but it was not a revolutionary doctrine. It demanded philosophic serenity on the part of its true-believers, and it collaborated, in effect, with existing social orders. The same might be said of Christianity at many times in its history, especially of ecclesiastical Christianity. But the primitive impulse in Christian teaching, which has never entirely lost its potency, partakes of a hope far more radical than anything envisioned by the Stoics. Christianity is "a movement of the lower classes, who are able to hope for and expect something quite fresh, and who, in their Myths and their Hero, have at their disposal energies of a very different kind which can exert a proper influence by mass-psychology."[17]

Initially, the Christian hope was perhaps much like the hope of post-exilic messianic Judaism. The first Christians believed that the Messiah had come, in the person of Jesus Christ, and would shortly return to inaugurate the millennium, a magical era of peace and harmony and freedom for the Jewish nation, after which the dead would be resurrected, and the peoples of all nations would be judged. Those found worthy would enter heaven, those found unworthy would descend into hell. Such a vision does violence to the strongly this-worldly Judaism of the Old Testament, but it was widely disseminated in the days when Jesus lived and taught, partly as the result of a powerful infusion of Zoroastrian ideas. Christianity thus brought with it two hopes, for personal immortality outside of time, and for a millennial utopia within the bounds of history.

Christianity also differed from Stoicism in its typically Jewish insistence on the primacy of moral imperatives proclaimed on divine authority, and its lack of interest in the philosophic search for truth. The great purpose of Greek philosophy was to know the world and nature and man, even if, as in Stoicism and Epicureanism, only to enable the individual to find his proper place in life. The Christian gospel began with acceptance of the fatherhood of God and the duty of all men to love their neighbors as themselves unconditionally. Like Judaism and Islam, it called not for philosophy but for submission to the will of God. Or, as an administrator at a prominent Fundamentalist university in the American Deep South recently told a television interviewer: "At this university we do not seek the truth: we have it." Such a statement may seem improper in the mouth of a spokesman for "scholars," but it discloses quite candidly the gulf between the Biblical world-view and Hellenism.

Although Jesus of Nazareth has been the subject of the most intensive historical research of any figure in ancient history, the results are so inconclusive that we may wonder if the man ever lived. But the New Testament offers a convincing word-portrait of a sharp-witted and benevolent teacher who gave up his career as a carpenter to bear witness to the voice of God within him, and who suffered martyrdom in Jerusalem, betrayed to the Roman authorities by his own people, in 29 A.D.

The Jesus of the synoptic Gospels of Matthew, Mark, and Luke devoted his ministry almost entirely to Jews. One is tempted to agree with Henry Bamford Parkes that Jesus may have "regarded himself not as the savior of all humanity but as a Jewish prophet [who] believed in the fulfillment of the Jewish national hope."[18] Yet the teaching of Jesus departed significantly from Pharasaic Jewish tradition, above all in its insistence that Jewish law had been transcended, although not abolished, by a higher law of love given to man directly by his heavenly Father, and fulfilled not by deeds but by the inward disposition of the heart. Whether the "historical" Jesus intended his words for Jewish ears alone or not, he had already begun the de-Judaization of Judaism by attaching supreme importance to an ethical world-view that bore no connection with the ritualism of the orthodox Jews, and could be accepted by all men regardless of race just as they found it in the books of the New Testament. At the same time, of course, Jesus took from the Old Testament its view of God as one, absolute, and universal, and its demands for righteousness and obedience to the divine will.

After the death of Jesus, if indeed there was such a man, the Christians divided into two factions, those who wished to continue as a Jewish sect, and those who wished to convert the Gentiles, even if it meant the abandonment of circumcision, Jewish dietary laws, and most of the other special features of Jewish piety. The former, led by Jesus's reputed brother James, flourished for a time with headquarters in Jerusalem, but gradually declined after a major Jewish uprising against Rome prompted the destruction of Jerusalem by the future emperor Titus in 70 A.D.

Meanwhile, the catholic faction, headed by St. Paul, established missions and Christian congregations in many of the towns of the Mediterranean world, converting both Jew and Gentile, and giving to the

Christian faith the status of a universal religious brotherhood as indifferent to national boundaries as the early Stoics. Paul is legitimately regarded as the second founder of Christianity, not only because his epistles in the New Testament represent a body of teachings comparable in depth of insight to those of Jesus himself, but also because it was he who transformed Christianity into a world religion.

The Acts of the Apostles and Paul's Epistles offer two views, not necessarily incompatible, of the relationship between Jew and Gentile. In the first view, expounded by Paul in his letters to the Romans and the Ephesians, God had formerly chosen to reveal his word to the Jews alone. Paul reminded the Gentiles that at one time "ye were without Christ, being aliens from the commonwealth of Israel, and strangers from the covenants of promise, having no hope, and without God in the world."[19] Christ "in his flesh" had destroyed the wall between the two worlds: through him, both now enjoyed access to the Father. Yet most of the Jews had refused to embrace Jesus as their messiah, and Paul, seeking to make sense of this ironic reversal of fortunes, suggested that the Jewish denial of Jesus had been necessary in order to stimulate the propagation of his gospel in the Gentile world. The Jews stumbled, he wrote in Romans, so that "through their fall salvation is come unto the Gentiles." He hoped, as a Jew, that the good example of the Gentiles would some day be emulated by "them which are my flesh."[20] But the whole passage seems to imply that if the Jews had all accepted Jesus of Nazareth as their savior in the first place, he would have become known essentially as a national prophet, and the rest of the world would have remained in darkness.

In any event, the providentially appointed role of the Gentile was to build a new Israel. The Jews as a nation, said Paul, had broken the law, and forfeited their special place in God's eye. The Gentile who became a Jew inwardly, by accepting God's will and salvation through Christ, was truly a Jew, and truly circumcised, while the Jew who merely conformed to Jewish tradition was not a Jew at all. The new chosen people were the Christians, the Jews of the spirit, no matter what their national origins, and all Christians alike could be described as "Abraham's seed, and heirs according to the promise," as "fellow-citizens with the saints, and of the household of God."[21]

In addition to the doctrine of Jewish national forfeiture and Christian inheritance, another view of the relationship between Jew and Gentile appears in the New Testament, which sought to minimize even the historic differences between the two peoples. Thus we read in Romans that "there is no respect of persons with God." He rewarded and punished men not according to whether they had heard his law (*i.e.*, whether they were Jewish), but according to whether they had lived justly, as many Gentiles had done. "For when the Gentiles, which have not the law, do by nature the things contained in the law, these, having not the law, are a law unto themselves: Which shew the work of the law written in their hearts, their conscience also bearing witness."[22] The influence of the Greek concept of a universal law of nature is unmistakable.

A similar point is made in Acts xvii:16-34, the memorable account of Paul's visit to Athens and his conversation with "certain philosophers of the Epicureans, and of the Stoicks." Referring to an altar he had seen inscribed "to the unknown God," Paul proclaimed that the God of Christ had created the world and "of one blood all nations of men for to dwell on all the face of the earth, and hath determined the times before appointed, and the bounds of their habitation; That they should seek the Lord, if haply they might feel after him, and find him, though he be not far from every one of us: For in him we live, and move, and have our being; as certain also of your own poets have said, For we are also his offspring."[23] Similar words had been used by Cleanthes of Assos in his "Hymn to Zeus," which Paul doubtless knew.

But whatever the past nature of the relationship between God's chosen people and the Gentiles, and whatever the sins of the Jewish nation as the executioner of its savior Jesus Christ, Paul's epistles affirmed unequivocally the unity of mankind under God in his own time and for all time to come. "For by one Spirit we are all baptized into one body, whether we be Jews or Gentiles, whether we be bond or free; and have been all made to drink into one Spirit." Or, as he wrote to his followers in Colosse, a new man had been born, in whom "there is neither Greek nor Jew, circumcision nor uncircumcision, Barbarian, Scythian, bond nor free: but Christ is all, and in all."[24]

Paul was executed as a trouble-maker by the Romans after more than a quarter-century of faithful service to the young Church, which included three extensive missionary tours to the cities of Greece and Asia Minor. Throughout his career, we may assume that he expected the imminent coming of a messianic kingdom of righteousness, of which the king would be Jesus Christ himself, restored to life, and whose subjects would be the whole body of Christendom, rather than Jews alone, as the popular Jewish eschatology of Christ's own time had specified. The hope of an imminent millennium generally faded in the second and third centuries A.D., although it has been periodically revived many times in the history of Christian faith. But Christianity enjoyed steady growth, in numbers of converts, and also in its appeal to the intelligentsia of the

Roman *imperium*, not to mention its institutional progress and its eventual triumph as the official state church under Constantine the Great in the 320's. The "fathers" of the Church during these first centuries included many of the greatest minds of late antiquity: Irenaeus, bishop of Lyons; Clement and Origen of Alexandria; Tertullian and Cyprian of Carthage; Eusebius of Caesarea; Ambrose, bishop of Milan; Jerome, the monk of Bethlehem; and Augustine, bishop of Hippo.

The claim of Christianity to the souls of all men and its vision of a world spiritual order was expanded in the fourth century A.D. to include both the concept and—at least in some degree—the reality of a Christian world state. So long as Rome remained a citadel of paganism and Christianity was persecuted by Rome's emperors, many Christians not unnaturally despaired of the empire, and even prayed for its eventual overthrow. But during the reign of Constantine, their attitude changed abruptly. The first Christian emperor made a point of cultivating prominent churchmen and Christian scholars, who looked on him as the founder of a whole new order in human affairs, calling to mind Virgil's praise of Augustus three centuries before.

One of Constantine's eulogists was Eusebius of Caesarea, the finest church historian of antiquity, and the author of a life of Constantine which saw the emperor as God's champion, who had conquered the world for Christ and would bestow upon it the blessings of true justice and peace. C. N. Cochrane concludes that "what Eusebius looked for in the age of Constantine was nothing less than a realization of the secular hope of men, the dream of universal and perpetual peace which classical Rome had made her own, but of which the *Pax Romana* was merely a faint and imperfect anticipation." Christianity alone provided the basis, "hitherto lacking, for human solidarity." The rival national and local deities of paganism had been toppled, and the ruler of the world now framed "his earthly government according to the pattern of the divine original, feeling strength in its conformity with the monarchy of God."[25] Further support for the Constantinian empire came from Lactantius, a Christian apologist of strongly humanistic leanings who was a member of the emperor's household and the tutor of his oldest son. Lactantius also prophesied the achievement of a Christian millennium of love and equality very much unlike his own world, but for which Constantine's reign, he believed, had prepared the way.

An optimistic and progressivist outlook that assigned to the Roman empire the providential task of unifying all mankind is frequently encountered in apologetic literature for many years after Constantine's death. As late as 403 A.D., the poet Prudentius contended that Rome

owed her worldly success to divine protection. "In all parts of the world
men live today as members of the same city and children of the same
hearth. . . . From the mingling of so many different bloods a single
race is born." The world had been put in readiness for the reign of Christ;
Rome's mission was only now approaching its fulfillment.[26]

But history—or providence—decreed otherwise. The sack of Rome by
Alaric the Visigoth in 410 and all the disasters that befell the empire
during the rest of the fifth century conspired to discredit the movement
in Christian thought initiated by Eusebius, at least for Western churchmen. Ruled from Constantinople, the eastern half of the empire survived
for another thousand years, harassed by enemies on all sides, but fashion-
ing its own version of world order modeled somewhat after the omni-
potent monarchy and the subordination of church to state of the old
empire. In the West, the imperial idea did not by any means perish. But
for several centuries it became difficult to sustain the hope of a great
world state that would literally restore the peace of Rome and assemble
all men in a single polity under a single law. As wave after wave of barbarians washed over Britain, Gaul, Spain, Africa, Italy, and central
Europe, the unity once provided by Rome disappeared, a fact too vast to
be ignored by the most sanguine of Christians.

More acceptable to early medieval thought in the West than the teachings of Eusebius and Lactantius were those of Augustine of Hippo, who
had only just reached the peak of his powers as a Christian theologian
and philosopher when the Visigoths captured Rome. In his greatest work,
The City of God, which he began writing in 413 as a refutation of the
argument that the Christian church was to blame for Rome's woes, he
set forth a world-view not dependent on the vicissitudes of states,
churches, or any other earthly institutions. Augustine's thought, for all
its virtuosity, drew inspiration from many sources, both pagan and Christian. His approach to the problem of human unity betrays the influence
of Stoicism and Manicheism, and also the image of the "household" or
"kingdom" or "city" of God frequently used in Biblical and patristic
literature. But it is primarily from Augustine that medieval Western
thought took its formulation of the Christian doctrine of the unity of
mankind.

Most pertinent here is Augustine's concept of the two *civitates*: the
civitas Dei and the *civitas terrena*. The former is invariably rendered "the
city of God"; the latter means "the earthly city," but earthly in a
pejorative sense, which it did not always have in Augustine's writing. The
civitas terrena was, in fact, the *regnum diaboli*, the realm of Satan, a portion of God's kingdom that had chosen to rebel against the divine govern-

ment in order to pursue its own self-appointed ends. But since all men and all angels owed absolute fealty to their creator, the secession of the damned was foredoomed to failure. Just as, in the Stoic philosophy, only the world-city of the wise conformed to the divine *logos*, or in Platonism only the ideal was real, so in Augustine's Christian dualism, only the city of God constituted a true commonwealth, and only the city of God enjoyed eternal life.

The rebellion against God, Augustine taught, had begun before history when certain of God's angels willfully turned away from his light and fell from grace. It continued with the fall of Adam, whose sin deprived mankind of immortality and introduced labor, lust, crime, and suffering into human life. The first state was founded by Adam's son Cain, a murderer, and coercive polities had been necessary ever since to keep earthly peace, because of fallen man's bad will. Yet the human race had not been converted *en masse* into a tribe of irredeemable devils by the circumstances of the fall. The *civitas Dei* also had its representatives on earth, in the stream of historical time; its citizens were pilgrims passing through the world on their way to eternity, whose archetype was Cain's victim Abel, an invisible republic of the saved and the blessed. Whether they suffered or prospered here below made no difference, yet they might be found in all walks of life, just as the citizens of the *civitas terrena* had infiltrated every human institution, not excluding the Christian church. The difference between the two cities was a difference of love. The earthly city had been formed "by the love of self, even to the contempt of God; the heavenly by the love of God, even to the contempt of self. . . . In the one, the princes and the nations it subdues are ruled by the love of ruling; in the other, the princes and the subjects serve one another in love, the latter obeying, while the former take thought for all. The one delights in its own strength, represented in the persons of its rulers; the other says to its God, 'I will love thee, O Lord, my strength.' "[27]

Augustine was careful not to confuse the *civitas terrena* with earthly states, just as he did not confuse the visible Church with the *civitas Dei*. Both cities, for that matter, were "invisible"; both consisted of souls, whether damned or saved. He also adopted from Greek thought the view that God had endowed mankind with reason and a social disposition. Both human depravity, therefore, and man's created nature demanded that he live in organized communities; nor did anything prevent citizens of the city of God from serving in earthly governments. Although Augustine ridiculed the popular fourth-century idea that Christian rulers invariably triumphed over their enemies and enjoyed long and happy reigns, he held as steadfastly as any Stoic to the conviction that rulers could be good men. Thus, in the fifth book of *The City of God* (v:24), it was no problem for him to offer a description of the ideal Christian emperor, which became a standard text for the admonition of princes in the centuries that followed. Augustine opposed not the world as such, but rather worldliness, in the sense of an exclusive lust for the ephemeral things of this world, for power and glory and wealth. The world had its own natural good, its own lesser peace, its own order and its own place in the economy of salvation, which no Christian could ignore.

At the same time, Augustine did not make the success of the city of God dependent in any way upon the success of earthly empires. The human race, or rather the elect of God, constituted a commonwealth beyond the power of anything that men might do within history. Nor did it matter if men lived under various terrestrial laws instead of one. "This heavenly city," he wrote, "while it sojourns on earth, calls citizens out of all nations, and gathers together a society of pilgrims of all languages, not scrupling about diversities in the manners, laws, and institutions whereby earthly peace is secured and maintained." The only *sine qua non* was that men not be hindered in their worship of God, for the goal of the pilgrim was nothing terrestrial, but the heavenly peace at the end of time, when "this mortal life shall give place to one that is eternal, and our body shall be no more this animal body which by its corruption weighs down the soul, but a spiritual body feeling no want, and in all its members subjected to the will."[28]

Augustine died in 430 A.D. By the end of the fifth century, the empire in the West was no more, and in the lands it had once ruled, a new kind of Western civilization gradually emerged, partly Judeo-Christian, partly Helleno-Roman, partly Germanic, partly Celtic, which lives on to the present day. Yet for its first eleven hundred years, a very long time in the history of any civilization, it took its intellectual and spiritual nourishment almost exclusively from what remained of the culture of antiquity. These are the eleven centuries of the "Middle Ages," the "Renaissance," and the "Reformation," from 500 to 1600 A.D., periods of great vitality and richness, of splendid architecture, art, and poetry, of commercial revival and expansion, of encyclopedic scholarship, of ingenious syntheses of law, philosophy, and theology, of advances in technology and methods of government: but not a time of fundamentally new departures in the realm of world-views or values. The most one can discover is new variations on old themes, or new ways of reconciling the Judeo-Christian and the classical elements in the Western tradition.

Still, the search for unity and the celebration of unity continued. Western Christendom, conscious of living in the aftermath of a great society that had spanned the whole world, whose technical accomplishments it needed several hundred years of growth even to equal, hungered after ecumenicity. Not only did it seek to emulate Rome; as a Christian civilization, it recognized only one God, one truth, one church. Nothing appeared more scandalous to the medieval mind than schism, at least in spiritual or ecclesiastical matters.

In some respects, post-classical Western Christendom did achieve organic unity almost from the beginning. The barbarian conquerors of old Rome were easily won over to the culture of the dead empire. They soon embraced to the best of their ability its literature, philosophy, science, and faith. A unified body of tradition emerged, with Latin as its *lingua franca*, differing little from Ireland to Italy or from Sweden to the Pyrenees. The "intellectuals" of the new civilization, its priests and monks, made their vows to the same universal church. Inspired by Christian universalism and by the powerful examples of Augustine in his *City of God* and Augustine's disciple Orosius in his *Seven Books of History against the Pagans*, scholars wrote histories of all mankind, an approach to the past unthinkable for the classical historian, but conventional throughout medieval and early modern times.

Yet politically Western Europe had been broken into a thousand pieces during the era of the *Völkerwanderungen*. The folk-law of the Germanic barbarians resisted Romanization far more stubbornly than their gods. Although doctrinal heresy and schism were uncommon in the Middle Ages, jurisdictional disputes between the Roman church and the secular sword occurred with great frequency, as barons, kings, and emperors sought jealously to preserve their local authority against all challenges from within or without.

At first, therefore, Europeans had little choice but to think of Christendom as a loose confederation of feudal monarchies held together by ties of faith and by memories of the *Pax Romana*. Even the power of the bishops of Rome was negligible in the early Middle Ages. But in due course, the growth of dynastic and papal ambitions gave rise to projects for making Christendom not only a single spiritual community, but a single state as well.

As early as 800, after successful military campaigns in Spain, Italy, and Germany, the Frankish king Charles the Great (Charlemagne) was crowned emperor in Rome by Pope Leo III, reviving the idea of a Roman *imperium* in the West. Although his empire, like Alexander's, collapsed after his death, it helped to keep alive the imperial tradition, and served as the precedent for a much longer-lived experiment in Christian imperialism, the "Holy Roman Empire" founded in 962 by Otto the Great of Saxony. Seldom more than an uncertain union of the principalities of Germany and northern Italy, the Holy Roman Empire reached its apogee under the house of Hohenstaufen in the twelfth and thirteenth centuries; but the idea of a Christian world state was long in dying. The Hohenstaufen emperors were succeeded by the house of Hapsburg, which ruled continuously from 1438 until 1740.[29] Even in the nineteenth century, vestiges of the imperial idea lived on in the career of Napoleon Bonaparte, who insisted on having himself crowned emperor of the French by the reigning Pope in 1804, and, rather more modestly, in the Austrian (or "eastern") Empire of the Hapsburgs, which ended only in 1918. Nor should it be forgotten that Byzantium endured, much diminished in size in its latter days, until 1453.

But kings were not the only claimants of imperial authority in the Middle Ages. Popes could also see themselves as world rulers, and perhaps with better cause. If the first rulers of united Christendom had been Constantine and his successors, the fall of the empire in the West had left the Roman church as the only institution representing the whole of occidental Christendom. Nor had Charles or Otto or the Hohenstaufens succeeded in literally re-creating the Roman *imperium*. The Pope alone spoke for all Christians. By the early thirteenth century, the papal court and its theological supporters had begun to claim for the Roman pontiffs sovereignty not only in the sacerdotal realm, but in the secular realm as well. In effect, writes John B. Morrall, the thirteenth-century papalists had transformed the early medieval concept of a Christian commonwealth into the vision of a full-fledged corporate polity, a state in the Aristotelian or Roman sense, "but under papal monarchy and with the secular rulers degraded to the rank of subordinate assistants to the papal world government."[30]

While popes such as Gregory IX, Innocent IV, and Boniface VIII contended with kings and emperors for the temporal overlordship of Europe, and found articulate supporters in theologians such as James of Viterbo and Giles of Rome, another party of apologists appeared who argued on behalf of the claims to world sovereignty of the Holy Roman emperors. One of these was Engelbert, abbot of the Cistercian monastery of Admont in Styria, who argued that the only guarantee of the peace and security of Christendom lay in the establishment of a world-encompassing empire ruled by a single supreme monarch. God in his infinite wisdom had ordained such an empire, for he knew that in no other way could concord be instituted among the various nations of man. Engelbert's world state, as Ewart Lewis observes, was a "philosopher's empire, based on the ultimate unity of human nature and its purposes, comprehending all mankind as a single people consenting to a common law, carrying to its perfect logical conclusion the principle of order attained through hierarchical subordination."[31]

Perhaps the most powerful of the defenders of secular imperialism was the poet Dante, in his treatise On Monarchy, written between 1310 and 1312. By this time the Hohenstaufen dynasty had long since passed away, the papacy had lost its battle with the French royal house and temporarily transferred its seat from Rome to Avignon, and the Holy Roman Empire had entered on a long period of progressive decline and enfeeblement. It was not unnatural for Italian and German thinkers, in particular, to lament the decay of imperial power and to hope for its restoration. But Dante's arguments went far beyond the practical politics of the moment.

In form, On Monarchy is a severely logical treatment of the problem of empire in the style and spirit of Aristotle, although the Philosopher himself would certainly have dissented from Dante's conclusions. A great variety of "proofs" are offered for the thesis that the proper ordering of temporal affairs requires monarchical world government. Some are pragmatic, such as the argument that when princes disagree, a supreme ruler is needed to resolve their differences. Others are purely religious, such as the claim that mankind is best when it is most like God: "But mankind is most like to God when it enjoys the highest degree of unity, since He alone is the true ground of unity—hence it is written: 'Hear, O Israel, the Lord thy God is one.' (Deut. vi:4) But mankind is most one when the whole human race is drawn together into complete unity, which can only happen when it is subordinate to one Prince, as is self-evident."[32]

The most strongly argued proof for world government that Dante presented in his treatise, however, rests upon his quasi-Aristotelian demonstration of the natural end of mankind. It was the peculiar nature of the human race, wrote Dante, to realize to the fullest possible degree its intellectual powers, something which no individual man in his short life could hope to do. Therefore, God permitted men to prolong their collective existence through many thousands of years, in order that their understanding might be perfected in the course of time. Such was the temporal happiness of mankind.

But mankind could not pursue its happiness without earthly guidance. Just as the body needed its mind, and the family its paterfamilias, so mankind as a whole needed a universal monarch, to lead it to its goal of intellectual self-realization. Just as the Roman pontiff guided mankind toward eternal life and heavenly concord, so the Roman emperor took responsibility for mankind's temporal happiness. "None would reach this harbour . . . unless the waves of alluring cupidity were assuaged and mankind were freed from them so as to rest in the tranquillity of peace; and this is the task to which that protector of the world must devote his energies who is called the Roman Prince. His office is to provide freedom and peace for men as they pass through the testing-time of this world."[33] Some scholars see in this sharp distinction between the temporal and heavenly goals of mankind the beginning of modern secularized politics, to which Dante's countryman Niccolò Machiavelli made such an important contribution more than two hundred years later.[34] In any event, Pope John XXII ordered the burning of Dante's work in 1329 and for more than three centuries after 1554 it appeared on the papal index of forbidden books.

More dangerous to Dante's thought than papal displeasure was the simple fact that a universal monarchy had become pragmatically impossible. The national and territorial monarchy was the wave of the future. No less a thinker than St. Thomas Aquinas, writing in the middle of the thirteenth century, failed even to mention the Holy Roman Empire in his chief work on politics, *De Regimine Principum*. By Dante's time, able opponents of the imperial idea had begun to speak out in defense of a plurality of sovereign states, such as John of Paris, who quite properly cited the authority of Aristotle and Augustine. All the same, it is impossible not to agree with Robert Folz that the vision of a Christian world state, no matter how strenuously it came to be opposed by the apologists of national polities or the prophets of *Realpolitik*, reflected "one of the most profound traits of the medieval mind, its aspiration to unity, its need of the *ordinatio ad unum*."[35]

The medieval concept of human unity, it may be concluded, based itself both on the Christian doctrine of the fatherhood of God and brotherhood of man, and on the classical doctrine of a common human nature. Thinkers tended to look for ways of harmonizing the two traditions, and in an age without a strongly developed historical consciousness, this was not as difficult a task as it would seem today. Classical philosophers had generally accepted the idea of a supreme creative intelligence or rational principle in the cosmos, from which human rationality sprang; Christian theologians, for their part, were quick to see that the Hellenic concept of the unity of human nature did not contradict Biblical anthropology. If all men were God's children, and Christ had died for all men, their possession of common faculties, needs, and predispositions was certain, and logically implict in Christian teaching. The theory that Athens and Jerusalem stand irreconcilably opposed to one another is more typical of modern than of medieval thought.

The same search for the harmony of religion and philosophy continued beyond the Middle Ages into the Renaissance of the fifteenth and sixteenth centuries. Indeed, from the point of view of the history of ideas, both the Renaissance and the Reformation are—as Herbert Butterfield has written—"mere episodes, mere internal displacements, within the system of medieval Christendom."[36] The efforts, for example, of Marsilio Ficino and his fellow Florentine Platonists to demonstrate the congruence of the Platonist tradition, including the neo-Platonism of Plotinus, with Christianity differ very little in their essential thrust from the efforts of the medieval philosophers to reconcile Aristotle and Christian teaching. The only difference is a small but perceptible shift in emphasis from the Christian to the classical part of the Western tradition, a stronger enthusiasm for classical learning, and—inevitably—a somewhat deeper respect for natural man. But the fascination exerted upon Renaissance scholars by antiquity was not limited to pagan antiquity. They also displayed a new interest in the Bible and the mystics and fathers of the early Church, including St. Augustine; and when they quarrelled with the medieval schoolmen, it was the alleged corruption and over-intellectualization of the Christian message carried out by men such as Aquinas, Scotus, and Ockham that earned their opprobrium above all, not the Christian inspiration of medieval thought as such.

A far more radical attempt to purify the Christian message was mounted by the Protestant Reformers, many of whom had been well schooled in the reverent humanism of the Renaissance. At their most fanatic, the reformers totally rejected classical philosophy and stressed the vileness of unredeemed man. Reason alone, even good works alone, profited a man nothing in their eyes. Yet, as Christians returning single-mindedly to Augustine, Paul, and Christ, they shared the early Christian conviction of the unity of mankind, a unity impaired only by human sin, and of the need to glorify God on earth by bringing all men under a common spiritual rule of life. Protestants, no less than Roman Catholics, insisted on the oneness of truth and faith. Some, such as the Calvinists and the Baptists, made strenuous efforts to establish millenarian republics that would call the peace of heaven to earth.

It is true, of course, that both Renaissance and Reformation in practice rendered aid and comfort to the movements in early modern Western society that tended to disrupt the universalism of medieval civilization. The modern absolute monarchy and sovereign nation-state, the ecclesiastical fragmentation of Western Christendom, and the attack on the organic order of medieval society by private capitalism all can be blamed, to some extent, on aspects of Renaissance and Reformation thought. But very little of this had been anticipated or intended by the humanists or the reformers themselves, and most of it would have happened sooner or later without their help.

Nor were the thinkers of the late Renaissance and the late Reformation indifferent to the anarchy that the events of the immediately preceding centuries had seemed to introduce into European life. Plans abounded for leagues of princes, the arbitration of international disputes, and permanent high councils to keep the peace of Europe. The prototype of such peace plans was perhaps Erasmus's *Querela Pacis* (1517), but more elaborate projects were published in the seventeenth century: Emeric Cruce's *Le nouveau Cynée*, Tommaso Campanella's *Monarchia Messiae*, the "Grand Design of Henry IV" included by the duc de Sully in his memoirs, and William Penn's *Essay toward the Present and Future Peace of Europe.*

Even more remarkable were the ideas of the seventeenth-century Moravian churchman and philosopher Jan Amos Komenský, better known as Comenius, who summed up all the most humane and cosmopolitan tendencies in the thought of the Renaissance and the Reformation. Born in 1592 and forced to leave Moravia during the Thirty Years War, Comenius was active in many countries in later life, including Poland, England, Sweden, and Holland. The disunity of Christendom troubled him profoundly. A bishop of the Moravian and Bohemian Brethren, he urged the convocation of an ecumenical council of all Christian confessions to restore the unity of the Church, after which, he predicted, a vast missionary effort would achieve the conversion of all men everywhere to the Christian faith.

Comenius also hoped to bring about the total integration of religion, philosophy, and the natural sciences. He termed his system "pansophy." Since truth was ultimately one, and revelation, reason, and observation were only different avenues to knowledge of the same indivisible truth, their unification in a single higher pansophist science posed no insuperable problems. A series of textbooks would be written synthesizing all knowledge encyclopedically, and a uniform system of schools using them would be established throughout the world. All men would speak a universal language and, understanding one another, they would become "as it were one race, one people, one household, one School of God." Yet another proposal made by Comenius was for a world conference of churches and nations to forge a common policy for promoting the peace and welfare of mankind. "We are all fellow-citizens of one world," he wrote in his

Panegersia in 1666, "all of one blood, all of us human beings. Who shall prevent us from uniting in one republic?"[37]

Some of the same hopes may be found in the writings of two other major thinkers of the seventeenth century, Francis Bacon and G. W. Leibniz. But with Bacon and Leibniz, rather more than with Comenius, we see at work the influences of a new force in thought that in time displaced classical philosophy and Biblical faith as the central inspiration of Western culture: the natural sciences conceived as autonomous disciplines, no longer subordinate in any way to metaphysics and theology. The cosmopolitanism of the eighteenth and nineteenth centuries depended heavily on the new views of nature, society, and man generated by the scientific outlook. In effect science usurped the functions of religion and philosophy. So did the integral nationalism of the nineteenth century, a regression to the polytheistic civic cults of pre-Alexandrian and pre-Christian antiquity, yet a potent substitute for religion in its own way.

But neither the scientific cosmopolitanism of the Enlightenment nor the nationalist counter-cosmopolitanism of the nineteenth century belongs to the traditional West as we have defined it in this chapter. The rise of modern science marks the beginning of a whole new era, not only in Western, but also in world history. In this modern era, all the traditional civilizations, Eastern as well as Western, have been suddenly hurled together. In the heat and fury of their confrontation, the great traditional doctrines of the unity of mankind assume new meaning and new relevance.

NOTES

1. See Mason Hammond, *City-State and World State in Greek and Roman Political Theory until Augustus* (Cambridge, Mass., 1951).

2. See Karl Jaspers, *The Origin and Goal of History,* tr. Michael Bullock (New Haven, Conn., 1953).

3. Xenophanes, "The Fragments" in Charles M. Bakewell, ed., *Source Book in Ancient Philosophy* (New York, 1907), p. 8.

4. Mario Untersteiner, *The Sophists,* tr. Kathleen Freeman (Oxford, 1954), pp. 252, 254, 283-284.

5. See W. W. Tarn, *Alexander the Great* (Cambridge, 1948), II, 399-449; and cf. T. A. Sinclair, *A History of Greek Political Thought* (London, 1952), pp. 240-242.

6. Nor should it be forgotten that Alexander, for his part, had been tutored by Aristotle!

7. Diogenes Laertius, "Life of Zeno," tr. C. D. Yonge and Moses Hadas, in Hadas, ed., *Essential Works of Stoicism* (New York, 1961), p. 4.

8. Two brief but provocative interpretations of Stoicism are Edwyn Bevan, *Stoics and Sceptics* (Oxford, 1913) and Ludwig Edelstein, *The Meaning of Stoicism* (Cambridge, Mass., 1966).

9. Cleanthes, "Hymn to Zeus," tr. James Adam, in Hadas, *Essential Works of Stoicism*, pp. 51-52.

10. Diogenes Laertius in Hadas, pp. 4-5.

11. Hammond, *City-State and World State*, p. 48.

12. Hadas in Hadas, *Essential Works of Stoicism*, p. xiii.

13. George H. Sabine, *A History of Political Theory*, 3d ed., (London, 1951), p. 142.

14. Hans Kohn, *The Idea of Nationalism: A Study in Its Origins and Background* (New York, 1944), p. 65.

15. Marcus Aurelius Antoninus, *Meditations*, 6:44, tr. G. Long, in Whitney J. Oates, ed., *The Stoic and Epicurean Philosophers* (New York, 1940), p. 533.

16. See M. I. Clarke, *The Roman Mind* (Cambridge, Mass., 1956), pp. 113-114.

17. Ernst Troeltsch, *The Social Teaching of the Christian Churches*, tr. Olive Wyon (New York, 1931), I, 67-68. Cf. Charles Norris Cochrane, *Christianity and Classical Culture: A Study of Thought and Action from Augustus to Augustine* (New York, 1944), p. 243.

18. Henry Bamford Parkes, *Gods and Men: The Origins of Western Culture* (New York, 1965), p. 388.

19. *Ephesians*, ii:12.

20. *Romans*, xi:11, 14.

21. *Romans*, ii:28-29; *Galatians*, iii:29; *Ephesians*, ii:19.

22. *Romans*, ii:11, 14-15.

23. *Acts*, xvii:26-28.

24. I *Corinthians*, xii:13; *Colossians*, iii:11.

25. Cochrane, *Christianity and Classical Culture*, p. 185.

26. Prudentius, *Contra Symmachum*, quoted in John T. McNeill, *Christian Hope for World Society* (Chicago, 1937), p. 10. See also Theodor E. Mommsen, "St. Augustine and the Christian Idea of Progress" in *Journal of the History of Ideas*, XII (June 1951), 346-374.

27. St. Augustine, *The City of God*, 14:28, tr. Marcus Dods (New York, 1950), p. 477.

28. Ibid., 19:17, pp. 696-697.

29. But Robert Folz notes that in the late Middle Ages the idea of an authentically universal empire gave way, for the most part, to the idea of a national empire, a territorialized empire taking its place as one sovereign state among others. Folz, *L'idée d'Empire en Occident du Ve au XIVe siècle* (Paris, 1953), pp. 171-178.

30. John B. Morrall, *Political Thought in Medieval Times* (New York, 1962), p. 81.

31. Ewart Lewis in Lewis, ed., *Medieval Political Ideas* (London, 1954), II, 446.

32. Dante, *Monarchy*, tr. Donald Nicholl (New York, 1954), p. 13.

33. Ibid., p. 93.

34. See Morrall, pp. 95-103, and A. P. d'Entreves, *Dante as a Political Thinker* (Oxford, 1952).

35. Folz, *L'idée d'Empire*, p. 190.

36. Herbert Butterfield, *The Origins of Modern Science* (London, 1950), p. viii.

37. Quoted in Matthew Spinka, *John Amos Comenius: That Incomparable Moravian* (Chicago, 1943), p. 83; and in Eduard Beneš, "The Place of Comenius in History as a Good European" in Joseph Needham, ed., *The Teacher of Nations* (Cambridge, 1942), p. 6.

PART 2

THE MODERN WORLD

SIX

Nationalism
and Internationalism

HANS KOHN

Emeritus Professor,
Department of History
The City College of New York

I

INTERNATIONALISM CAN BE DEFINED IN TWO WAYS, EITHER AS a form of a supra-national organization of society which includes, preserves and at the same time controls and limits nation-states, or as a state of mind which tries to visualize mankind as a whole, as a unit transcending all parochial (national or otherwise) groupings. Thus internationalism is an "idea," as nationalism was at its beginning, an *idée-force* which, also, seeks its realization in the political, cultural and economic order. But nationalism has found, beginning with the modern period of European history and in ever widening circles, its outward institutionalization, and this sometimes even in extreme forms of political, cultural and economic self-sufficiency. The fate of internationalism has been so far very different. In its first definition, it has found only in the twentieth century an imperfect institutionalization in the League of Nations and a more perfect yet still very inadequate one in the United Nations; yet none in its second definition. The possibility of an institutional objectivization of internationalism depends, of course, as that of nationalism, on the technological advance of communications to a degree which has been achieved only in the post-1945 era. Nevertheless, internationalism as a vision of the unity of mankind, frequently called cosmopolitanism or universalism, is a concept much older than nationalism is.

Nationalism as an idea dominant among the intellectual classes and as a movement (though not necessarily as a sentiment) was born, as far as historical trends or movements can be limited by precise dates, in the second half of the eighteenth century. But that century was also the time of a conscious cosmopolitanism, *Weltbürgertum*, among the educated classes in the Western world.

The century of the Enlightenment conceived history as a universal evolutionary process. Biblical concepts of the unity of mankind, descending from one and the same couple, being guided through Providence toward a common goal, were now secularized. In 1784 Immanuel Kant wrote his "Idea for a universal history from a cosmopolitan point of view" in which he put forward the thesis that "The greatest problem for the human race, to the solution of which Nature drives men, is the achievement of a universal civic society which administers law among men." And an early nationalist like Herder forsaw in the 16th book of his "Ideas for the History of Mankind" not the victorious rise of nationalism but the approaching end of nationality. "The scholars who study [the] customs and languages [of the European nationalities] must hurry and do so while these peoples are still distinguishable: for everything in Europe tends toward the slow extinction of national character. . . . The whole civilization of northern, eastern and western Europe has grown out of seeds sown by Romans, Greeks and Arabs. It took a long time before this plant could grow in the hard soil and could produce its own fruit which at first lacked sweetness and ripeness. A strange vehicle, an alien religion, was necessary to accomplish by spiritual means that which the Romans had not been able to do through conquest. Thus we must consider above all this new means of human education, which had no lesser aim than to educate all peoples to become one people, in this world and for a future world, and which was nowhere more effective than in Europe."

The cosmopolitanism of the eighteenth century was the legacy of the Stoics and of the Stoic-Christian Roman Empire. Probably similar universalist "ideas" have existed in Buddhism, in the Chinese and in other traditions, but I am confining my observations to the Western world. For the twentieth-century forms of nationalism and internationalism on a global scale derive from the Western tradition in its modern secularized form with its recognition of pluralism or diversity within a growing unity of a globe unified in the astonishingly short period of less than a century by Western technology. Nothing of this technological advance existed in the eighteenth century though the idea was there, f.i. when Oliver Goldsmith ended the last letter of his "The Citizen of the World" (1760), the observations of a wise Chinese visitor to Europe: "As for myself, the world being one city, I do not care in which of the streets I happen to reside."

Cosmopolitanism, the vision of and sometimes even the approximation to an open interdependent society, has dominated much of Western thought for over 1500 years. The Greek historian Polybius who lived in the second century B.C. described in his "Universal History" the consequences of the rise of the Roman empire: "Formerly the things which happened in the world had no connection among themselves. Each action interested only the locality where it happened. But since then all events are united in a common bundle." And fourteen centuries later Dante expected the salvation of mankind, torn by wars, from a universal monarchy, a world government, which would establish peace, justice and earthly happiness. Very different from nineteenth century Italian nationalists, Dante welcomed as the world ruler of his day a non-Italian, a German.

The same eighteenth century which emphasized in its educated classes an internationalist consciousness—the masses still thought and felt within a purely local context—witnessed also the first expressions of modern nationalism. Yet the later antagonism between nationalism and internationalism was widely unknown. They formed two aspects of the same movement; both were manifestations of the great moral and intellectual crisis through which the Western world passed in the second half of the eighteenth century and which I tried to describe in the last chapters of my *The Idea of Nationalism*. It was a search for regeneration, for better foundations of social life, for new concepts of public and private morality. The French Revolution was only the terminal focal point of a general movement, which can be called a populist and yet cosmopolitan nationalism or democracy, both taken in a broad sense, implying a struggle against the existing traditional and by now obsolete forms of government and hierarchical social order.

Government and society, state and people were arraigned in the eighteenth century against each other: the movement of renovation strove to fuse them in the name of liberty. The concept of political liberty and human dignity united internationalists and nationalists alike. As H. N. Brailsford pointed out, Benjamin Franklin's epigram, "Where liberty is, there is my country," and Thomas Paine's crusading retort, "Where liberty is not, there is mine," sum up the spirit of the new cosmopolitan patriotism of the later eighteenth century. It was the same spirit which is basic to Kant's "Zum ewigen Frieden." Cosmopolitanism or internationalism, and patriotism or awakening nationalism intermingled in that age of promise and hope under the aegis of liberty and peace.

The "fathers" of modern nationalism, Jean Jacques Rousseau and Johann Gottfried Herder, were at the same time cosmopolitans or internationalists. Deeply attached to their *patrie* or their native language and tradition, to their "amour de la patrie," they regarded at the same time the whole of mankind as a greater and higher fatherland and were also attached to the love of liberty and of peace. Rousseau followed the example of Plato and of Sparta in regarding the love of the *patrie* the most heroic of all passions and in stressing the distinctive self-being and self-centeredness of each [small] people. But different from Plato or Sparta, he extolled the rural population, the common man of his time, not the educated classes or philosophers or a warrior nobility as the matrix of national life and genius. Though Rousseau insisted on universal military service for patriotic and moral reasons, his ideal nation had to renounce all thought of military glory or expansion. The true nation, according to Rousseau, "ne sera point illustre, mais elle sera heureuse. On ne parlera d'elle; elle aura peu de considération au dehors; mais elle aura l'abondance, la paix et la liberté dans son sein."[1] This peaceful static nation was full of an intense inner life, of a great emotional love-force.

Herder, a non-political man in the non-political Germanies of his time, was a humanitarian democrat and a cosmopolitan pacifist as Rousseau was, in spite of some contradictory statements in their rich and not always systematic thought. More strongly even than Rousseau, Herder saw in Roman pride and lust of domination, in the glorification of the sword and of war, the evil inheritance of Western history. "Immer mehr muss sich die Gesinnung verbreiten, dass der Länder erobernde Heldengeist nicht nur ein Würgengel der Menschheit sei, sondern auch in seinen Talenten lange nicht die Achtung und den Ruhm verdiene, die man ihm aus Tradition von Griechen, Römern und Barbaren her zollet."[2] Herder discovered the "folk," the national community based upon what has been called the lower classes, as a genetic, developing and creative unit. By this discovery he gave a new perspective to our understanding of history, of civilization, the letters and arts. But he never raised the folk to an absolute or ultimate value, an important fragment of reality into a sovereign totality. The objectivity with which he viewed in his "Ideas for the History of Mankind" the peoples of northern Europe is remarkable and has not found many imitators. His description of the Slavs and Latvians, among whom he grew up and liked to live, has become famous. Peaceful, charitable and industrious, the Slavs and Latvians "have been sinned against by many nations, most of all by those of the German family." Herder was convinced that with the progress of civilization—and that meant for him, peaceful intercourse—these "submerged peoples" will come into their own. He saw European civilization as the work of all of them and of their intermingling. He warned "the historian of mankind to beware lest he exclusively favors one nationality and thereby slights others who were deprived by

circumstances of chance and glory." For Herder this principle was true beyond Europe, too. Like Kant, he castigated the colonial expansion of the
white race of his time. "Das Menschengeschlecht ist ein Ganzes: wir arbei-
ten und dulden, säen und ernten für einander . . . Das Gesetz der Billig-
keit ist keiner Nation fremd; die Übertretung desselben haben alle gebüs-
set, jede in ihrer Weise. Wenn intellektuelle Kräfte in mehrerer Ausbil-
dung der Vorzug der Europäer sind, so können sie diesen Vorzug nicht
anders als durch Verstand und Güte beweisen. Handeln sie...in niedrig
vermessenem Stolze, so sind sie die Tiere, die Dämonen gegen ihre Mit-
menschen."[3] Rousseau, Kant and Herder were conscious of the dangers
contained in a nationalism that does not treat all other peoples, whatever
their power or their degree of development, as possessing equal status and
equal right.

II

The project of an organization which would institutionalize the solidarity
of free peoples above all inevitable national conflicts and rivalries goes
back to the Enlightenment. It found its first concise and realistic formulation in Kant's brief pamphlet "Zum ewigen Frieden." The Napoleonic
wars, designed to establish French hegemony in Europe and the two German wars for European and global hegemony in the first half of the
twentieth century seemed to contradict Kant's expectation of an international order. Do not Nietzsche's famous words, written in admiration of
Napoleon and in contempt of the liberal pacifism of his age, appear prophetic today: "We owe to Napoleon...that several warlike centuries un-
equalled in history will now follow each other, in short, that we have
entered the classical age of war...to which thousands of years will look
back with envy and awe as to something perfect...a Napoleon who
wanted a unified Europe and this Europe to be the master of the globe."
Did the events of 1914 to 1945 not bear out Nietzsche's prophecy? Nietzsche himself was not a nationalist, least of all a German nationalist, and no
admirer of any state, least of all of Prussia or of Bismarck's Reich. Nevertheless, his extremism, his contempt for moderation and liberalism, his
apparent glorification of war, violence and hardness, so opposed to his own
nature, influenced the rise of an authoritarian, militant nationalism.

Yet the idea of internationalism remained always alive in the nineteenth
century. In the early part of the century Christian conscience mitigated
the concern of nationalism with power as its chief aim and substance, and
the rational cosmopolitanism of the Enlightenment survived in many
thinkers and scholars even in a period of aroused nationalist passions. The
German philosopher Karl Christian Friedrich Krause elaborated in 1808

a plan for a federation of mankind (Menschheitsbund) and published in 1814 a draft of a constitution of a European federation which he considered as a regional system within a future world government. During three months he published a "Tagblatt des Menschheitslebens," probably the first journal dedicated to the cause of mankind. The Göttingen historian Arnold Hermann Ludwig Heeren praised the German Bund as the "Friedensstaat von Europa." A centralized German nation-state in the heart of Europe appeared to this German patriot as the potential "Kriegsstaat von Europa." In anticipation of Toynbee and the post 1945 world, he was convinced that future historians would deal with a Welt-Staaten-System and that an era of sea-power and of liberal world-order would secure a happier future for mankind.

In 1814, a German, living in Paris, Count Gustav Schlabrendorf, speaking of the failure of the French Revolution to E. A. Varnhagen von Ense, explained it by the lack of a broader framework for the democratic movement which started in 1789: "As little as individuals, can states form themselves and prosper in isolation; they succumb to dull inertia or wild fury; they lack a thousand qualities which are produced and preserved by neighborly competition. That was the reason, why the French Revolution could not immediately succeed: one people alone can not carry through such a task. One used to say that France was too large [for a democracy]; I say to the contrary, it was too small. But now the revolution is no longer an isolated French fact, because the whole of Europe has taken part in it, willingly or otherwise, and will take part even more. Now [democracy] can succeed as the work of so many people. . . . But I demand that the form of the [future] states be such as to allow everyone, without being a hero and ever ready to fight for it, to live always as a free man and with dignity; such a liberty is England's great advantage, it was entirely absent in old France."

Professor Theodor Schieder has recently expressed his surprise how favorable the political literature of the nineteenth century judged the supranational state. "Selbst bis weit in den Liberalismus hinein wird der politische und ideelle Vorrang des Nationalstaates bestritten und ist die grundsätzliche Überlegenheit eines über den Nationalitäten stehenden Staatsprinzips behaupten worden."[4] The same can be said of many poets and writers. When in 1840 nationalist passion ran high on both sides of the Rhine, Lamartine wrote his "Marseillaise de la Paix"; fifteen years later he affirmed "Homo sum, voilà ma patrie." Early in the nineteenth century an organized peace movement arose in the West; it started in 1815 with the founding in the United States of three peace societies; Noah Worcester in his "A Solemn Review of the Custom of War" (1814) was, according to Norman Angell, the first specifically to advocate joint action against war through peace societies; he urged a confederacy of nations with a high court of equity for the settlement of national controversies. In 1828 the local American peace societies joined to form the American Peace Society. Soon they began to cooperate with the British Society for the Promotion of Permanent and Universal Peace, founded in London in 1816; under their influence the Société des Amis de la Morale Chrétienne et de la Paix came into being in Paris and Count Jean Jacques de Sellon, Cavour's uncle, founded the Société de la Paix de Genève.

Through men like Richard Cobden and John Bright an international attitude expressed itself in England not only in demands for free trade and intercourse but also in pacifism. They and Elihu Burritt, the learned blacksmith from Connecticut, made the first proposals for close Anglo-American-French cooperation. They warmly supported George McGibbs when he suggested founding in Paris, in 1842, a daily paper in French; in the following year, on June 28, 1843, the first international pacifist conference met in London, attended by delegates from the United States, the United Kingdom and France. On September 20, 1848, the first international peace congress in Brussels was hopefully greeted by the American poet John Greenleaf Whittier in a poem "The Peace Convention at Brussels":

Evil shall cease and violence pass away.
And the tired world breathe free through a long Sabbath day.

The Congress favored simultaneous reduction of armaments, a congress of nations, and education toward the eradication of national prejudices. Huge popular demonstrations in London and other English cities preceded the Second Peace Congress which met in Paris in August 1849 and was officially received by the then Foreign Minister, Alexis de Tocqueville. From Britain alone came 670 delegates. Victor Hugo was its president, Cobden its vice-president. In his opening address, on August 21, the French poet insisted that peace was a practical and inevitable goal, and that arbitration would take the place of war. Pointing to the example of the French provinces which had replaced wars of former ages by the ballot box, he predicted that the European nations would similarly fuse in a higher unit while preserving their distinct individualities. "A day will come," he concluded, "when we shall see these two immense agglomerations, the United States of America and the United States of Europe, facing each other and stretching out their hands across the seas in close cooperation." Two more peace congresses were held, in 1850 in the St. Paul's Church in Frankfurt—but the first peace society formed in Germany in Königsberg was soon suppressed by the Prussian authorities on the ground

of its having conducted a correspondence with the London Peace Society
—and in London in 1851, at the time of the Crystal Palace exhibition.
Peace societies continued active in Britain and the United States. An international peace congress met in Geneva in 1867, but ended in dissensions between radicals under Garibaldi's leadership and moderates. In the
same year the League for Peace and Liberty met in Berne and began to
publish its weekly "Les États Unis d'Europe." But the international movement was revived on a broader basis only around 1890, with the Inter-
Parliamentary Union and the Universal Peace Congresses, the first of
which met in Paris in 1889.

Yet even in the difficult period between the early 1850's and 1889, when
aggressive and self-centered nationalism grew strong in Europe, international cooperation and peace continued to be discussed and favored by
some of the foremost thinkers of the time. Among the jurists proposing
the institutionalization of supranational law, James L. Lorimer (1818 to
1890) may be cited, who held the chair of the Law of Nature and of Nations, a name derived from Grotius, in the University of Edinburgh. In
1872 he published a draft scheme for a permanent congress of nations and
for an international court of justice. The international Congress was to
consist of a Senate and a Chamber of Deputies who were empowered to
settle the political disputes of Europe. A similar scheme was worked out
in 1881 by the Swiss jurist Johann Kasper Bluntschli, then professor at the
University of Heidelberg, in his book "Die Organisation des europäischen
Staatsvereins." He, too, proposed a bicameral representation, a Council of
governmental delegates and a Senate of parliamentary representatives, to
settle European problems.

Starting from a broad historical rather than from a concrete juridical
basis, Ernest Renan analyzed the European situation at the end of the
war of 1871 in an open letter to David Friedrich Strauss. After reflections
on the role of Britain, France and Germany in their relationship among
themselves and with the United States and with Russia, reflections which
are even today of highest interest, he continued: "Peace cannot be established and maintained except by the common interest of Europe or, if
one prefers it, by a league of neutral powers ready to enforce peace. Justice
has no chance to triumph between two contending parties, but between
ten contending parties justice wins out, for she alone offers a common
basis of agreement. The only force capable of upholding a decision for the
welfare of the European family against its most powerful member state
lies in the power of the various states to unite, to intervene and to mediate.
Let us hope, that this force will assume ever more concrete and regular
forms and will lead in the future to a real congress, meeting periodically if

not permanently. It will become the heart of the United States of Europe, bound by a federal pact."

A new internationalism, based this time upon mass-parties, emerged in 1889, the centenary of the French Revolution, when the Second International of Socialist and Workers Parties was founded. Most members officially adhered to the orthodox Marxist point of view, as expressed at the Congress of Brussels in August, 1891, that "There could not be for them any antagonism or struggle of race or nationality, but only the class struggle between proletarians of all races and capitalists of all races." This stand was taken in connection with the rejection of a motion by Jewish Socialists from the United States concerning anti-semitism. But soon the International had to recognize the urgency of national problems and conflicts and the prevention of war between nations became one of the main tasks of the International. Many workers and their leaders changed, as the economic situation of the working classes improved and their stake in the existing economic and political structure grew, from their theoretical class-internationalism to an acceptance of the realities of the late nineteenth century nation-state. Understandably some socialists in the then politically and economically backward countries like Russia did not follow this trend; the situation of the working class there at the beginning of the twentieth century recalled the European conditions of the 1840's rather than those of the contemporary Europe. In some continental countries the compulsory military service influenced many workers, at least subconsciously, in taking pride in the military tradition and in the greatness of the fatherland. A recent book by Hans-Ulrich Wehler, "Sozialdemokratie und National-staat," gives a convincing analysis of the shift in the German Social Democratic party from internationalism to the full acceptance of the reality of the German nation-state. In 1871 Karl Bebel and Wilhelm Liebknecht protested against the annexation of Alsace-Lorraine and Bebel called the annexation "ein Verbrechen gegen das Völkerrecht" and "ein Schand-flecken in der deutschen Geschichte."[5] In January 1886 Liebknecht still insisted in discussing Bismarck's anti-Polish policy that a nationalism by which a nationality oppresses another or drives it from the land was barbaric and that the principle of humanity (Humanität) ranked high above that of nationality: "Erst sind wir Menschen und dann Glieder einer Nation. Die Nationalität ist das Zufällige und das Menschsein ist das Wesentliche."[6] But from 1890 on more and more concessions were made to the "normative power of the factual situation" (die normative Kraft des Faktischen) and the socialist party began to feel responsible for German interests (die deutschen Belange) in Alsace-Lorraine and in the Polish lands under Prussian rule.

The decline of internationalism in the International, and especially the role played in this process by the German Social Democrats has been brilliantly analyzed by Professor James Joll. Yet the majority of socialists continued to believe in the power of the united European proletariat to prevent or stop wars. This confidence was strongly expressed at the last Congress of the International, called to Basel in November 1912 at the outbreak of the Balkan war. Edouard Anseele declared there: "The proletariat, which from today henceforth must be recognized as the herald of world peace, demands peace in the Balkans, republican autonomy for the Balkan peoples, the abandonment of alliances and of diplomatic intrigues which carry with them the seed of every war. Austria-Hungary must not try to rob the Balkan peoples of the fruit of their victories, and, if Russia attacks, the Russian proletariat itself will rise and support it [the international proletariat] enthusiastically and admiringly. For France and Germany the hour of reconciliation has struck. There is to be no more war between Germany and France. (There was particularly excited applause at this point.) Great Britain and Germany should arm but not in a race to build warships for a war that will bleed them white, but arm to overcome misery and oppression. The International is strong enough to speak in this tone of command to those in power and if necessary to follow up their words with deeds. War on war, peace for the world, hurrah for the workers' International!"

The socialist leader of the period who was most concerned about the preservation of peace, Jean Jaurès, stressed that the socialists were not alone in their struggle for peace. Christianity—the Congress was held in the Cathedral of Basel—or at least some of its representatives, too, stood for international conciliation. In his generous and undogmatic spirit Jaurès exclaimed: "In this very church I heard just now as it were a call to general reconciliation—the sound of the bells that welcomed us. It reminded me of the motto which Schiller set at the head of his wonderful Song of the Bell: Vivos voco: J'appelle les vivants pour qu'ils se défendent contre le monstre qui apparaît à l'horizon. Mortuos plango: je pleure les morts innombrables couchés là-bas vers l'orient et dont la puanteur arrive à nous comme un remords! Fulgura frango: je briserai les foudres de la guerre qui menacent dans les nuées."[7]

The year before, on December 20, 1911, at the occasion of the ratification of the Franco-German treaty on Morocco, Jaurès spoke in the French Chamber of Deputies on the bases of international peace. He warned of the danger of war brought about by mutual suspicions and by pessimistic acceptance of the inevitability of war. "When one sometimes speaks lightly of the possibility of this horrible catastrophe, one forgets the hitherto unknown extent of the horror and the greatness of the disaster that would occur. . . . The present-day armies of each nation represent entire peoples, as in the times of primitive barbarism; but this time they would be let loose amidst all the complexity and wealth of modern civilization. . . . Do not imagine that it will be a short war, consisting of a few thunderbolts and flashes of lightning. . . . This terrible spectacle will over-stimulate all human passions." Against this danger, Jaurès saw "three active forces working for peace today." The first was, in his opinion, the International of the working classes of all countries. But a similar force for peace was modern capitalism with the global interaction, fluidity, and entanglement of business interests. "There is, however, a third force for peace in the world: it is Anglo-Saxon America, reborn from the old Puritan ideals. We do not know the great American people or the American conscience. . . . Should Europe be foolish enough to divide and tear itself apart tomorrow, this great enlightened American idealism would shame it with its proposals for arbitration."

Three years later Europe was at war. The Congress of the Socialist International was to meet late in summer, 1914, in Vienna to celebrate the 50th anniversary of the founding of the First International (1864) and the 25th anniversary of the founding of the Second International (1889). The Congress, of course, never convened. In August 1914 the overwhelming majority of the working classes in the warring nations joined the armies; the nationalism of the masses proved stronger than internationalism or class solidarity. In the critical hour, the threatened general strike against the mobilization order did not materialize. On the eve of the outbreak of war, Jaurès was assassinated by a French nationalist. On August 4, the Socialist parties in Germany and France voted for the war-appropriations.

III

In all the upsurge of nationalism in our century the spirit of universality has not been drowned. Some African writers, for example, have rejected the claims of *négritude* and have insisted on individuality and on their right to participate in Western civilization. M. F. Dei Anang warned in the *Présence Africaine* (1959) that "Il existe deux dangers à considérer dans notre retour vers le passé. . . . Le danger interne découle de la satisfaction qu'on éprouve à l'évocation du passé, manifestation d'un chauvinisme étroit qui applaudit sans discussion les conceptions démodées de la vie indigène. Ceci est quelquefois le résultat d'un certain complexe d'infériorité qui déteste l'étalage des faiblesses à l'encontre des nouvelles impulsions et des compétitions, et préfère rester pieusement dans les bosquets inchangés de la tradition. Les puristes du langage, les tradionalistes en musique et en art et les conservateurs en matière d'habillement, tous appartiennent à ce groupe. . . . Il y a aussi l'espèce également destructrice des critiques de l'extérieur qui considèrent la civilisation dite greco-romaine comme le rempart exclusif du monde occidental."[8]

In *Black Orpheus* (Ibadan) appeared in June 1961 a poem "Négritude," in which F. A. Imokhuede defended his individuality against nationalist art:

Poor black Muse, since we must, under newlaid laws
worship at your altar,
Before true acclaim and recognition can come our way,
I have no other
Course than to dance to puppet tunes and 'gainst all
conscience
force on your new-tuned ears melody that's strange
and strained . . .
. . . Why can't you leave the black Muse alone? Must
you make rules
And thus to standardise and commercialise that which
differs from prophet to prophet?
I want to be known myself but this is not the means
to that end
I don't care what people think of my verse, for what
I write is me—négritude or not.

In a similar spirit, at the meeting of the Rumanian Writers Union Executive Committee in March 1964, the late Academy member Professor Tudor Vianu stressed the growing "affinity" of the literatures of East and West born out of their "same feeling of seriousness toward our times and the desire to overcome the tragedy of man's condition." In his view, although the Eastern and the Western writers see different solutions to the human condition, the fact of the search itself brings them together. "We are citizens of our country, but we are also citizens of the world. We must be citizens of the whole wide world."

Internationalism has grown simultaneously with the world-wide spread of nationalism. Their growth is closely interrelated. It was the response to native nationalism which evoked a new international spirit in the Christian missionary movement. In the nineteenth century this movement was often instrumental in communicating the cultural attitudes underlying the growth of modern nationalism. But at that time the missionaries lacking historical perpective saw in the present stage of Christianity and of European civilization the final achievement and the absolute norm of civilized life. The Easter, 1928, meeting of the International Missionary Council in Jerusalem "tried to break away from this attitude and to discover new ways founded upon rapprochement and equal rights and future unity." There the representatives of the "young" Asian and African churches won equal standing with those of Europe and America. At the International Missionary Council in Edinburgh in 1910 there were only 20 representatives of non-white races amongst 3000 delegates. In Jerusalem, eighteen years later, more than a third of the participants were natives of Asia or Africa, "and it is worthy of remark that alike in theological questions and in the debates devoted to political and social problems the representatives of the non-white races took the intellectual lead. . . . The East has become the schoolmaster of the West, has widened the missionaries' field of vision and forced them into serious self-examination."

It is noteworthy to recall that the Christians in Asia and Africa stood, together with their non-Christian fellow citizens, in the foremost ranks of the native nationalist movements. It was this nationalism, this striving for equality of status, which brought the Western missionaries to a realization of the growing oneness of mankind. The missions' task, it was declared, "was to impress on men's hearts the idea of the oneness of the human race and its united labor for the salvation of mankind. It was not for the mission to divide but to unite, not to point out what is negative in others, but to lay stress on what is positive."

Archbishop William Temple regarded his emerging "universal fellowship" as "the great new fact of our era." The Third Assembly of the World Council of Churches, which met in New Delhi in 1961, called for a strengthening of the United Nations within the framework and spirit of the Charter. The non-aligned countries, the appeal stressed, can contribute to this goal by their impartiality; with others they can be the champions of the Charter. "A creative strategy for peace with justice requires universal recognition of the claims of humanity—of all people, whatever their status, race, sex or creed." The twentieth century witnessed not only a rejuvenation and adaptation of Christianity to rapidly changing conditions but also a similar invigoration of Islam and Buddhism which entered a new stage of activity in their consciousness of world religions in a growing universal order.

Internationalism on a new scale manifests itself also in the rapidly growing number of professional, scientific, and scholarly meetings held in a great variety of countries. Meetings of this kind announced and stimulated in the first half of the nineteenth century the growth of nationalism in Germany and Italy. They may, under the changing conditions of the second half of the twentieth century, contribute to the growth of internationalism. There are common interests and loyalties among scientists which transcend national boundaries. Historiography, which in the last one hundred years has been primarily nation-oriented, has in some cases lately tried to broaden its vision and to be on guard against national or parochial prejudices or preferences. The problem of teaching universal or world history in a true sense of the word has been discussed in many meetings of historians.

But the most important sign of the growth of internationalism in a world of juridically equal nation-states of various civilizations and ideologies is the vitality of the United Nations. Founded in 1945, it has barely come of age. But twenty years after its start, the League of Nations was dead, whereas the United Nations, partly thanks to its universal character, is still growing. In July 1963 Pope Paul VI well defined the nature of the United Nations when he assured its Secretary General (characteristically for the organization's universal character a Buddhist Burmese), that the Holy See "considers the United Nations as the steadily developing and improving form of the balanced and unified life of all humanity in its historical and earthly order. The ideologies of those who belong to the United Nations are certainly multiple and diverse, and the Catholic Church regards them with due attention. But the convergence of so many peoples, so many races, so many states in a single organization, intended to avert the evils of war and to favor the good things of peace, is a fact which the Holy See considers as corresponding to its concept of humanity."

The United Nations has helped to smooth the transition of many colonies to national statehood and thus fulfilled the task which at the end of 1918 Jan Smuts assigned to the League of Nations as the heir of the crumbling imperial order. The United Nations accepted the democratic principle of the legal equality of small and great nations alike and provided each one of them with a voice in world affairs. Thereby it contradicted both the concert-of-great-powers concept which prevailed in nineteenth-century Europe, and fascist disregard for the rights of "weak" or "small" states. The often clashing interests of nations find in the United Nations a forum, in which they can be discussed according to the procedures developed by the Western parliamentary tradition. With all the difficulties involved in a rapid revolutionary transformation, the United Nations represents the first realization of internationalism which promises a hope of divesting the clashes of nationalist and ideological aspirations of their extremist character while recognizing their intrinsic validity.

It is not the task of the historian to foresee the future of nationalism. Undoubtedly, it is a divisive force in a world growing more and more interdependent, a force capable of producing bitter tensions and one-sided, selfrighteous judgments, that threaten the rational solution of international conflicts. But nationalism, if controlled by regard for fellow-nationalities, represents also a form of resistance to imposed uniformity, a bulwark of diversity, individuality, and liberty of collective groups. The conditions of the post-1945 world—the existence of weapons of a formerly unknown destructive capacity and the new neighborly interdependence of all, even the formerly most remote and secluded, peoples—may help to bring about a change of temper in respect to the role of nationalism and the nation-state in international relations.

More than forty years ago I compared this change to the change brought about in eighteenth-century Europe, which replaced the age of religious wars and intolerance with a period of uneasy and distrustful but generally peaceful coexistence of formerly mutually exclusive absolutist claims on the part of conflicting religions, which had been regarded as the legitimate basis of political and territorial organization and as the beneficiary of man's supreme loyalty. This change did in no way imply the end of religion and of religious influence on the life of peoples, but it progressively diminished religious aggressiveness and exclusiveness. This process began as a protest of intellectuals against the changes and chaos which the religious wars and religious intolerance brought upon the cohesion of society and the creativity of cultural life, and it reached its contemporary high point in the encyclical "Pacem in terris" by Pope John XXIII. Such hopes as I expressed in 1922 were premature, yet today the possibility is growing that a similar process, on a worldwide basis, may transform the age of nationalism and of warring nation-states into an age of an uneasy but on the whole peaceful coexistence of various civilizations, traditions, and ideologies, which like everything in history, are subject to change and transformation, and may share more and more in regarding mankind as a whole and themselves as parts and partners in this common humanity.

NOTES

1. "will not be at all renowned, but it will be happy. It will not be spoken of; it will have little esteem abroad; but it will have ample resources, peace and liberty in its bosom."

2. "Evermore the conviction must spread that the land-conquering heroic spirit not only is a destroying angel of mankind but also does not nearly merit for its talents the respect and the fame which it receives in the tradition of the Greeks, the Romans, and the barbarians."

3. "The human race is a whole: we work and suffer, sow and reap for one another. ...The law of equity is not alien to any nation; its transgression all have atoned for,

each in its way. If intellectual powers of higher development are an advantage enjoyed by Europeans, they cannot give proof of this advantage in any other way than through understanding and kindness. If they act...with basely arrogant pride, then they are animals and demons toward their fellow-men."

4. "Even liberalism to a considerable extent attacked the political and ideal preeminence of the national state and asserted the basic superiority of a state-principle standing above the nationalities."

5. "a violation of the law of nations" and "a blemish upon German history."

6. "First we are men and then members of a nation. Nationality is the accidental and humanity is the essential."

7. "Vivos voco: I call upon the living to defend themselves against the monster who appears on the horizon. Mortuos plango: I weep for the many dead lying there in the east, whose stench reaches us like remorse. Fulgura frango: I will shatter the thunderbolts of war that hang threatening in the clouds."

8. "There exist two dangers to be considered in our return to the past....The internal danger flows from the satisfaction that one experiences in evoking the past, the manifestation of a narrow chauvinism which commends without discussion the outmoded conceptions of native life. This is sometimes the result of a type of inferiority complex that abhors the exposure of weaknesses to new impulses and to competition, and prefers to remain piously in the changeless thickets of tradition. Linguistic purists, traditionalists in music and art, and conservatives in matters of dress, all belong to this group....There is also the equally destructive class of critics of foreign countries who consider the so-called Greco-Roman civilization as the bulwark only of the Western world."

SEVEN

Science, Technology, and the Unity of Mankind

MELVIN KRANZBERG

Chairman, Program in the History of
Science and Technology
Case Western Reserve University

WHEN WE SPEAK OF LIVING IN A "SCIENTIFIC AND TECHNOLOG-
ical age," we assume that science and technology are properties of our
own times, without recognizing that they helped shape the past as well.
We also take the parochial view that Western civilization is the only one
worth studying. We fail to realize that modern scientific and industrial
society is largely confined to the Western world and that the mass of mankind today lives in a pre-scientific, pre-industrial society.

Yet the statement that ours alone is a scientific and technological world
catches us in a paradox. How can we point to the universality of science
and technology throughout history—in all times and all places—and at
the same time claim that the non-Western portions of the world fail to
share in it? The resolution must lie in recognition that both science and
technology are developing processes. Although both reach back to the
very beginnings of mankind and played a major role in the development
of society and the directions of civilization, only within the past three
centuries has their influence become dominant in any society. Indeed,
only within the past few decades have we become aware how influential
they are. Science and technology have permeated the institutions of
modern life and created our contemporary world. At the same time we

can recognize that they have not yet assumed the dominant role in most of the rest of the world.

The Scientific Revolution and the Development of Political Democracy

The Scientific Revolution of the 17th century, so intimately connected with the names of Galileo Galilei (1564-1642), Sir Isaac Newton (1642-1727), and other great, but perhaps less well-known, scientists, created the major divergence between West and East and marked the beginning of modern Western civilization. True, there were differences between East and West long before the 17th century began; historians can trace the divergences far back into antiquity; for example, the conflict between Greek and Persian in the 5th century B.C. is interpreted as an East-West conflict. The Renaissance in Europe in the 15th century marked another break. Nevertheless, the Scientific Revolution was more radical. It was a break with past scientific ideas as well as the culture and philosophy of preceding eras. It provided man with new ways of looking at the universe, the physical environment, himself, and society.

The scientists themselves were little concerned with man and society. Their concerns, in the 16th and 17th centuries, were celestial mechanics and terrestrial physics. The older science held that the earth was the center of the universe. This view had the authority of Aristotle and Ptolemy and common sense observations. The earth did seem to stand still at the center of things while heavenly bodies appeared to move about pursuant to their own laws of perfect "circular" motion. The Aristotelian concept of the universe was reinforced by its incorporation into medieval Christian theology. The idea fitted well with the Christian notion that man was the special target of God's concerns. It also helped explain the imperfections of man on earth compared with the more perfect qualities of Heaven. Christian theology became inextricably committed to a set of physical concepts about the universe, which explains a good deal of the opposition to acceptance of the "new" science.

Nicolas Copernicus (1473-1543), the Polish astronomer, was not the first to question the ancient Aristotelian view, nor was he the first to recognize that the Ptolemaic geometry was very complicated and probably mistaken. Copernicus postulated a simpler hypothesis in which the sun stood still while the earth and the other planets moved about it. Observations of planet position, comets, and novae supported the Copernican scheme, but it was largely the telescope, first used by Galileo, that shattered Aristotelianism. The immutability of the heavens became impossible to sustain, and the earth, different from the other heavenly bodies, was like the moon and the planets. Galileo reinforced the Copernican view. His challenge of Aristotle put him in trouble with the Church, but his recantation could not reverse the ideas and the evidence.

Although doubt has been cast upon Galileo as an experimenter,[1] there is no doubt that he fostered the notion that science should be concerned with measurable qualities and that the physical universe is describable by the interplay of calculable forces and measurable bodies. Equally important was Galileo's conviction that the universe is mechanically, structurally, and physically uniform; the same principles of movement extend to the heavenly bodies as exist on earth. This changed the kind of knowledge scientists would henceforth seek; mechanical and measurable principles applied alike to the movements of the heavens and earth, and all parts of the physical universe were mechanically interrelated. These became fundamental axioms of modern science.

Although Galileo laid down fundamental principles and challenged the views of the old science, he himself was unable to create a new physics. He took the first steps, but the man who actually created it was Isaac Newton. Newton saw that the force causing a stone to fall is the same as that moving the planets. He first clearly stated the laws of motion, applicable both to celestial bodies and objects on earth. He showed how human reason, employing mathematics, could determine the principles of the natural universe. He completed the dethronement of Aristotle and destroyed the medieval picture of the theological universe and replaced it with the natural universe. No First Mover accounted for the universe, but physical mechanisms operating according to simple natural laws. Newton himself would have avoided this statement, but, all the same, this is what he did.

His mathematical laws as applied to the physical universe were immediately taken up in the other sciences and even applied to man and society. Perhaps the extreme example was the attempt by Spinoza (1632-1677) to reduce ethics to geometrically stated principles. Newton's friend, John Locke (1632-1702), attempted to carry Newtonian principles into a science of human nature. Newton's concepts thus had influence in economics and politics, although Newton limited himself to physical nature.

Voltaire was much taken with Newton's work and introduced it to the French. Newton became a symbol of the French *philosophes*. Popular writers like Henry Pemberton, capitalized on Newtonianism, which also found its way into the physico-theology of William Derham, the Clarke-Leibniz exchange of letters, and Pope's "Essay on Man." Concepts of progress through knowledge and understanding of the physical universe prospered, though actual material foundations of progress had to wait until the Industrial Revolution in the latter 18th century. An intellectual revolution was in motion, with repercussions for the unity of mankind.

The break with the religious tradition was important, for it weakened faith in authority of all kinds. David Hume's writings manifested a general skepticism which lowered the prestige of religion and weakened the notion of a divinely constituted social order. Political thought became secularized. Locke's *Two Treatises on Civil Government* (1690), for example, addressed the reactionary and the progressive: One treatise used old arguments based upon Biblical authority, and the second, justly the more famous and significant, provided a secular defense of representative government.

The idea of laws of nature, characteristic of 18th-century political, economic, and social thought, derived from Newtonian concepts. "Social Newtonism" asserted that laws of nature applied to society as to the physical universe. If men could organize society in accordance with these laws, they would lead a harmonious existence. Unfortunately, absolute monarchy and the established church interfered with the rational organization of society, but nature was brought to the support of revolution. The American and the French Revolutions appealed to the laws of nature, and reordering of the political structure was justified by the structure's defiance of natural law.

Rousseau, one of the most influential of 18th-century thinkers, asserted man's natural virtue had been destroyed by civilization: "Man is born free, but everywhere he is in chains." Man could guarantee his natural rights by entrance into a "social contract" freely agreed to by the people, and their "general Will" rivalled the Trinity and the Virgin Birth for mysticism. Though Rousseau was essentially a poet, the majority of the philosophers of the Enlightenment believed in the power of human reason to develop social and political systems consonant with nature, and they used the test of reason to heap scorn upon the Church and State. The unity and equality of men, whatever their station in the sight of God, was transferred to politics. Men had rights, not by virtue of birth and rank, but because they were men.

It is not surprising that the men who took the leadership in forging independence in the United States and the revolutionary movement in France were well versed in the new science. Indeed, some were respectable amateur scientists themselves. Benjamin Franklin, Thomas Jefferson, and the French Encyclopedists like Diderot (1713-84) and D'Alembert (1717-83) united interests in the new science with their efforts to liberate the people from outmoded political and social systems. Newton's science not only stimulated an enormous outburst of scientific work, but also deep thought about society, emphasizing the equality and unity of mankind.

Concepts of the laws of nature also produced a new economics. The Physiocrats in France, in the 18th century prior to the French Revolution, believed that natural economic laws were prevented from operating by outmoded political, economic, social institutions, governmental controls and monopolies, tolls and taxes, and guild regulations from the Middle Ages. They believed in a policy of *Laissez-faire*, wherein government would keep hands off economic activities and free them to function in accordance with natural economic laws.

Adam Smith's *Wealth of Nations*, published in 1776, the same year as the American Declaration of Independence, inquired into the nature and causes of national wealth. Smith viewed man in economic terms, living by labor and by exchanging the products of his labor with his fellowmen. These activities had been corrupted by mercantilist regulations dating from the 17th century and by even older feudal, manorial, and guild regulations. Smith called for an economic order in accordance with laws of economics. Each man should pursue his own self-interest, and, as all did so, they would be led by "an invisible hand" to promote the good of all. Here, too, was a powerful concept for the unity of mankind stemming from scientific—that is to say, Newtonian—leads.

The idea of inexorable law operating in the political, social, and economic sphere in order to secure human happiness was a liberating idea which freed men from the grasp of superstition and the rule of aristocratic institutions based upon the essential inequality of mankind. Human liberties and self-expression as well as social, educational, and material progress became the vision of man, a logical outgrowth of Newtonian conceptions in the physical world applied in social spheres.

Although great and liberating doctrines, natural rights in politics and law, the economy and society, did not always lead in practice to unity nor, indeed, to the goals the original formulators anticipated. Doctrines of political rights led to the strengthening of the nation-state and ultimately to the development of modern nationalism. This turn of affairs ultimately became the source of national rivalries, warfare of the most brutal type, and a chief deterrent to the progress toward the unity of mankind. Similarly, doctrines of economic freedom from restraint were used to justify the unconstrained freedom of the industrialist to exploit his workers and despoil the natural environment. Hence old types of social divisions among the people were replaced by new social distinctions based on wealth and position in productive systems. Yet the seeds of political democracy, sown by the application of natural rights philosophy, derived from the natural philosophy of the Scientific Revolution, provided bases for the development of the democratic constitutions in the 19th and 20th centuries. Once enunciated, these ideas were too powerful to be denied, and they were reinforced by the Industrial Revolution of the 18th century, which linked up with the same outburst of human energies and freedom which characterized the Scientific Revolution of the preceding century.

Technology and the Development of Social Democracy

Just as the Scientific Revolution laid the groundwork for the political philosophy of the American and French Revolutions, so the Industrial Revolution founded social democracy. Legal equality and civil rights without a concomitant growth in social rights and elevation of the working man in society could have become quite meaningless. Social democracy still lags even in the most industrially advanced countries, and the lag has prevented the full achievement of political rights, even when embodied in the laws of a nation. Still, the eventual outcome is not in doubt.

At the beginnings of industrialization, however, it scarcely seemed that the pressures of technology were forcing society into the direction of a more democratic way of life and a higher standard of living for all. The degradation and exploitation of the workers in the mines and factories of the early Industrial Revolution seemed to point, indeed, in the opposite direction.[2] The division between the "haves" and the "have-nots" was deeper than the chasm between master and slave in ancient societies. Nevertheless, the long-term impact of industrialization narrowed the gap and opened up possibilities for closer cooperation of all segments of society. Industrialization fostered the growth of social democracy by (1) increasing enormously the production of goods and services to meet basic human needs, (2) elevating the status of the working man, and (3) providing the conditions necessary for the political effectiveness of the masses.

Political concepts of democracy would perhaps have remained little more than theoretical constructs had they not been founded on material conditions which made them practical. This is not to say that industrialization inevitably brings about social democracy. There is a "cultural lag" in human affairs. Even in 20th-century United States, social practice does not always correspond with political and legal pronouncements. The plight of the Negro, rural and urban, suggests that legal rights are not easily transformed into equal social and economic opportunities. Yet, as we shall see, technological developments eventually overcome the lag. They always have. Let us identify the technological elements which characterized the Industrial Revolution and how that revolution affected the development of democratic doctrine and practice.

As is the case with most historical developments of so far-reaching a nature, the identifications are not simple. Industrialization is a complex phenomenon; some consequences are direct and immediate; others are indirect and subtle: still others are contradictory in nature. The technological developments of an industrial revolution always advance the arts of war, for instance; yet the very same developments increase the potentialities for the peaceful progress and the ultimate achievement of man's unity. Similarly, industrial development can lead to the organization of a factory system which engenders exploitation and brutality, but unionization and economic considerations for the productive system as a whole can transform the factory and its products into liberating social forces which help guarantee social equality and a higher standard of living for all. Workers, it is at last understood, must be able to purchase what they produce.

The complexity of the Industrial Revolution changed all dimensions of human life. It wrenched man and woman from hearth and home and farm. Agriculture, though still of basic importance in satisfying human needs, was replaced by industrial production and services; the factory replaced the farm as the locale for man's working hours. The Industrial Revolution was no simple matter of a few machine inventions of the 18th and early 19th centuries—spinning and weaving devices, James Watts' steam engine, the railway locomotive, the steam boat, and the factory system—instead, it involved every aspect of human life and work.

It is not generally recognized that the Industrial Revolution in 18th-century Britain rested on an agricultural base. Profound transformations had begun as early as the 17th century in English agricultural production.[3] They stemmed not only from new agricultural implements and devices but also from the enclosure system. The larger fields could be farmed more efficiently, and some of the lands could be used for livestock. The new size of the agricultural units and the switch from subsistence to animal and cash crops were accompanied by changes in method and tools. Crop rotation systems replenished nutrients with clover and turnips instead of allowing the land to lie fallow for long and unproductive periods of time. Improved farming tools and implements eased the work and increased crops. Empirical methods of breeding and soil culture improved quality and quantity; the use of wind and water power on farms did likewise. The result was a striking increase in agricultural productivity which steadily accelerated throughout the 19th and 20th centuries, then stepped up in another Agricultural Revolution following World War II.

The effects of these agricultural transformations on the development of industrial technology were manifold. Sharp increases in agricultural productivity fed large numbers of people living in the cities and engaged in industrial work. Factory organization and urban concentration of the population would have been impossible without the increase in food supplies for those no longer engaged in food production. Ex-farmers joined the labor pool for burgeoning industries. The demand for more efficient farm implements and machinery stimulated industrial production and increased the production of foodstuffs and other agricultural crops. Agricultural revolutions thus became both source and stimulant for industrialization.

Other technological elements in the Industrial Revolution have been objects of much more study and are more clearly seen. There were changes in the basic materials used. Over the millennia, wood had been the primary source of man's fuel and tools and equipment. Prehistoric metallurgy introduced bronze, copper, and iron, but these remained expensive, difficult to work, and restricted to needs that wood could not possibly meet. The Industrial Revolution converted to metals as the basic material for tools, machines, and devices. In the early stages, wrought and cast iron began to be used where wood had been employed before. Later, steel emerged as the chief building and tool material for mankind. During the 20th century, a materials revolution took place. Steel was alloyed for various specialized and desirable characteristics. New and lighter metals such as aluminum and magnesium came into use for particular purposes. New synthetic materials—plastics, polymers, abrasives, and ceramics— whose form was first developed in scientific laboratories, fully deserved the title of "man-made" materials. These new synthetic materials tremendously enlarged human technical capabilities. Today it can be fairly claimed that men can devise new materials to fit virtually any characteristics required for the particular job at hand.

There was a revolution, too, in energy sources and power devices. Before industrialization, natural power sources such as wind, water, and muscle—both human and animal—were the basic power sources. Indeed, they still provide much of the power and energy in industrialized countries as well as in underdeveloped areas of the 20th century. Yet new fuels, engines, and systems came to augment and, in some cases, replace entirely the primitive power sources. Fossil fuels—coal, petroleum and natural gas—powered the machines, including the electrical. Then in the mid-20th century nuclear power has raised the potential for man's use of energy to virtually infinite limits and removed the fear that fossil fuel resources would be exhausted.[4]

These new sources of energy were invariably linked with devices for conversion of energy from one form to another, such as heat to kinetic energy. The new sources of motive power—the steam engine, the internal combustion engine, the electric motor—took the burdens off men's backs and freed productive activity from confinement to sites of steady water and wind streams.

The Industrial Revolution also witnessed the mechanization of many processes previously performed by human hands. In the 18th century the invention of the spinning jenny and the power loom permitted vastly increased production of cloth with a smaller expenditure of human energy. These were but the forerunners of a very large group of machines of all sizes, types, and functions which quickened and multiplied the work of man's mind and hands, culminating in the electronically automated machinery of the 20th century.

Intimately connected with the new machines was the factory system exploiting division of labor and specialization of function. The worker, no longer a craftsman working with hand tools, became a machine operator subject to factory discipline. Division of labor, specialization, and discipline of the work process resulted in a rising tide of production. Although there had been division of labor and specialization before and something resembling factory organization had been seen in workshops since classical antiquity, the impetus given these developments by specialized machinery was revolutionary. The constant flow of raw materials to feed the machines and their enormous capacities led to wholly new concepts of the worker's position and relation to his work as well as a tremendous flow of goods meeting man's needs. To move the flow at accelerating rates, financial, commercial, and trading institutions developed; communication and transportation facilities were built and rebuilt; and modern advertising, assisted by the behavioral sciences, provided techniques for creating new needs.

In transportation and communication, developments seemed to strike some instinct in the human animal for speed and reached the crescendo of invention we live through today. Out of the steam engine came the steam locomotive and the steamship; then the internal combustion engine for the automobile and the airplane; then the jet engine for the airplane and rocket propulsion for space vehicles. Electricity made possible the telegraph, telephone, radio, and television.

The sociocultural consequences of the technological developments which entered into industrialization were immense. Standards of living for populations of the industrialized countries rose sharply for workers as well as managers and owners. It became wholly reasonable—say, 66 percent correct—to refer to the United States as an "affluent society." Except for an uneducated poverty class, the abundant national economy was here. Citizens in the industrially developed countries of the world have so much in the way of material goods that they can and do assist men in other parts of the globe who still labor under primitive technological systems deficient in productive capacity.

The ancient religious notion of charity—sharing material sustenance—had but limited application in the centuries before industrialization. Men usually had so little left over from the results of their labor that they had little to share. By the mid-20th century, industrialization allowed some peoples such a surfeit of material goods that they could afford to share it without having to forego any of life's material necessities themselves. This made possible the emergence of a new freedom in man's age-old attempt to enlarge human liberties.

That freedom was enunciated formally for the first time in the Atlantic Charter by President Franklin D. Roosevelt and Winston Churchill in World War II as freedom from want. The advances of science and technology made it possible to banish forever the spectres of starvation and misery which had so long haunted mankind. The ancient charitable religious injunctions were no longer pious hopes but practical political goals. Thus the material foundations for the unity of mankind have been laid by an advancing technology which promises to free men everywhere from material deprivation.

Within the highly industrialized countries, the advances of technology helped to erase social differences and the inequalities which had long hampered democratic principles and institutions.[5] The "haves" and "have-nots" still remained, but the sharp antitheses in material standards of living were blunted. The poor in industrially advanced countries could enjoy adequate amounts of food and clothing; enjoy the same entertainment as the rich merely by the flicking of a switch and the turning of a dial; and transport themselves from one place to another by automobiles quite as serviceable as those of the rich. Except for small pockets of poverty, even the very poorest members of industrialized society have enough to eat; in many cases, their standard of living judged by food supply, the quality and variety of amusements, entertainment, and basic comforts of life are comparable to those enjoyed by aristocracies of earlier dates. Technology has obliterated some major social differences which, throughout history, inhibited feelings of unity among men, even in the same region.

Factory organization of work and machine methods of production, with their accompanying social and political changes, have elevated the status of the worker in society. Throughout history, manual labor had been derogated by the educated. Plato made a distinction between the hand and mind, and ancient Greek society, even in its most glorious period of philosophic insight, was based upon the distinction between manual laborers and those who worked with their minds. Farmers were regarded with pity, if not scorn, and the hardest labor was allocated to slaves. Aristotle denied slaves the virtues of men, because hard manual labor demanded only obedience and did not allow the use of the mind, which he regarded as the supreme human quality. This ancient aversion to manual labor persisted in Western history throughout the Middle Ages. The elite classes of society were priests and soldiers; manual workers were "serfs," a word having the same root as "servile." This low regard for the people actually performing the tasks enabling society to subsist became embodied in educational systems and still persists in many universities today. The humanist looks down upon the engineers; liberal arts pretends to Greek and medieval superiorities over the sciences; the rigors of mathematics and physics are despised by "intellectuals."

In the course of history, manual workers, including women and children, worked long hours at miserable wages. As industrialization began, they were unprotected from the whirring belts and cogs of the machinery, and accidents were frequent. In the ups and downs of the business cycle, they were thrown out of their jobs without compensation. Sickness, accident, and old age were sufficient cause for dismissal. Workers lived in drab tenements, without adequate lighting, sanitation, or other facilities. The social reformers of the 19th century—English, American, and European—painted a dismal picture of the plight of workers.

Subsequent historical investigation indicates that this picture of the plight of the working man may have been overdrawn.[6] Miserable working conditions were apparently not universal, and in certain types of industry living standards of the workers actually rose. There is also reason to believe that even the early factory system at its worst represented a slight improvement over the conditions of the workers in the previous system of home and cottage industry, which in turn may have represented an advance over serfdom. Even if workers' circumstances were black and dismal as pictured, the factory system was not the sole cause; economic doctrines of laissez-faire and ignorant oppression by the inexperienced ruling classes of the period seem to have played roles. Not technology, but the way in which it was applied, was at the bottom of the injustices Karl Marx so ably exploited.

Although historians may never reach agreement on the short-range effects of the Industrial Revolution on the working man in the early factory system, there is general agreement that the long-range impact raised the standard of living of the workers. Their very plight in documented instances gave rise to effective social reform movements throughout the 19th century. The worst abuses of the factory system, like woman and child labor, were eventually proscribed by law. First the humanitarian impulses of the proprietary and professional classes, then the organization of the workers themselves improved their lot. The most powerful theory underlying the reforms proved to be the Marxian concepts of social revolution.

Though Marxian ideas seemed to call for disunity by the stress on the class struggle, and for violence through uprisings of the proletariat, they also had significance for the concept of unity. The recognition that workers everywhere had common interests and concerns was a unifying principle, and the Marxian emphasis on the universality of the workers' interest was spread by socialist political parties and the trade unions of a socialist nature. To these organizations war was part of bourgeois capitalist exploitation, and they were strongly pacifist in orientation. They contributed greatly to international peace movements, firmly based upon unity of interest among very large majorities of mankind.

Technology contributed indirectly to socialist ideologies just at it had to capitalist development. It brought workers together into one place of employment, and it congregated them in cities; these factors assisted in the communication of injustices and in organization for effective political and social action. The clamor resulted in popular pressure for giving a greater political voice to the lower orders of society. The franchise was extended to propertyless citizens and to women. The sheer numbers of workers, concentrated by technology, won political power. They acquired economic power through the strike, a direct gift of technology managed under a profit system. They became a force to be reckoned with in the policies of the industrialized nations, and they raised their own status within society.

The strike and work-stoppage of entire plants was a powerful weapon handed the workers by technology. Peasants in the earlier agrarian, semi-manorial productive system were scattered. Effective action was virtually impossible, as the many ill-fated peasant revolts in previous centuries of European history testify. Factory workers concentrated in towns had only to throw a wrench into machinery to halt a plant, whereupon organization based on grievance became easy. So did revolution, and the workers, particularly in the 1848 revolutions throughout Europe, played decisive roles in overthrowing and changing governments.

Thanks to division of labor and specialization, almost any small group of workers in one specialized branch of industry could disrupt an entire industry. This done, the interrelationships to other industries, technological and economic, did the rest. They could, with persistence, disrupt entire economies.

Technology also created needs for more skilled and educated workers. The early machinery had been simple to operate. Women and children were as proficient—and cheaper—than men. But as the machinery became more complex, more highly skilled classes of laborers to maintain the machines and guide operations were required. When the skill was built into the machine, its maintenance and operation required high orders of training and education. Mechanics' institutes were founded during the early 19th century, and the widespread development of compulsory primary school education began. Illiteracy became intolerable, and as the technology became more complex, simple literacy was not enough; vocational and technical skills also had to be taught. The countries most advanced in industrialization, indeed, were the most advanced educationally. Western European countries almost succeeded in wiping out illiteracy and developed large, but never sufficient, pools of skilled workers whose wages depended more upon demand than upon unionization. Today in 20th-century America, shortages of skilled labor coexist with unemployment among the educationally underprivileged. Those missing out on proper education are effectively deprived of participation in a highly developed industrial system.

The impact of education on the concept of the unity of mankind hardly needs repeating. Instead of dispossessed, ignorant, and illiterate masses, the industrialized nations have educated—at least up to a point—workers. The educational imperative of technology and industrialization served well, and will serve better, the cause of education as a barrier-breaking force toward the unity of man. Educated workers demand and receive higher rates of pay. Their purchasing power tends to unite them with the wealthier citizenry. Social distinctions blur. Privileges based on wealth, rank or birth largely disappear.

Yet the second-class citizenship which is still the lot of the American Negro suggests how, even in a highly industrialized society, a cultural lag runs counter to the tendency of the technological imperative. The Negro, brought to this country as a slave, was fitted into the plantation economy of the agrarian South. When slavery became first technologically then legally obsolete as a result of the Civil War, the social and economic system which gave rise to slavery persisted. When the South began to industrialize, Negroes were called upon to man the factories. The machine itself was colorblind; it required only that the hand which operated it be trained. But the South could not survive industrially if it continued to adhere to the social system denying the Negro educational and economic opportunities. When the South responded too slowly, the Negro, in an effort to improve his opportunities, moved to the northern urban industrial centers. Here the educational and social deprivations which had been his lot prevented him from taking his rightful place in the industrialized economy. The frustrations of the Negro, combined with the ignorance, fear, and social stupidity among elements of the northern white population, produced civil strife and breakdowns in law and order in major American cities in the 1960's. The spectacle certainly supports the disunity of mankind in cities which are technological centers in the most advanced country of the world. Yet the demands of an advancing technology will inevitably require equality of social, educational, and economic opportunity for the Negro population of the United States.

Perhaps the Industrial Revolution's most significant contribution to the unity of mankind is intangible. By shifting men from traditional pursuits, places, and ways of living, industrialization broke "the cake of custom" and opened men's minds to the possibilities of change and betterment. When men tilled the same plots of ground in the same manner as their ancestors had done for centuries before, their lives were narrow and their vision circumscribed. They were subjected to the authority of the local lord and priest. Industrialization wrenched them from traditional places, thoughts, and activities. It broke the bonds of the old authorities and enormously enlarged associations. Man's outlook was no longer confined to people in the village and its immediate vicinity, but to the factory, the city, and eventually to all the people in the entire world. It is hard to exaggerate the consequences of this shift. The change from the narrow, parochial world of the past is incalculable and not yet complete. Completed and in perspective, the transformation may one day be viewed as the historical process that inexorably unified mankind.

Technological Interdependence and the Unification of Mankind

Economic interdependance dates back to the cities of prehistoric times, if not earlier. Primitive divisions of labor must have arisen at a very early date, and so did trade. Both waxed and waned over epochs and in regions, favorable and unfavorable, because men, even if only semi-civilized, never achieved self-sufficiency either as individuals or together in any one place. There were always certain commodities—metals and salt are instances—which could not be produced locally and which, where produced, required at least primitive divisions of labor. The international division of labor which accompanied the Industrial Revolution was therefore not new to history. What was new was the extent and magnitude of this economic phenomenon in which entire regions, not to say nations, became dependent upon international trade.

The cotton textile industry in Britain during the latter part of the 18th and the beginnings of the 19th centuries demonstrated the absolute necessity of international economic interdependence. Cotton could not be grown in England. At the same time, the British factories with their mechanized facilities produced goods in greater quantity than could be consumed in the home markets, and England had to sell textiles abroad. Furthermore, Britain had to produce and sell her surplus in order to purchase foodstuffs from abroad for a rapidly-growing population concentrated in factory production. The viability of Britain's industrial economy could only be assured by close economic and commercial ties with other nations. Industrialization thus linked together people throughout the world. Autarchy—that is, self-sufficiency—attempted under pressures of war, currency exchange, and nationalism, never achieved more than limited success. As technology increased in complexity and sophistication, scarcely any country commanded sufficient natural resources within its own territory to keep its industrial machine working profitably, nor could even the largest home markets take the immense production created by skilled workers in mechanized factories using the latest equipment.

One of the most cherished myths of underdeveloped countries is the notion that industrialization will free them from dependence upon more highly industrialized nations. Yet the long-range effects of industrialization always increase interdependence. Almost without exception the greatest amount of trade is among nations already highly industrialized; there is less between industrialized and the underdeveloped nations. The efficient exploitation of the resources demanded by advancing technology requires that mankind function together as an economic unit, and this surely is becoming the basis for the unity of mankind in other terms.

Transportation and communication advances of the Industrial Revolution, and subsequently, represent a remarkable interaction with the necessities of economic interdependence. At the beginning of the 18th century men could not travel faster nor communicate more quickly than at the dawn of history. On land they were limited by the speed and durability of the horse, and on the sea, by the speed and capacity of the sailing vessel. The printing press in the 15th century widened the possibility for the dissemination of information, but these potentialities could not be fully realized until the development of high-speed presses, inexpensive inks, and cheap paper—and a large literate public—in the 19th century. Nowadays, communication, not only written but oral and visual, has become virtually instant throughout the entire globe. Transportation has quickened to the point where no man is more than 24 hours distant by jet commercial plane from any point on earth—though he may still have to finish the journey by oxcart. The transportation and communication developments of the past crowded century and a half make an impressive list: the steamship, the railroad, the automobile, the airplane, space vehicles and telegraph, telephone, radio, phonograph, motion pictures, television, communications satellites.

Of course, it can be argued that the spectacular advances in communication have not improved what man has to say to man, and man can travel more quickly only to quarrel more bitterly with man. Furthermore, improved methods of transportation and communication and other technological gear enabled Western nations during the latter part of the 19th century to subdue vast colonial domains. Modern rascals of history like Adolf Hitler and Gamal Abdel Nasser used radio effectively in order to spew hatred and to incite their countrymen to violence against neighboring states. The motion picture and television are frequently used for propaganda, the dissemination of lies and misinformation. Yet the potential for the unity of man is there, in the systems and devices. What one thinks man will do with them depends upon one's view of man.

Those of us who believe man is salvageable can point to the production and distribution of books to mass markets and to the impressive news services of newspapers, radio, and television—national and international from exotic lands and faraway peoples—to vast audiences. We point to the moral and political instruction, the immediacy and unforgettable learning, of the television coverage of the Negro revolution, South and North in the United States. We also note the television coverage of Vietnamese peasants victimized by warfare in their country; the place is no longer so far off, and many Americans question the nature and justice of our intervention there. Here are remarkable evocations of sentiment regarding the unity of mankind made through 20th century communications.

In the dissemination of knowledge generally, the development of printing in the 15th century rivals the invention of writing during the third millennium B.C. At the outset books were expensive, and their circulation was limited. During the 19th century, with a growing literacy, itself partially a product of the demands of industrialization, the market for printed matter and illustrations in books and magazines grew apace. It was met by a myriad of technological aids such as the linotype machine and the rotary press. Compulsory public education, free public libraries, the penny newspaper, the dime novel, and the magazine stand became Western institutions. The so-called "mass media" came into their own.

Far behind commercial newspapers, magazines, radio, movies, and television came audio-visual aids to supplement traditional teaching methods within the schools. This technology is progressing, and educators are rethinking conventional attitudes on the educational efficacy of the mass media, and on the challenges posed by automation.[7] The educational function of communications technology has probably laid the foundations for a new element in the cultural life of mankind and in the extension of democratic concepts. We shall call it "cultural democracy."

Technology and Cultural Democracy

When we speak of cultural democracy, we use the word "cultural," not in its anthropological sense, but in a more restricted sense—as the knowledge and appreciation of the humanities. By cultural democracy we mean the extension of that knowledge and appreciation to the entire population.

Throughout most human history, this type of culture has been largely an aristocratic monopoly. Enjoyment of the arts was limited to a small segment of the population; only the higher social orders had the leisure to enjoy the arts and humanities and the wealth to support them. With wealth and leisure they acquired the necessary educational background. The masses of mankind had neither time nor money for these pursuits. Even when nature was bountiful and their labors blessed, they had little opportunity to learn to read and write, which alone could have opened the doors of knowledge.

Technological developments changed this situation. Industrialization raised the standard of living of the working classes, giving them time, money, and literacy; and technological developments lowered the costs of books, newspapers, and magazines.

Of course, the printed word is not the only medium for the dissemination of culture. Art works must be seen; music, heard; and drama both seen and heard. Photography, color photography, and improved methods of printing color reproductions of works of art brought the masterpieces into many homes. The phonograph, high fidelity, and stereophonic records and record players for voice and instrumental music brought to the masses the finest symphony concerts and operatic performances. The movie and television relayed dramatic and musical performances to millions of people. It is claimed that a single performance of one of Shakespeare's plays on network television in the United States reaches more people than all stage performances of all Shakespearean plays on the stage from the time they were written over three centuries ago. If this is not true, it soon will be. Technology has democratized culture.

There are, of course, those few who believe "mass culture" is debasing the arts. The fact that many more people listen to classical music and see reproductions of great works of art does not mean, it is said, that they truly appreciate, or even understand what they have heard or seen. Cultural snobs accept no halfway houses in the learning of culture, nor evidences of genuine interest in literary, musical, or fine arts. They continue to declaim against the baseness of popular tastes. Snobbery as a career seems to have private rules. The fact remains that technology has introduced the people to the heritage of the best. Culture is no longer the property of hoi aristoi, but belongs to hoi poloi, breaking down old barriers and creating the cultural unity which is surely precedent to the unity of mankind.

Parenthetically, the development of a mass culture has also led to a greater appreciation of folk art and foreign art. Folk culture was local, aristocratic culture, cosmopolitan; folk art was for the lower classes, fine arts, for the upper classes. Yet today folk art has become the property of all. Likewise, the art work of exotic and distant peoples was long unappreciated. With modern means of communicating, this art has diffused through the world. The eclectic and experimental nature of modern art embraced foreign art forms simply because they, to the Western eye, were new and exotic. And so again, the potential cultural unity of mankind through the medium of technological development is confirmed.

We may deplore the disappearance of regional subcultures and handcraft arts as primitive peoples take to the products of Western industrialism, and we can hope that technological imperatives will not homogenize culture throughout the world. Yet they do make possible universal acquaintance with diversity throughout the world. This is the prelude to an increasing respect for human dignity and the creative abilities of mankind everywhere.

Science and Technology in Emergent Nations

For the unity of man, the great obstacle—and opportunity—lies in the underdeveloped nations. Many of these suffered under colonial domination, but casting off the imperial yoke has not put an end to their problems. Their economies provide inadequate standards of living for their people; their lack of political experience, well-founded institutions, and economic stability produces internal turmoil and sore spots on the body politic of the world. The wide gap between them and industrialized nations foments jealousy and envy. Furthermore, their rivalries and aspirations have been exploited by the superpowers looking for spheres of influence. Drawn into the Cold War competition between the Soviet Union and the United States, their threat to the existence, not to mention the unity, of mankind, is dangerous. In their areas, great power confrontations can occur—indeed, have almost occurred—leading the world to the brink of war.

The late President Kennedy referred to the aspirations of the former colonial peoples as "the revolution of rising expectations," but the path to political stability and economic well being has proved difficult. "Instant industrialization" has not proved possible. Instead, internal strife and conflicts with neighbors have resulted and have imperilled international peace.

Yet the problems are not insoluble. The emergent nations are proud peoples with long histories and cultural heritages of which they need not be ashamed. The word "underdeveloped" refers solely to scientific and technological levels as compared with the West. Scientific knowledge and technological development are therefore keys to the solutions.

One problem crying for solution is the explosive increase in population in these underdeveloped areas, making even the present low standard of living difficult to sustain. Approximately 2.1 billion people—70 per cent of the world's population—live in the emergent countries. If the trend continues, about 4.6 billion people—80 per cent of the world's population—will be living in them by the 21st century. Since the majority now live in desperate squalor, their misery can be expected to grow. World tensions and the threat to all mankind will increase.

The United States, by underwriting the efforts of the United Nations and by its own efforts, has improved public health, nutrition, and disease control in these areas. Death rates have been slashed to about 17 per 100 per year, without compensating reductions in birthrates, which remain at approximately 43 per 1000. This will double the populations in about three decades, and the pressure on food supplies will surely lead to turmoil. Obviously, something must be done to increase the food supplies, and this can be done only by widespread and unprecedented applications of science and technology.

Four major difficulties stand in the way: (1) the ambivalence of the emergent nations toward Western science and technology; (2) the difficulties inherent in the diffusion of scientific knowledge and the transfer of technology; (3) economic, political, and sociocultural factors within these countries themselves; and (4) the inadequacy of foreign aid and technical assistance programs of the industrialized nations.

The ambivalence is easily understood. Western technology was the instrument of conquest by the Western nations—in the 16th century, Central and South America; in the 17th, the Indies; the 18th, North America and India; and in the 19th, Africa.[8] The economies of these regions were used for supplying raw materials, and their peoples were regarded as consumers for the product of European factories. This type of imperialistic domination and exploitation resulted in the American Revolution and left other peoples permanently resentful. Only one nation—Japan—appropriated Western science and technology; in all other cases, they were rejected as foreign influences of a baneful nature.

At the same time the artifacts of Western technology and the benefits of Western science became highly desired. The subjected peoples could see their colonial masters enjoying the material benefits of industrialized society and wished to obtain them. They also recognized the achievements of Western science in wiping out disease. Abhorring the West—its values, standards, political institutions, and ethical norms, all of which appeared to them as hypocrisies—the non-Western nations nevertheless desired the West's hardware.

Yet Western science and technology could not be appropriated simply; they could not easily be separated from the matrix from which they had emerged—the education and skills of Western peoples, their institutions, and even their climates. Western science and technology rest upon deep cultural foundations. It has not so far been possible to appropriate certain elements of Western science and technology without taking the rest, and the cultural baggage appeared heavy and alien.

So Arabian sheiks prefer air-conditioned Cadillacs to tractors and irrigation works. Juke-boxes, Coca-Cola, and other trivia were more welcome than tools and machines. Nuclear reactors became status symbols when fertilizers would have been more useful. Worst of all, the emergent nations wanted planes, tanks, and guns. The Japanese at the end of the 19th century, for example, appropriated some of the most malevolent aspects of Western culture—autocracy, militarism, imperialism—and so did other emergent nations of the mid-twentieth century.

Complexity is also an obstacle to a direct transfer of Western technology. Industrially advanced technology such as steel mills and nuclear reactors is too sophisticated to transfer to rural peoples. These require capital funds, highly skilled workers, available resources, a developed transportation and communication network, and consumers with buying power. The emergent nations usually lack them all.

The spread of the Industrial Revolution from Britain to other Western nations during the 19th century took a century and was not accomplished without difficulty. Yet this represented a spread of technology among nations possessing a similar cultural background. How much more difficult to effect transfers when the cultural background differs so greatly as it does between the Western and the emergent nations!

Sir Eric Ashby[9] points out that it might seem simple to develop an air transport network in Africa, then spells out the difficulties: soil mechanics for airstrips, fuel supply and storage problems, knowledge of meteorology, radio communication, and so on. Hundreds of skilled men —technologists—are required to design the systems and maintain them. Soon the emergent nation finds it must reorganize its entire educational system, universities and technical colleges, apprenticeship systems, and trade schools. The condition precedent is making whole tribes literate. Yes, there is a great deal more to transferring technology than simply importing the products.

There is the quantum jump problem, too. Can emergent nations move from a technical base at about the level of Stone Age man to sophisticated 20th-century technology, or must they pass through the intermediate stages of industrial revolution recapitulating the industrialization process of the West? Can a country move from oxcart to jets without passing through, say, the railroad stage of transportation? The answers are by no means clear. Perhaps the questions do not admit of simple answers, or perhaps historians have not investigated these problems sufficiently to provide guidance. Technological lags occur, moreover, like cultural lags. African or Asian natives can flick the switch of a transistor radio, one of the most sophisticated and advanced products of Western technology, while tilling their fields with tools dating from time beyond memory and history.

Both the Soviet Union and Communist China attempted to telescope the industrial revolution which had taken a century and a half in Britain, Western Europe, and America. This brought about enormous dislocations and was done only with severest coercion and social unrest. Only 50 years after the Bolshevik Revolution did the tensions in Soviet society seem to relax. The Chinese experience seems even harsher and less successful, though we do not know enough about it to draw any confident conclusions. The Russians, however, cut the British and American time by two-thirds, an impressive accomplishment. The promise of short-run, effective industrialization is part of the competition between East and West among the emergent nations.

Besides education, the chief problem that is a function of time is capital funds and how to sweat them out of the labor of the people. No matter how capital is acquired, socialist or capitalist, history tells us the process is painful. Both change and hard work for little pay are painful. Yet, if standards of living are to be raised, adherence to old methods and tools must be broken and antiquated landholding systems must go. Educational opportunities for all must be instituted. Perhaps some kind of authoritarian productive institution, like the U.S. corporation or the Soviet commissar system, must be established, wherein punishment for the crime of loafing will be immediate, severe, and rehabilitative.

Pride must give way to lowly hopes of gain. Fierce national honor must be recognized as a luxury of wealthy nations. Military establishments must be reduced to constabularies. Steel mills, nuclear reactors, national airlines, and large-scale computers must be eschewed in favor of tools suitable to actual conditions of scarce capital and skilled labor shortage. These are imperatives for emergent nations; but most Western technological specialists coming from heavily industrialized environments in technical assistance programs, if they ever knew the imperatives, have forgotten them.

They introduce technologies beyond the reach of the underdeveloped economies. The United States and the Soviet Union often regard assistance projects as part of the international political struggle and ignore the interests of the people they purport to be assisting. Ritchie Calder gives a contemporary example.[10] While driving over an excellent road through the northern teak forest of Thailand, he congratulated the Thailander who accompanied him.

"This is an American road," said the Thailander. "They built it."

Calder remarked that it was thoughtful of the Americans to give the Thais a road on which to haul their teak.

"This is not our road. It is the strategical road to the Mekong and Laos."

"Never mind. The road will still be there when the emergency is over."

"They built it. They taught no one how it was built. They taught no one how to maintain it. To us, building a road means mechanical shovels, bulldozers, concrete mixers—all things we have not got."

The difficulties in applying science and technology to the underdeveloped lands are enormous. Yet the Western world has the scientific knowledge, the technical expertise, and—yes—even the human understanding to do it. Here lies the road toward the unity of mankind. The real question is whether we possess the tact and the foresight.

Science and Technology in the Future

We do not lack the scientific and technological knowledge to advance the unity of mankind. We lack the political wisdom. Science and technology, in this situation, provide benevolent potentialities. We could, if we would, eliminate misery, starvation, and deprivation. The cost, though great, would be less than dealing with well-ripened human discontents, guerrilla warfare, and total war. Yet accelerating advances of science and technology in the West are bringing sharper divisions between "haves" and "have-nots." What should unify man is actually contributing to disunity. No moratorium on scientific and technological developments is possible, but their spread to all peoples of the earth is eventually feasible.

Certain developments in contemporary science and technology can assist us. Advances in cultural anthropology and political science, for example, are giving us more sophisticated and knowledgeable approaches. The computer, handling large quantities of statistical data quickly, can assist in decision-making. The new administrative and management sciences, such as operations research and systems research, can help us take into account many more parameters of human conduct. In computational capabilities and dynamic modeling, the social sciences have powerful new tools for analyzing a society and determining the probable results of plausible decisions. If these new tools are correctly used, they can do much to translate ideas into action, to apply science and technology to elementary economics, and to promote the unity of mankind.

To an extent never before possible in human history, science and technology have given man the opportunity to determine his own destiny, to guide his own social evolution, and to construct a civilization, at once unitary and diverse, which embraces all mankind. They have also given mankind the opportunity to destroy itself and the world in which we live. The ultimate decision will, of course, rest upon man himself.

NOTES

1. Alexander Koyré, Études Galiliennes (Paris, 1939).

2. J. L. and Barbara Hammond, The Town Labourer, 1760-1832 (London, 1917) and The Bleak Age (London, 1934). See also E. Royston Pike, Hard Times: Human Documents of the Industrial Revolution (New York, 1966).

3. N. S. B. Gras, A History of Agriculture in Europe and America (New York, 1954); B. H. Slicher von Bath, The Agrarian History of Western Europe (London, 1963); R. E. Prothero (Lord Ernle), English Farming, Past and Present (New York, 1936).

4. S. H. Schurr, B. C. Netschert et al., *Energy in the American Economy, 1850-1975* (Baltimore, 1960).

5. David M. Potter, *People of Plenty* (Chicago, 1954).

6. Colin Clark, *The Conditions of Economic Progress* (London, 1940); T. S. Ashton, *The Industrial Revolution, 1760-1830* (Oxford, 1948); F. A. Hayek, ed., *Capitalism and the Historians* (Chicago, 1954).

7. Luther H. Evans and George E. Arnstein, eds., *Automation and the Challenge to Education* (Washington, D.C., 1962).

8. William Woodruff, *Impact of Western Man: A Study of Europe's Role in the World Economy, 1750-1960* (New York, 1967).

9. Eric Ashby, "The Administrator: Bottleneck or Pump," *Daedalus*, 92 (1962), 264-278.

10. Ritchie Calder, "Technology in Focus," *Technology and Culture* III, 4 (Fall 1962), 569.

BIBLIOGRAPHY

J. D. Bernal. *Science in History.* 3d ed. New York: 1965.

John G. Burke, ed. *The New Technology and Human Values.* Belmont, Calif.: 1966.

Sigfried Giedion. *Mechanization Takes Command.* New York: 1948.

Gerold Holton, ed. *Science and Culture.* Cambridge, Mass.: 1965.

Norman Kaplan, ed. *Science and Society.* Chicago: 1965.

Melvin Kranzberg and Carroll W. Pursell, Jr., eds. *Technology in Western Civilization.* 2 vols. New York: 1967.

Margaret Mead. *Cultural Patterns and Technical Change.* New York: 1955.

Lewis Mumford. *Technics and Civilization.* New York: 1934.

Gerard Piel. *Science in the Cause of Man.* New York: 1961.

Charles R. Walker, ed. *Modern Technology and Civilization.* New York: 1962.

EIGHT

Race:
Unity in Diversity

ROBERT A. LYSTAD

School of Advanced International
Studies
The Johns Hopkins University

The Concept of Race

THE VARIOUS POPULATIONS OF MANKIND, LIKE THE POPULATIONS of other organisms, differ from each other in the frequency of certain genes. The observation of these differences and of the visible or measurable (phenotypic) differences between populations has provided the empirical basis for the concept of race.

Throughout the lifetime of an organism, the genes operate to determine its physical structure and the manner in which its various parts function. Because each of these elementary particles operates in an environment influenced by other genes and by other factors internal and external to the organism, the effects of most of the genes are not absolute but are modified from what they would otherwise be. Nutritional, maturational and pathological states affect their performance, and external ecological, social and human cultural factors also alter their visible or measurable effects. The genes themselves, however, are not modified. They are reproduced and transmitted from generation to generation as discrete, stable entities, each giving the same directives within the changed environment of the offspring as it did to the parent.[1]

Why, then, is there such variability between the observable effects of identical genes within populations and even between parents and offspring? One reason, of course, is that as the total organism matures the changing environment of some genes retards, accelerates or otherwise alters their effects. Because genes always act in an environment, and because each individual organism has its own special environments, no two members of a population are ever quite identical to each other.

Another reason for this variability is found in the process by which the organism acquires its own particular set of genes. These genetic units are organized into pairs; that is each unit characteristic is the result of the operation of two separate genes with identical functions. A few characteristics are determined by a single pair; most are the result of the work of a complex of paired genes. All except single-celled organisms inherit their genes from two sources, usually two separate parents. Each parent contributes one of each pair, that is a complete set consisting of one half of its total number of genes, to its offspring. These recombine in the new offspring to produce a different blend of effects. The genes themselves do not blend or change in any way. Each particle retains its separate entity and integrity and goes about its work. But the new blend of characteristics is different from that of either of its parental sources. Because it is a matter of sheer chance that one rather than the other of the pair is transmitted, and because the number in each half set is so large—one estimate for man is between 20,000 and 45,000—the possibilities are virtually nil that any two individuals would ever receive identical complements of paired genes and hence be genetically or phenotypically identical.[2]

Despite this observable variability within a population, even between offspring of the same parents, many members of one population do resemble each other more closely than they resemble members of other populations. And that is a non-genetic way of saying that certain genes occur more frequently and operate in similar environments within one population than in another.

The Study of Human Races

Anthropologists, geneticists and others who study race as a human phenomenon attempt to describe and explain the differences in the phenotypes (observable characteristics) and genotypes (gene frequencies) between the various human populations. Students of race try to relate these differences to their possible genetic and environmental origins and causes, and to determine the processes by which they have come about. What are some of the widely-accepted findings about the phenomena and the concept which make them relevant to the intelligent appreciation of the mankind concept?

An excellent summation of the areas of agreement between representatives of the sciences concerned with various aspects of the concept is found in the *Statement on the Nature of Race and Race Differences.*[3]

1. Scientists are generally agreed that all men living today belong to a single species, *Homo sapiens*, and are derived from a common stock, even though there is some dispute as to when and how different human groups diverged from this common stock.

The concept of race is unanimously regarded by anthropologists as a classificatory device providing a zoological frame within which the various groups of mankind may be arranged and by means of which studies of evolutionary processes can be facilitated. In its anthropological sense, the word "race" should be reserved for groups of mankind possessing well-developed and primarily heritable physical differences from other groups. Many populations can be so classified but, because of the complexity of human history, there are also many populations which cannot easily be fitted into a racial classification.

2. Some of the physical differences betwen human groups are due to differences in hereditary constitution and some to differences in the environments in which they have been brought up. In most cases, both influences have been at work. The science of genetics suggests that the hereditary differences among populations of a single species are the results of the action of two sets of processes. On the one hand, the genetic composition of isolated populations is constantly but gradually being altered by natural selection and by occasional changes (mutations) in the material particles (genes) which control heredity. Populations are also affected by fortuitous changes in gene frequency and by marriage customs. On the other hand, crossing is constantly breaking down the differentiations so set up. The new mixed populations, in so far as they, in turn, become isolated, are subject to the same processes, and these may lead to further changes. Existing races are merely the result, considered at a particular moment in time, of the total effect of such processes on the human species. The hereditary characters to be used in the classification of human groups, the limits of their variation within these groups, and, thus the extent of the classificatory subdivisions adopted may legitimately differ according to the scientific purpose in view.

3. National, religious, geographical, linguistic and cultural groups do not necessarily coincide with racial groups; and the cultural traits of such groups have no demonstrated connection with racial traits. Americans are not a race, nor are Frenchmen, nor Germans; nor *ipso facto* is any other national group. Muslims and Jews are no more races than are Roman Catholics and Protestants; nor are people who live in Iceland or Britain or India, or who speak English or any other language, or who are culturally Turkish or Chinese and the like, thereby describable as races. The use of the term "race" in speaking of such groups may be a serious error, but it is one which is habitually committed.

4. Human races can be, and have been, classified in different ways by different anthropologists. Most of them agree in classifying the greater part of existing mankind into at least three large units, which may be called major groups (in French grand-races, in German Hauptrassen). Such a classification does not depend on any single physical character, nor does, for example, skin colour by itself necessarily distinguish one major group from another. Furthermore, so far as it has been possible to analyse them, the differences in physical structure which distinguish one major group from another give no support to popular notions of any general "superiority" or "inferiority" which are sometimes implied in referring to these groups.

Broadly speaking, individuals belonging to different major groups of mankind are distinguishable by virtue of their physical characters, but individual members, or small groups, belonging to different races within the same major group are not so distinguishable. Even the major groups grade into each other, and the physical traits by which they and the races within them are characterized overlap considerably. With respect to most, if not all, measurable characters, the differences among individuals belonging to the same race are greater than the differences that occur between the observed averages for two or more races within the same major group.

5. Most anthropologists do not include mental characteristics in their classification of human races. Studies within a single race have shown that both innate capacity and environmental opportunity determine the results of tests of intelligence and temperament, though their relative importance is disputed.

When intelligence tests, even non-verbal, are made on a group of non-literate people, their scores are usually lower than those of more civilized people. It has been recorded that different groups of the same race occupying similarly high levels of civilization may yield considerable differences in intelligence tests. When, however, the two groups have been brought up from childhood in similar environments, the differences are usually very slight. Moreover, there is good evidence that, given similar opportunities, the average performance (that is to say, the performance of the individual who is representative because he is surpassed by as many as he surpasses), and the variation round it, do not differ appreciably from one race to another.

Even those psychologists who claim to have found the greatest differences in intelligence between groups of different racial origin, and have contended that they are hereditary, always report that some members of the group of inferior performance surpass not merely the lowest ranking member of the superior group, but also the average of its members. In any case, it has never been possible to separate members of two groups on the basis of mental capacity, as they can often be separated on a basis of religion, skin colour, hair form or language. It is possible, though not proved, that some types of innate capacity for intellectual and emotional responses are commoner in one human group than in another, but it is certain that, within a single group, innate capacities vary as much as, if not more than, they do between different groups.

The study of the heredity of psychological characteristics is beset with difficulties. We know that certain mental diseases and defects are transmitted from one generation to the next, but we are less familiar with the part played by heredity in the mental life of normal individuals. The normal individual, irrespective of race, is essentially educable. It follows that his intellectual and moral life is largely conditioned by his training and by his physical and social environment.

It often happens that a national group may appear to be characterized by particular psychological attributes. The superficial view would be that this is due to race. Scientifically, however, we realize that any common psychological attribute is more likely to be due to a common historical and social background, and that such attributes may obscure the fact that, within different populations consisting of many human types, one will find approximately the same range of temperament and intelligence.

6. The scientific material available to us at present does not justify the conclusion that inherited genetic differences are a major factor in producing the differences between the cultures and cultural achievements of different peoples or groups. It does indicate, on the contrary, that a major factor in explaining such differences is the cultural experience which each group has undergone.

7. There is no evidence for the existence of so-called "pure" races. Skeletal remains provide the basis of our limited knowledge about earlier races. In regard to race mixture, the evidence points to the fact that human hybridization has been going on for an indefinite but considerable time. Indeed, one of the processes of race formation and race extinction or absorption is by means of hybridization between races. As there is no reliable evidence that disadvantageous effects are produced thereby, no biological justification exists for prohibiting inter-marriage between persons of different races.

8. We now have to consider the bearing of these statements on the problem of human equality. We wish to emphasize that equality of opportunity and equality in law in no way depend, as ethical principles, upon the assertion that human beings are in fact equal in endowment.

9. We have thought it worthwhile to set out in a formal manner what is at present scientifically established concerning individual and group differences.

(a) In matters of race, the only characteristics which anthropologists have been able to use effectively as a basis for classification are physical (anatomical and physiological).

(b) Available scientific knowledge provides no basis for believing that the groups of mankind differ in their innate capacity for intellectual and emotional development.

(c) Some biological differences between human beings within a single race may be as great as, or greater than, the same biological differences between races.

(d) Vast social changes have occurred that have not been connected in any way with changes in racial type. Historical and sociological studies thus support the view that genetic differences are of little significance in determining the social and cultural differences between different groups of men.

(e) There is no evidence that race mixture produces disadvantageous results from a biological point of view. The social results of race mixture, whether for good or ill, can generally be traced to social factors.

Text drafted at Unesco House, Paris, on 8 June, 1951 by: Professor R. A. M. Bergman, Royal Tropical Institute, Amsterdam; Professor Gunnar Dahlberg, Director, State Institute for Human Genetics and Race Biology, University of Uppsala; Professor L. C. Dunn, Department of Zoology, Columbia University, New York; Professor J. B. S. Haldane, Head, Department of Biometry, University College, London; Professor M. F. Ashley Montagu, Chairman, Department of Anthropology, Rutgers University, New Brunswick, N.J.; Dr. A. E. Mourant, Director, Blood Group Reference Laboratory, Lister Institute, London; Professor Hans Nachtsheim, Director, Institut für Genetik, Freie Universität, Berlin; Dr. Eugène Schreider, Directeur adjoint du Laboratoire d'Anthropologie Physique de l'Ecole des Hautes Etudes, Paris; Professor Harry L. Shapiro, Chairman, Department of Anthropology, American Museum of Natural History, New York; Dr. J. C. Trevor, Faculty of Archaeology and Anthropology, University of Cambridge; Dr. Henri V. Vallois, Professeur au Museum d'Histoire Naturelle, Directeur de Musée de l'Homme, Paris; Professor S. Zuckerman, Head, Department of Anatomy, Medical School, University of Birmingham; Professor Th. Dobzhansky, Department of Zoology, Columbia University, New York, and Dr. Julian Huxley contributed to the final wording.[4]

Mankind Is One Species

The two innovators of ideas responsible for the great breakthrough in knowledge of hereditary biological relationships and the processes by which organisms have become differentiated are Charles Darwin and Gregor Mendel. Other significant contemporaries, intellectual descendants, independent discoverers, and subsequent pioneers have added to the understanding of the biological unity of mankind and its position in the organic scheme of things, but the publication of Darwin's *Origin of Species* (1858) and the delayed discovery of Mendel's *Investigations in Plant Hybridization* (1865) prepared the way for the great flowering of knowledge about evolution, human or otherwise, during the past century.

About a century before their works appeared, the originator of the modern taxonomial system, Linnaeus, had devised a scheme which summarized observations about the probable relationships between living organisms. The criteria for his classification were similarities and differences of form. He assessed the degree to which the form of an organism differed from man's and resembled that of other organisms which he then placed in the same category. On his recognition of a great degree of mutual similarity he classified man, the great apes, the monkeys and several other animals in a single order, called primates. The order of primates, along with other orders of the animal kingdom, was assigned a position within the infraclass eutheria (including rodents and carnivores). This infraclass constituted one subdivision of the subphylum Vertebrata (including fishes, amphibians, reptiles, and birds). The phylum Chordata (including a few animals which were not quite similar enough to be classed with other vertebrates), and the grade Metazoa (including all except the single-celled animals) comprised the successively more general and inclusive categories within the Animal Kingdom.

Within the order of primates, man stands in varying degrees of relationship to the other animals. This simplified chart indicates his taxonomic position in these respects and suggests his biological, evolutionary affinities and his unique position among the other related animals.

Within the genus *Homo*, as among most other genera in the taxonomic system, certain finer distinctions are possible. To these several subcategories the term *Species* is given, and there is practically universal agreement on the designation of all modern men as species *Sapiens*.

There have been some terminological and classificatory differences between the taxonomists, however, over the proper placement of the various pre-modern types of *Homo* that have appeared—most of them to disappear or be absorbed—in the course of perhaps 1.8 millions of years of man-like hominid habitation of the earth. Not all of the aspects of the debate are directly relevant to the understanding of the taxonomic position of modern man, although some of them have at least indirect

FORMAL TAXONOMY

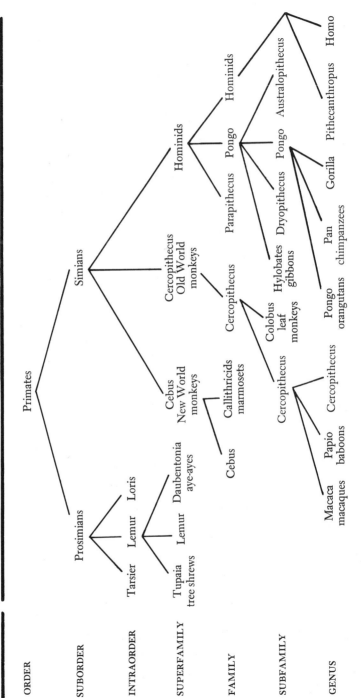

CATEGORY

ORDER

SUBORDER

INTRAORDER

SUPERFAMILY

FAMILY

SUBFAMILY

GENUS

Adapted from Lasker (1961:30)

relevance to the comparison of the modern races. What is important here is the unanimity with which scientists agree that all modern men can be classified as one at the level of the species.

Despite the apparent differences between the various human populations in form—ranging in height, for example, from the smallest Pygmy to the tallest Nordic Caucasoid or Nilotic Negroid, and including physical characteristics invisible to the naked eye—all are capable of interbreeding with each other and producing offspring who themselves are interfertile. This capability essentially is what distinguishes one species from another; its membership is closed to the members of any other species—regardless of how similar in form the species may appear to the eye—because there is no means of genetic ingress.[5] The races of mankind suffer no such disability and, as the history of the mixing between human populations reveals, man has in fact exploited his single species capability when the opportunity has presented itself.

When populations mix, genes are said "to flow" between them. Within the species, each individual can carry genes which in some previous generation have flowed from a population other than his own present one. And he can transmit these to his offspring. In a sense, then, a person could be classified as "belonging" to two or more races simultaneously. But he could never be classified as belonging to two or more species, or as belonging to any species other than *Homo Sapiens*, or as belonging more to some species other than *Homo Sapiens*.

How has this unity of the species *Sapiens* within the genus *Homo* come about? The taxonomic chart on page 166 suggests that there have been at least two genera of the family of hominids, one of which, *Pithecanthropus*, has long since become extinct. Still a third sub-family on the chart, the also extinct *Australopithecus*, is classified by some taxonomists as being more properly placed on the same stem or as an offshoot of the stem bearing the genus *Pithecanthropus*. Complicating a more complete chart would be the placement of a considerable number of other extinct members of the family of hominids. Many of these have been dignified with Latin names which suggest that they belonged to species different from *Sapiens* and even to genera different from *Homo*. The well-known *Homo Neanderthalensis* is an example of the former, *Sinanthropus Pekinensis* of the latter.

Carlton S. Coon (1962), an eminent physical anthropologist, has propounded a theory that prior to *Homo Sapiens* there existed a single hominid species, *Erectus* (of which *Sinanthropus* and *Pithecanthropus* are two of five racial populations) which evolved into *Homo Sapiens* at probably five different times and in five different localities. He argued that most of the distinguishing physical traits could have been caused by minor changes in endocrine balance and growth sequence and that relatively little genetic change was necessary. A major result of the different geographic locations and time lags between the changes was the differentiation of *Homo Sapiens* into five modern races, which is what he was primarily concerned to explain.

In the controversy which has ensued, various other respected scientists, such as Theodosius Dobzhansky (1963) and Ashley Montagu (1963) have argued that the chances of five different evolutionary processes producing a single species from an earlier species are so small as to be nil. Most scientists are in agreement with Coon that the populations of modern *Homo Sapiens* are so similar because they share the same evolutionary history of descent (or ascent) from an earlier hominid, such as *Homo Erectus*, but they cannot accept Coon's evidence for conclusions about the process of modern racial differentiation. Five origins, each independent in time and space, would be more likely to produce five different species which could not subsequently merge into one. If the details of time, place and processes by which the modern races within the species became differentiated cannot yet be determined, at least the broad outlines of the process of evolution by which an earlier species evolved into a biologically single modern species have been agreed upon.

The Causes of Similarities and Differences Between Races

If mankind is thus unique or "separated" from all other animals at the level of the species—as all species of organic life are unique—is it proper to think of the various racial populations as unique or separated from each other? They obviously cannot be very different from each other biologically because of their interfertility. But they obviously do differ in their forms, at least in some small degree. This degree, moreover, appears to be very considerable in the estimate of some largely non-scientific observers. How have these differences emerged? The answer to this question is found both in the genetic processes of evolution and in the different physical and social environments in which mankind lives.

The frequencies with which genes occur in a population change over a period of time. This is essentially what is meant by the concept of evolution; this is the process which has led to the differentiation of species; and this is the process which has led to the differentiation of races. Gene frequencies may be altered by any or several of these factors: mutation, natural selection, random genetic drift, and isolation.

The first factor, *mutation*, refers to the process by which the structure and hence the function of a gene may change. A new or structurally modified gene is introduced into a population's reservoir of genes (the total complement of genes from which an individual could acquire his personal set through the mating of members of the population). If the person who initially acquired this gene survives to produce one offspring, the chances are equal that the mutant gene will be transmitted to the next generation or be lost. If he produces more than one offspring, half of them are likely to receive the mutant gene.

Although mutations have been induced in plants and animals in the laboratory, little is known about the mechanism by which they occur in humans—although x-ray and other radiation including even natural or normal radiation, appear to be among the several possible causes. In the absence of extensive knowledge about the causes, mutations are frequently referred to as "accidental" or "spontaneous," but the rate at which they occur has been estimated at between 5 and 50 per million births under normal conditions.

When they do occur there is a great likelihood that they will have disadvantageous effects on the individual. If these disadvantages are lethal before the individual becomes sexually mature, or if they biologically or socially prevent him from breeding, they have no effect on evolution. The mutant gene is never transmitted to any offspring and is lost from the population's gene pool. Not all mutations are that disadvantageous, however, and at least one, that causing hemophilia, has become well recognized in consequence of its occurrence in Queen Victoria and its transmission to various of her descendants over several generations. Although not all mutations are disadvantageous, that the majority of them are is readily explainable. Any surviving species is the inheritor of an accumulation of advantageous genes over a long period of time. Any species represents a well-balanced adjustment between highly selected genes and the environment in which the species lives. A new gene, which modifies a gene the advantages of which have been proved in the test of survival, is more likely to upset the balance than to improve it and hence to be regarded as disadvantageous.

It must be recognized, however, that physical and social environments also change over time, and it is quite likely that a gene which placed an individual at a slight disadvantage in one environment may place him at an advantage in a changed environment. Within the species as a whole, then, genetic changes may occur through mutation which permit the modified species to survive in a changed environment, even while the formerly well-adjusted but now unfortunate non-mutant members may not survive.

When mutations have occurred in a radical fashion in one segment of a population over a short period of time, or when they have gradually accrued over a longer period of time and to a degree which makes the mutant segment incapable of breeding with the non-mutant segments of the population, a new species is said to have emerged. There is every reason to believe that this process of genetic change through mutation has been going on among men, even as it has among all other organisms, and that physically different racial populations are the outcome. This does not mean, however, that this factor in the process of evolution is working to produce new species of mankind out of the present single species. Several other factors, to be discussed below, have been operating simultaneously to reduce the possibility of such an occurrence to practically nil.

The second of the change-producing factors is *natural selection*. It is particularly for this conceptualization of an aspect of its heredity that mankind is indebted to Charles Darwin. Well-popularized, if often mistakenly so, in the phrase "survival of the fittest," the concept refers not to a brutish battle between individuals for survival but to the acquisition of a physical endowment which enables a species to survive in its environment. Darwin was unaware of the genetic mechanisms by which the appropriate physical characteristics were acquired, but his concept greatly clarified the manner in which the natural environment selected for survival those species best adapted to it and enabled them to transmit their characteristics to the next generation. In most of the animal world, those animals which acquired certain specialized features (particularly well-adapted to a few features of the environment) such as wings, claws, hoofs, armor plate, fins, long necks or camouflage, managed to out-survive less fortunate creatures inhabiting the same environment, which failed to acquire similar or other specialized features which could adapt them to it equally well.

Some early species of hominids encountered difficulty in these adaptive respects, for they are now extinct. Other hominids fared much better in the selection process, and of those which did, the species from which *Homo Sapiens* evolved acquired certain remarkably adaptive characteristics which were, at the same time, relatively unspecialized. The most distinctive of mankind's particular adaptations to his environment have been suited to living in an extraordinary number and types of environments. Although he shares many adaptive features with other primates and a decreasing number with all other members of the animal kingdom that appear in the formal taxonomy, not one of them has acquired the same combination of highly adaptive and relatively unspecialized characteristics. Central among these features are his eyes, hands, feet and a large, complex brain which enables him to create an enormous variety of linguistic and other symbols and to communicate, compare and share his adaptive (and ill-adaptive) experience. *Homo Sapiens* may not be able to escape directly by taking flight on land or in the sea or air, rout his attackers with a strong limb, a sharp claw, or a powerful jaw, crawl into a shell, fade into the background, or reach the topmost greenery, but he can create and manipulate tools and machines which can do all of these things and in a far greater range of environments than is available to the more specialized beasts.

Homo Sapiens cannot directly transmit these tools or machines to his offspring through his genes, but he can teach his offspring, who are remarkably educable, to re-create them. In certain circumstances, they can even improve upon them and invent new ones. Instead of awaiting new genes which will adapt him to his environment through the chance processes of mutation and selection, man alters his environments to fit the genes he has inherited. The factor of natural selection in determining gene frequencies in human populations has thus taken on a new meaning. It has operated to select a combination of genes so superbly adapted to its environments that *Homo Sapiens* has been lifted out of the ordinary selective process and been given a considerable measure of control over it.

What is true of the total species in these respects is true of every racial population within it. All possess the same comparatively unspecialized adaptive features. Nor do the physical differences between the races appear to have any important adaptive function which might justify some more radical kind of separate classifications for them. There is some evidence that dark-skinned, broad-nosed people are biologically better adapted to tropical environments than are light-skinned, narrow-nosed people, and there are a number of other characteristics that may adapt certain other human populations to their environments in a superior manner. But dark-skinned people are also well-adapted to living in temperate and arctic climates—as they do—not so much on the basis of their dark skins as on the basis of their eyes, their hands and feet, their brains, and their consequent ability to invent a culture which shapes the environment to their biological capabilities. It is highly unlikely, furthermore, that a dark-skinned human population could survive in the tropics without the cultural aids it has devised any more than could a light-skinned population in a temperate or a tropical environment.

Such slightly distinctive or specialized characteristics as appear in different populations in different environments may well help them survive the local rigors of the natural selection process. They may even more certainly be understood as helping the total human species adapt to its total world environment. This, more than the adaptation of a small segment to its particular area of the globe is the probable function of some of those racial differences.

The two remaining factors affecting gene frequencies, random genetic drift and isolation, are even more closely dependent upon each other, and the mechanisms of their operation are the same. The first, random genetic drift, occurs in a situation in which one breeding population has become isolated from others, and especially where it is a very small population (for example, about 50 people). The number of variants of a particular gene in the total pool of a small population is obviously limited; only a few persons in the group will have a certain variant. Even a particular gene may be present only in a few individuals. Should those few persons fail to reproduce, or should they produce smaller numbers of offspring than the others, their rare gene would either immediately or gradually disappear completely. It could never reappear unless the proper mutation occurred or it got reintroduced from the outside world—in which case the isolation would be broken. In larger populations, random drift does not occur, because a larger number, though not necessarily a larger proportion, of the population carry the more rare gene, and the chances are greater that the carriers will reproduce at about the same rate as all the other members of the group. The two critical features, then, are the size of the breeding population—all those who may be expected to mate with each other—and its isolation from other groups. In small, isolated populations the effects of random gene drift may show themselves clearly within the span of a few generations. In large populations, and especially in those in which the gene pool receives rather frequent infusions of genes from other populations, the effects of random drift are much harder to detect, if they are present at all.

Modern human populations, of whatever race, are usually neither small nor isolated enough for the process of drift to occur. In the early days of *Homo Sapiens*, however, it is likely that this factor was prominent in the creation of the various races. The total membership of the human species was small, the members lived in small, frequently isolated groups, and there were limited possibilities for the wide sharing of a gene pool or the infusion of genes into the pool. In such circumstances separate groups could acquire distinctive racial characteristics over a short period of time, and the genetic foundations of the modern races could quickly have been laid.

Geographic barriers have probably been the most important factors isolating potential breeding populations from each other during most of human history. Oceans, deserts and mountains have proved effective inhibitors of easy communication and affection between peoples. But each advance in technology has tended to make these barriers less formidable, from the time when men learned they could control fire, manufacture a bow and arrow, build and sail a boat, or domesticate a camel, to the present, when they are able to soar over nearly all physical obstacles and find potential mates in a different population practically at will. Such has been the ingenuity of *Homo Sapiens* during his recent history that no group has managed to remain sufficiently isolated from others to acquire or maintain more than minor differences from them. On the contrary, he has been so mobile that the crossing of population boundaries and the mixing of genes appears to have ended whatever chances for species differentiation there might once have been. This is not the same as saying that all men are genetically identical or draw their ration of genes from a common pool. It is merely to say that they are not importantly different from each other now and that the likelihood of their ever becoming so is very small indeed.

New races are in continual process of formation as a result of the reduction of isolation and the increase of mixing over much of *Homo Sapiens'* last 30,000 years of existence. Relative isolation and small degrees of mixing, however, are still characteristic of most of the world's populations. Physical factors, such as distance, still prevent members of most populations from breeding with outsiders in the same proportions as they mate with others of their own group. Social factors, such as caste and class, religion, ethnic ties, and even racial characteristics themselves, continue to restrain many people from blending their genes with those of another social group. Whatever the continuing barriers, it is unlikely that all members of *Homo Sapiens* will ever draw their genes from a common pool and that the species will ever consist of a single homogeneous group. As a consequence of these and of mankind's innumerable other marriage and mating customs, relative physical and social isolation continue to operate to produce new races. New genes may be added to a particular pool, but mixing stops short of the point where all persons are equally potential mates. Then some degree of isolation is maintained or reasserted, and a somewhat modified population with somewhat altered characteristics evolves. In the recent millennia of mankind's existence, his mobility and racial mixing have made impossible the formation of a new species, but they have not proceeded so far as to prevent the formation of new races.

The Significance of Racial Similarities and Differences

The existing races are merely the present end products of genetic and environmental factors which have operated since the beginning of *Homo*

Sapiens—and before—to produce the great similarities and the minor differences within mankind. But the different meanings various observers have read into these similarities and differences have been the source of considerable confusion about their significance. What are the causes of misinterpretations of the meaning of race that, in certain times and places, have fostered hostility and conflict, discrimination and recrimination on groundless bases?

There is no human group which does not distinguish between itself and others on one basis or another. Most groups, furthermore, distinguish different types or categories of people within their own group. There are many criteria which can be used individually or collectively for making such distinctions either within or between groups. Among those familiar to nearly everyone are the possession of relative degrees of power or authority, ownership of property or control of the means of production, income, consumption standards in housing, dress, transport or recreation, education, occupation, enviable achievement, acceptance into prestigious groups, morality, "family background" or ancestral position, ethnic origin, nationality, religious custom, language or dialect, geographical location, and many others, frequently including, of course, some "physical characteristics." Not all groups use all these distinctions for perceiving differences between themselves and others; some use very few. Many groups place great emphasis upon genetically determined racial phenotypes as important distinguishing criteria, some place only a little, and a few use that criterion not at all.

Distinctions between categories of people are not only inevitable, they are absolutely necessary for the conduct of human group life. Classification of groups based on such criteria helps the individual to sort out those persons and groups more likely than others to be congenial or appropriate to his needs. No person could survive long or well if forced either to choose at random or to subject to intensive personal scrutiny every individual upon whom he must depend. In part at least, he must make his selections on the basis of categories, not individuals. Discrimination in this sense is essential to group life. There is nothing inherent in human beings, however, which impels members of one category to be hostile or fearful toward members of other categories. Some animals appear to be inherently hostile to members of another species or even of another race or breed of their own species, but *Homo Sapiens* reveals great variability in this respect. Karl Marx, for example, seems to have felt that hostility between the owners of property and the propertyless is inevitable and inherent in the scheme of things. Types of relationships under which "haves" and "have nots" coexist indicate far more alternatives than he seems to have envisaged. Some societies seem to recognize racial characteristics as stimulants of hostility or fear, but even within those that do, there usually are sizeable groups that react to the presumed stimuli with far less intensity than the others. *Homo Sapiens* must learn his "proper" reaction patterns.

In addition to learning how to discriminate between categories, men also frequently learn to rank the categories as higher or lower, superior or inferior, better or worse. This ranking may be done on rational or utilitarian grounds ("category X is demonstrably more appropriate to my needs than category Y"), but it is often also done on non-rational or moral grounds ("category X is superior to category Y"). This tendency to rank categories is often accompanied by a tendency to assume that a person of high (or low) rank in one category must also be a person of high (or low) rank in other categories. Memberships in many categories frequently do overlap, especially when the activities of one are also appropriate to or dependent upon the activities of another category. If a, b and c are large-scale owners of means of production, they are likely also to possess large amounts of economic power, possibility of political power as well; they (or at least their children) are likely also to be well-educated,, enjoy considerable prestige, belong to "the upper class," and have other "superior" characteristics. But not all categories are likely to overlap so neatly. Must a, b and c all be French, or German, or American? Are they all likely to be Protestant, or Catholic, or Jewish, or Muslim? Do they necessarily have Caucasoid, Negroid or Mongoloid physical features? Obviously certain categories are less closely related to some than to others, and the tendency to confuse a person's membership in some with membership in others should be less strong. But in many societies at various times men have been taught to equate several which are not relevant to each other. *Homo Sapiens'* remarkably adaptive ability to classify and rank phenomena has at times been subverted by his remarkably ill-adaptive tendency to mis-classify and to err in his judgment of rank.

One of the categories which frequently has suffered violation of its integrity in this respect is race. The term which denotes that category has been equated with nationality (the "French race," the "German race"), with religion (the "Jewish race," the "Muslim races"), geographical location (the "Asiatic race," the "African race"), languages and language families (the "Aryan race," the "Bantu race") and with other categories. None of the foregoing categories has any necessary connection, either as cause or as caused, with the genetically inheritable characteristics or with the gene frequencies in a population denoted by the categorical term "race."

Theoretically there is no reason why a group of persons may not agree to give so arbitrary a symbol as the word "race" any meaning they wish. The word, however, has a long history of scientific usage as a reference for heritable physical characteristics (however much the processes of physical inheritance have been clarified during the past century). It is hardly advisable, therefore, to use a term for one phenomenon as a substitute for perfectly comprehensible terms traditionally used for other unrelated phenomena, terms such as nationality, religion, and language. Unless a large majority of the world's people who attempt to communicate precisely with each other agree to use the word "race" in these nonscientific ways, it is a disservice to mankind to do so. In view of the political and social passions its misuse and misinterpretation have aroused, it is even dangerous to mankind to do so.

The confusion over relationships between terms and categories has arisen, however, not so much because of mere historical or linguistic error or obtuseness as because many people attribute causal powers to the categories. This is particularly true when persons who occupy a position in a category they rank high rather than low, superior rather than inferior, better rather than worse, attempt to explain the behavior of their presumed subordinates. It requires a long, unjustified leap in logic to conclude that membership in one category causes membership in others. Large numbers of people, nevertheless, seem capable of making the leap, particularly when racial characteristics provide the springboard. At various times and places in mankind's history, members of all the races mistakenly have had their lowly or despised conditions—their enslavement, poverty, weakness, laziness, disorganization, criminality, ignorance—attributed to that "basic cause," their "race." Many wrongly-called racial groups have in time more or less escaped from their stigmata (for example, the "Irish race" and the "Italian race" in America), others have been stigmatized now and then (the "Chinese race" and the "Jewish race" in America) and still others have not yet escaped (the "Bantu race" in South Africa, the "Negro race" in America, and the "white race" in modern China). It is not inconceivable that at some time the condition of every human group has been explained in racial terms. Whenever it has, the explanation has been the infertile offspring of an imprecise definition and a false assumption.

Race Classifications

The similarities between all populations of mankind, the mobility of most of mankind and the blending of genes that has occurred whenever human groups meet under auspicious circumstances have produced a human population which is difficult to classify racially. Indeed, it is almost appropriate to say that there are as many racial classifications as there are anthropological classifiers. This is due not to technical incompetence but to the varying purposes of classifications, to the selection of criteria for classifying, and to the nature of the raw material, that is, the inheritable physical characteristics of populations. There are many traits, visible and invisible to the naked eye, which could be measured. Although a cluster of "typical" traits may be used to distinguish one race from another, considerable variations around the mean for any one trait and for all traits in the cluster inevitably are to be found. Between populations, furthermore, there is tremendous overlapping or mutual sharing of a large portion of the total range for any one characteristic. Finally, the composition of the pool of genes from which the traits are drawn is continually changing through the processes of mutation, natural selection, isolation and drift, and especially through the introduction and mixing of genes from the outside.

It is not surprising, therefore, that those scientists concerned with the study of the concept of race have tended to turn increasingly away from problems of racial classification to problems of genetic processes, the factors effecting gene frequencies, the causes and geographical distribution of single traits, genetic determinants of abnormal and normal behavior, patterns of growth and maturation in the individual, and other problems well outside the range of racial classification. It is felt that there is no longer anything to be learned from mere racial classification; that approach to race has reached a dead end.

Consider just a few of the many classifications that have been devised by anthropologists and geneticists. One classifies the principal racial types as Negroid, Caucasoid, Mongoloid, Australoid-Veddoid, Oceanic Negroid, and Polynesian-Micronesian. Another lists the eleven major races as Caucasoid, Mongoloid, African Negroid, Melanesian, Micronesian-Polynesian, The Congo or Central African Pygmy, The Far Eastern Pygmy, Australoid, Ainu, and Veddoid. Still another prefers a classification into Archaic Caucasoid (Ainu, Australoid, Dravidian, Vedda), Primary Caucasoid (Alpine, Armenoid, Mediterranean, Nordic), Secondary or derived Caucasoid (Dinaric, East Baltic, Polynesian), Mongoloid (Asiatic, Indonesian-Malay, American Indian), Primary Negroid (Forest, Negrito), and Derived Negroid (Bushman-Hottentot, Nilotic, Oceanic). A final example includes Caucasoid (Nordic, Alpine, Mediterranean, Dinaric), Mongoloid (Malayan, southern Chinese, northern Chinese and Mongolian, Siberian, American Indian, Eskimo), and Negroid (True Negro, Bantu-speaking Negro, Khoisan or Bushman-Hottentot, Nilotic, Hamite,

Pygmy, including those of the Congo forest, the Andaman, Vedda, Negritoes, Aeta, and others) and Melanesian.

These classifications—and there are many more—are based primarily upon visible and measurable physical characteristics such as various aspects of skin color, stature, head form, face form, hair, eye color and lid, nose form, and body build. Although genetically determined within the limits imposed by the physical and social environment, only that of eye color appears to be the product of the action of a single gene. These traits, therefore, do not readily permit the classification of races in terms of gene frequencies in a population, a disadvantage which William C. Boyd (1950) and others have attempted to overcome in the use of blood groups in racial classification. A typical classification based on the frequency of certain genes, the mechanism of inheritance of which is known, yields a classification like this: "1. Early European group (hypothetical) —Possessing the highest incidence (over 30%) of the Rh negative type . . . and probably no group B . . . Gene N possibly somewhat higher than in present-day Europeans . . . Represented today by their modern descendants, the Basques. 2. European (Caucasoid) group—Possessing the next highest incidence of rh (the Rh negative gene), and relatively high incidence of the genes Rh_1 and A_2, with moderate frequencies of other blood group genes . . . 3. African (Negroid) group—Possessing a tremendously high incidence of the gene Rh^0, a moderate frequency of rh, relatively high incidence of genes A_2 and the rare intermediate A ($A_{1,2}$, etc.) and Rh genes, rather high incidence of gene B. Probably normal M and N." (Boyd 1950:268). In similar fashion three other groups, Asiatic (Mongoloid), American Indian, and Australoid are identified by the geneticist.

Despite the differences between these attempts biologically to relate people to each other, several features are common to all of them. Three of the racial terms refer to very large human populations: Caucasoid, Negroid and Mongoloid; all the terms refer to groups of people who inhabit or have fairly recently migrated from particular or continuous geographic regions. The bracketed terms refer to subdivisions or embraces of the larger groupings and reflect an attempt to account for finer physical and regional differences within them. And some of the terms refer to relatively small and isolated populations.

These racial categories have had some value in the past in describing the physical differences between peoples from different regions of the world. The explanation of these differences may be summarized by stating that the breeding populations of the world have been somewhat isolated from each other at various times in their histories and that the normal genetic processes (mixture, mutation, selection and drift) have operated to yield different end products. But these comparatively isolative conditions no longer obtain for most of mankind, and one can presume that the degrees of isolation will progressively become smaller and the degrees of mixing greater. Even at the present stage of man's history the mixing has been such as to require the more or less arbitrary classification of many populations. As more mixing occurs the variations around the mean increase in diversity and scope, and racial categories become less and less useful as explanatory devices.

An increasing number of anthropologists have reached the conclusion that the racial categories have already outlived their usefulness as guides to further knowledge about human likenesses and differences (see for example Livingstone 1958, 1962; Newman 1963). They believe the search for explanations of the varieties of mankind must now focus on very small breeding populations, consisting primarily of those people who actually marry or mate with each other. Such studies are ideally conducted in small local groups where the genetic mode of inheritance is known and the selective or adaptive value of the trait can be demonstrated. One outcome of these studies is a map that shows the distribution of a single trait or of correlations between several traits. Scientists using this approach are interested not only in observing gene frequencies but in the specific mechanisms by which they fluctuate. Their maps resemble temperature maps, the clines showing the frequency of certain specific genes in adjacent populations. Explanations for the shifting clines are found in the recent spread of an advantageous gene, in the mixing of populations which previously had different frequencies for a gene, and in a gradual change in the value of a particular gene for a particular population. Some of these scientists question the value of the term race in any context and have dropped it from their vocabularies. Many others use it sparingly and in narrowly defined ways; nearly all who employ it more commonly justify its usage on the grounds that it is a traditional and widely used popular concept which deserves explanation.

On quite a different level, the concept of race is criticized as dangerous to human social relations because of the ease with which racial classifications of dubious accuracy and value come to be regarded as explanations of other differences and as justifications for harsh treatment of those who are different. The identification of a criminal as a Negro or a white man greatly narrows the search for him, but it does not explain the reason for the crime, nor does it justify the imputation of criminal tendencies to all or most members of his racial classification. In an attempt to avoid this error in social interpretations of what is merely a biological phenomenon and a taxonomic convenience, one anthropologist uses such terms as "divisions and ethnic groups of man."

"An ethnic group represents one of a number of populations comprising the single species *Homo sapiens* which individually maintain their differences, physical and cultural, by means of isolating mechanisms such as geographic and social barriers. These differences will vary as the power of the geographic and social barriers, acting upon the original genetic differences, vary. Where these barriers are of low power, neighboring groups will intergrade or hybridize with one another. Where these barriers are of high power, such ethnic groups will tend to remain distinct—or to replace each other geographically or ecologically." (Montagu 1942:44-45).

His classification is not radically different from those which do use the race concept.

However the problems may be defined, whatever the differences in the modes of studying them, however different the outcomes, there is near universal agreement that none of the races can be regarded as more advanced or more primitive, higher or lower, superior or inferior to the others. None is "closer to" or "farther from" *Homo Sapiens'* Neanderthal or other hominid ancestors or from non-human primate relatives. Common sense may suggest that this surely cannot be the case, and the observation of a few selected physical characteristics may seem to confirm it. But on the taxonomic tree, all the races—whatever the number—are growing at the end of the very same branch.

Caucasoids appear "more advanced" from earlier or other primate forms with respect to a few traits, such as their light skins, blue eyes, and vertical faces, since earlier men and other primates probably had dark skins, brown eyes, and prognathous jaws, characteristics shared in a general way by Negroids. But Negroids appear "more advanced" than Caucasoids with respect to their longer thigh bones and greater heel development. Negroids, furthermore, are "furthest removed" from non-human and less modern human types in their kinky hair, thick lips, and relatively hairless bodies and faces, and the blackest of the Negroes are as far removed from them as are the lightest Caucasoids. On the other hand, the Negroes' broad noses could be regarded as "less advanced."

Mongoloids, too, share in this mixed bag of irrelevancies. Their incisor teeth and eyefold are uniquely human, although their straight hair gives them less reason for misplaced racial pride than would the wavy or curly hair (but not the straight hair) of the Caucasoids or the woolly or kinky hair of Negroids. Heads that are proportionately long in comparison with their width are shared by Caucasoid populations in northern Europe (Nordics) and southern Europe (Mediterraneans, especially from Italy), Negroids in Ethiopia, and nearly all ancient hominid ancestors and non-human primates. Most modern men tend more closely to roundheaded-ness. Early hominids had thick cranial bones, but all modern skulls, re-gardless of race and despite slight and meaningless variations, are fragile in comparison.

In short, if one engages in fruitless comparisons along these lines, he must conclude that the only significant differences between hominids are those which determine the species, not those which distinguish the races. If one were to pursue these kinds of differences within each of the great racial categories, he would find that the differences between individual members of each are greater than the differences between the averages of the three categories. For these traits are neither dependent upon each other nor inherited together; they do not all evolve simultaneously nor at the same rates of speed. Each trait is the result of a gene or, in the traits discussed above, a complex cluster of genes, each of which is inherited as a unit distinct from all the others. The individual is a total organism, to be sure, but genetically he is a working unity constructed of many divisible entities. Their effects, while compatible, undergo changes as units, not as a totality. And these changes occur and are transmitted to the next genera-tion not in the population as a whole but only in those far smaller sub-groups which have experienced the genetic change and whose members breed together. A race after all is only an abstract, statistical generalization, the purpose of which is to report an observed fact that the people in one population biologically resemble each other more closely than they do others. There is nothing in such a statement to support the inference that some of those people or their populations as a whole are more advanced than or superior to others.

Finally, one must contrast the ridiculously minor differences upon which racial classifications are based with the impressively major similar-ities between all men: their stereoscopic vision; their dexterous hands; their magnificently arched feet which support completely upright posture; their comparatively huge brain which is capable of substituting symbols for experience and controlling the refined movements of the body parts, especially those which produce the sounds of human languages; and all the other intricate and distinctively human features shared by all mankind. It is clear that, on the level of race, all populations (though not all individual members of each population) are equal, and none is more equal than others.

Cultural and Psychological Differences Between Races

If mankind can be regarded as a unit in biological and evolutionary respects, can it also be regarded as a unit with reference to cultural and
psychological capacities for achievement and actual achievements? To
answer "yes" to both questions, at least without qualification, would certainly seem to fly in the face of common sense observation. The cultural
achievements of the world's populations are obviously dissimilar, and it is
beyond the scope of this paper to discuss the ways in which individual
cultures have come to be what they are. Whatever the processes of growth
and change, however, cultural and social anthropologists normally abstain
from comparative evaluations of cultures which place them in some kind
of ranked qualitative order. Anthropologists describe and compare cultures for the purpose of discovering possible relationships between various
sets of culture-determining variables, not for the purpose of designating
those which are superior or inferior, higher or lower, more civilized or
advanced than others. Such categories have the same disadvantages as
racial categories. They have no explanatory value; they fail to provide any
except the most general clues to the ways of life so labelled, fail to provide
any explanations of why a culture has become what it is, and fail to provide
any explanation for the tremendous differences between specific cultures
within each category or for the characteristics shared by cultures in
different categories.

One of the classical definitions of "culture," that by Clyde Kluckhohn
(1945:97), states that it consists of "historically created designs for living,
explicit and implicit, rational, irrational, and non-rational which exist at
any given time as potential guides for the behavior of men." Each
member of each human population enters the world equipped with his
own individualized set of distinctively human biological characteristics
and proceeds gradually to learn and possibly to modify somewhat the design historically adopted by the group into which he was born. Some individuals in each population are more richly endowed, more educable and
creative than others, but none can completely escape the confines of his
cultural heritage.

The designs for living devised and enjoyed by the many populations of
mankind differ greatly from each other, and non-anthropologists often
rank some as "more advanced" than others. The current fashion, for
example, is to classify countries as economically "developed" or "underdeveloped" or "developing." Theoretically there need be no objection to
using such terms, if the user clearly recognizes the selective and limited
nature of the criteria for his comparison and refrains from generalizing

about the total culture and its people. It can then validly be said that a particular design for living produces a higher gross national product, produces a higher per capita income, uses more energy from non-human sources, supports bigger armies with greater firepower, has more telephones and automobiles, publishes more books, builds miles of expressways, or yields lower infant mortality rates, higher life expectancies and larger population than another. Or it can be said that a design for living can produce a Shakespeare or a Beethoven or an Ian Fleming or the Beatles, and that other designs for living cannot produce those particular craftsmen and artists. Or it can be said that one design has produced a Confucius, another a Mohammed, another a Jesus, and no other design for living could produce these leaders. Many other criteria may be used to support the assertion that one culture is more "advanced" or "civilized" than another in some particular respect. But all the possible criteria are arbitrary and limited; none is absolutely valid or universally accepted, and none provides a basis for the sweeping generalization about the peerless achievements of an advanced culture and the inherent incapacities of the backward or primitive cultures.

Some of these criteria, or others like them, have come to be accepted—or are becoming accepted—in cultures other than those which have produced them, but their previous designs for living have not yet been sufficiently readjusted to make rapid "advances" probable. That many cultures of the "Third World" do accept them does not make the criteria any less arbitrary or any more universally valid. Many of the criteria, furthermore, are not even accepted by all members of the cultures which produce them, for in complex cultures, in which there are many different sub-groups and "all kinds of people," there are many who do not share equally in the "benefits" or even desire to do so. For these and other reasons, cultural achievements are viewed by anthropologists as objectively or structurally or functionally comparable but not as qualitatively comparable. Is an industrialized culture, whose people must "live with" the threat of self-destruction through nuclear energy, superior to a non-industrialized, quiet culture, whose people must "live with" the threat of famine or disease? No one can answer that question with other than a flat assertion. Certainly terms like "advanced" or "developed" must be used with utmost caution and with an attempt at specificity; they should never be used with reference to cultures as a whole. There simply are no universal criteria that can serve as a basis for making such general comparisons or evaluative judgments.

If populations do differ in their achievements, however, is it not likely that the reason is to be found in the incapacities of some to achieve anything much different from what they have? If by that question is meant that "some designs for living cannot achieve certain results," the answer is yes. This kind of social or cultural incapacity to achieve a particular result at any one moment of time can be readily understood. The chances of the contemporary American design—or any of its current variations—producing Genghis Khan, Gandhi, Queen Victoria, George Washington, or any known or unknown heroes of some past time and place must be practically nil. The chances of any of the many traditional African designs producing Albert Einstein, Henry Ford, Mary Baker Eddy, or Calvin Coolidge must also be practically nil. But if by that question is meant a genetic or racial incapacity to achieve something other than what they have, the answer is "no." A geneticist has summed up the conclusions of the modern scientific consensus in these words: "It is . . . a matter of elementary genetics that the capacities of individuals, populations, or races cannot be discovered until they are given an equality of opportunity to demonstrate these capacities. Wisely or otherwise, many people prefer self-government even to good government. To demonstrate 'equal' capacities for cultural achievement, all races need not reproduce copies of whatever civilization we happen to regard as the quintessence of enlightenment and discernment. Given an opportunity, people may arrange their lives in different ways. Without adopting the viewpoint of extreme cultural relativism, one may nevertheless hope that mankind may profit by this diversity more than it might gain by a monotonous sameness, even of the most 'advanced' kind." (Dobzhansky: 1961:317).

Designs for living are not inherited as are the biological potentialities of the individual and the group. The former are far more plastic than the latter, far more subject to factors and fluctuations in the social environment, the social heritage, the physical environment and the technology available for exploiting the environment. Populations acquire their cultures through creating and learning them rather than through the transmission of genes, and the limits of *Homo Sapiens'* capacities to innovate and to learn are unknown but undoubtedly great. The ingenuity displayed by the populations of mankind in adapting an unspecialized physical organism to the varied environments of land, sea and space by means of culture is a continually astonishing testimony to their capabilities.

Populations do not learn their genetically inherited physical characteristics; they are derived from the gene pool from which each individual's genes fortuitously have been drawn. Exploitation of the full potentialities is also limited and channelled by the physical environment. Populations may also modify their appearance and composition through their nutritional habits, lack of scientific medical knowledge, curling their hair, smoking cigarettes, lifting weights and other forms of social behavior, but the genetic limits of development at any one time are given. There are also genetic limits to learning, but these limits are remarkably expandable. That they normally expand in the directions prescribed by and foreshadowed in the prior cultural design for living does not preclude their expansion in quite different directions when new or altered cultural factors are introduced into the culture. A mid-twentieth-century A.D. Caucasoid may resemble a mid-twentieth-century B.C. Caucasoid, and his inheritable intellectual endowments may be no greater, but there is little resemblance in their designs for living. That comparison could be drawn for any of the races.

Most people seem to be acutely aware of the plasticity and expandability of intelligence; this is evident in their almost universal demand for superior educations for their children. Nonetheless, there remains a suspicion, sometimes amounting to a conviction, among many many people that members of races other than their own are inherently "less intelligent," less culturally expandable, and less educable. Several types of evidence have been advanced in support of these suspicions.[7] One consists of data from the comparison of cranial capacities. Comas (1961: 307) for example, reports the following series taken by K. Simmons:

Mean capacity of 1179 White male skulls	1517.49 cc.
Mean capacity of 661 Negro male skulls	1467.13 cc.
Difference between the series	50.36 cc.
Mean capacity of 182 White female skulls	1338.82 cc.
Mean capacity of 219 Negro female skulls	1310.94 cc.
Difference between the series	27.88 cc.

The differences of 3.3% between the male skulls and of 2.1% between the female skulls could hardly support the kinds of claims to superiority that are sometimes heard. Had cranial capacity any significance for intelligence, furthermore, both White and Negro males would be more intelligent than either White or Negro females. W. D. Hambly's (in Comas: 307-8) findings on male cranial capacities in various populations included the following examples among others: Europeans (Czechs), 1438 cc.; Europeans (Old English), 1456 cc.; Melanesians, 1463 cc.; Europeans (French), 1473 cc.; North American Indians, 1514 cc.; Central Eskimos, 1558 cc. Fortunately for Negro females, white females, and Czechs, though unfortunately for the Central Eskimos, these data simply mean that some populations have more space for "gray matter" than others; they do not mean that those populations are less or more intelligent than the others.

The evidence from studies of cerebral structure and complexity is less clear, and unfortunately does not yet permit generalizations about comparative intelligence. This assessment by Coon, Garn, and Birdsell (1950: 101; in Comas, 1961: 308) is widely accepted by anthropologists: "In these and other anatomical factors, one might look for differences between the brains of men of living races, but actually too little inter-racial anatomy has been done to warrant generalizations. . . . It may be apparent why differences between races in brain activity and ability cannot yet be determined and why the evolutionary position of the brain has not been studied in living people. That some individuals exceed others in ability is well known, but neurologists do not consider it likely that gross differences in the capacity for 'intelligence,' however defined, will appear. What they expect to see will be racial differences in specific functional areas, in metabolism, and in the degree of development of the association systems. This, the most important part of evolution, and the one in which the most significant racial differences are likely to appear, has not yet even been tackled." Here, then, is an area of knowledge which needs objective research; it is not an area of knowledge on which pronouncements of racial superiority or inferiority can be based.

One final area of research, that of psychological testing, also presents findings that are subject to different interpretations. A small minority of social scientists interpret intelligence and other psychological test scores conducted on various American "Negro populations" and American "white populations" (using social rather than genetic definitions) in the following manner: "The remarkable consistence in test results, whether they pertain to school or preschool children, to high school or college students, to drafts of World War I or World War II, to the gifted or the mentally deficient, to the delinquent or criminal; the fact that the colored-white differences are present not only in the rural South and urban South, but in the border and northern areas; the fact that relatively small average differences are found between the I.Q.'s of northern-born and southern-born Negro children in the northern cities; the evidence that the tested differences appear to be greater for abstract than for practical or concrete problems; the evidence that the differences obtained are not due primarily to a lack of language skills, the colored averaging no better on non-verbal tests than on verbal tests; the fact that differences are reported in all studies in which the cultural environment of the whites appeared to be no more complex, rich, or stimulating than the environment of the Negroes; the fact that in many comparisons (including those in which the colored appeared to best advantage) the Negro subjects have been either more representative of their racial group or more highly selected than have the comparable white subjects; all points to the presence of some native differences between Negroes and whites as determined by intelligence tests." (Shuey, 1958: 318).

The great majority of anthropologists, on the other hand, do not consider intelligence or temperamental characteristics as variables affecting racial classification. Nor have they yet engaged in the study of what appears to be methodologically a highly, if not impossibly, difficult problem, that is, the study of the evolutionary significance of possible population differences in cerebral structures and functions. Because of the policy-making and other social significance of these matters, however, many anthropologists have felt impelled to declare their opinions about the results of tests and interpretations by other social scientists. A statement of the considered view of a large majority was approved at the annual meeting of the American Anthropological Association (1961). It reads in part: ". . . there is no scientifically established evidence to justify the exclusion of any race from the rights guaranteed by the Constitution of the United States. The basic principles of equality of opportunity and equality before the law are compatible with all that is known about human biology. All races possess the abilities needed to participate fully in the democratic way of life and in modern technological civilization."

Although this is a policy statement rather than a scientific judgment on an issue of great significance to a particular society, there is a consensus in the scientific community that underlies it. This consensus may be summarized in this way: Scores on intelligence tests have consistently been higher for whites than for members of other "races." ("Races" in this context refers to socially rather than rigorously genetically defined groups; persons of mixed "white" and other racial ancestry are usually classified as non-white, Negro, American Indian, etc., rather than as white.) The differences between populations are not large, and the differences between them are smaller than the differences between the highest and lowest scores within each population. If scores overlap in this manner, explanations other than heredity must be of far greater significance. Tests also indicate that the differences within and between groups diminish when the groups are matched for socio-economic background and educational opportunity. Intelligence, therefore, appears to be highly modifiable and plastic rather than relatively rigid and narrowly limited by inheritable factors. In addition to their susceptibility to change with changes in socio-economic and educational environments, scores are also influenced by language facility, motivation of the members of the group, the rapport that exists between the tester and his subjects, and the speed of completion required of the subjects.

So complex is the problem of intelligence measurement when so-called racial groups are being compared, that anthropologists and many other social scientists forego using test scores for such purposes. Intelligence tests are useful for discriminating between more capable and less capable individuals when a specific practical goal is to be achieved. When, for example, previous testing has established that there is a positive correlation between test scores and probable success at some specified task, an intelligence test or some other test of temperament or "personality" may aid materially in the selection of the persons most suited for the task. Within an understood margin for error, tests can help to choose the more able people to fill some job, be admitted to college or to qualify for a particular kind of special training. But to use tests in more general or theoretical ways is clearly unjustified by present knowledge.

One of the consequences of these findings has been a realization that intelligence is not a unitary *thing.* American parents of children aspiring to college have become aware—sometimes painfully—of college entrance exams, a type of intelligence test in which basic scores are given for verbal and for mathematical abilities. These two scores may vary widely for any one individual, and girl's and boy's scores are frequently reversed in rank. Which score indicates "intelligence"? Is it the one or the other, or is it the average of the two, which, of course, is neither of the two? And are the boys or the girls more intelligent? Would an Australian Bushman, a Swiss cowherd or a Chinese peasant be "proved" less intelligent if they performed badly on them? The concept, "intelligence," in fact, has no clear-cut reference. It is one of those many concepts that can only be defined arbitrarily and operationally and for certain specific purposes in the mind of the tester. It has no tangible existence in the individual like the pituitary gland; it has no existence in a population like an Rh gene. And if that be the case, of what validity are measurements of a doubtful "basic" or "inherent" intelligence applied to people who come from different backgrounds within one culture or who come from far different cultures?

The tests themselves and the very notion of intelligence testing are the products of certain subgroups of certain "Western" populations and cultures and are not readily transferable to other populations and cultures. Thus the concepts of intelligence and of intelligence-testing—except under the most carefully defined and controlled conditions—have undergone searching criticism. Neither concept has proved useful in disentangling the network of inherited and environmental factors which operate to produce those most intelligent of living organisms, *Homo Sapiens,* the human race.

Nor are the grounds for distinguishing the "temperaments," national or group characters, tendencies toward criminality, musicality, athletic ability or other special aptitudes any more solid. Although it is a common sense and, to some extent, "scientific" observation that social groups differ in their values, in behavior patterns, in the personality traits they desire to have, and in their psychological designs for living, there are as yet no valid reasons for concluding that these differences are caused by a high frequency of distinctive genes in the population or by any other inherent biological systems. There seems to be no more reason to search for racial explanations of such group differences than there is to search for genetic explanations of differences in musical tastes between adolescent and adult generations or of differences in attitudes toward labor organizations between employers and employees.

Race now appears irrelevant as a factor in intelligence, temperament or other so-called psychological qualities of groups. Certainly the proved capacity of all normal, and even of many abnormal or subnormal, people to learn new skills and tastes as they are nurtured and mature suggests strongly that the crucial factors to be analyzed are environmental. It is not necessary to rule out the possibility, even the likelihood, of genetically determined differences between populations. But until such time as they are discovered and verified, the more parsimonious and comprehensive theory, compatible with the available data, is that the populations of mankind are insignificantly different in their capacities to think, feel and act.

In his extensive review of psychological research conducted in Africa on Negroid and Caucasoid subjects, and in many instances compared with research on Caucasoid subjects in Europe, Leonard Doob (1965: 375-6) writes: "From a political standpoint the most impertinent variant of the basic (psychological) question is: are Africans genetically different from Europeans? Of course they are with respect to certain physical attributes such as skin colour and type of hair. But are they born with bodies that cause them to behave differently from Europeans regardless of, or in conjunction with, cultural factors? The answer must be, as it has been for a generation or more in scientific circles, No. At the same time the possibility cannot be excluded for all eternity, and the precise way in which so-called culture functions to produce the obtained differences is by no means completely clear."

Societies and cultures and natural environments shape the expression of these psychological capacities into patterns that are not easily or often drastically changed by many members of a group after their childhood. But this built-in tendency toward conservatism does not mean that a population need wait for some fortuitous genetic mutation or some inflow of migrant genes for superior intelligence or personality to enable it to be or become whatever is possible for it within its environment.

The Ideology of Race and the Concept of Mankind

Despite the overwhelming consensus of scientists who have investigated and reached similar conclusions about the meaning of race and the utility or disutility of the concept, controversy about it periodically flourishes. It is inaugurated from time to time by a small minority of scientists and especially by amateur students of the phenomenon. A recent example of the latter genre is *Race and Reason, A Yankee View*, by Carleton Putnam (1961); an example of the former is the work by Audrey M. Shuey (1958). Both authors appear to be inheritors of lines of argument that had their inception in the 19th century about the time of and shortly before Darwin's evolutionary theory made its appearance. There have been many accedants to this heritage of speculation (see Comas, 1961: 303), and the journal *Current Anthropology* has devoted many thousands of words to the issues since 1961. Most scientists would react to the arguments with silent disdain were they not moved by consideration of the misguided political and other social actions that sometimes flow from ideological statements such as these.

Manning Nash (1962: 285-88) has made a distinction between the study of race and the "ideology of race" in his analysis of the issues. The former, he points out, "is the pursuit of knowledge about a biological phenomenon," the latter is "a system of ideas which interprets and defines the meaning of racial differences, real or imagined, in terms of some system of cultural values. The ideology of race is always normative: it ranks differences as better or worse, superior or inferior, desirable or undesirable, and as modifiable or unmodifiable. Like all ideologies, the ideology implies a call to action; it embodies a political and social program; it is a demand that something be done. The ideology of race competes in a political arena, and it is embraced or rejected by a polity, not a scientific community."

Because the study of race and the ideology of race are only indirectly related, arguments on the basis of scientific evidence or "facts" are fruitless. Ideologies persist because they serve psychological and social needs, and, therefore, "no amount of evidence (even were it scientifically impeccable) will destroy an ideology, or even, perhaps, modify it." Racial ideologies will always reappear when political or social circumstances make it necessary to justify an existing social order that is threatened or that some people would prefer to establish. In the history of the West, it was the expansion of Europe into the New World and later into Africa and Asia that provided the stimulus for racial ideologies. As Nash argues, these ideologies provide a moral rationale for systematic deprivation of certain socially designated ethnic or racial groups; they allow members of the dominant groups to reconcile their values with their activities; they discourage the subordinate groups from making claims on the society; they rally the believers to political action "in the interests of all mankind"; and they defend the existing division of labor as eternal. In these and other respects, all racial ideologies resemble each other regardless of their date and the circumstances in which they have been propounded. Their disappearance into "wherever it is that historical curiosa are stored" depends on the achievement of social conditions of fuller democracy and equality of opportunity.

Racial ideologies, as they appear in the Western world, are undoubtedly the product of Europocentric thinking. Europeans began to spread into the wider world in the 15th century on the wings of a technology that surpassed all others, and they gradually came to confuse their real technological superiority with other presumed superiorities in their designs for living. In the absence of verifiable data which might explain the differences between their dominant and the subordinate cultures, they seized upon the immediate and highly visible evidence of differences in physical characteristics. From that point and in a setting of conflict and conquest, it was but a simple step to project the explanation into a theory of inherent racial superiority and inferiority. In a way they were abetted in this respect and desire accorded their technology by many of the exotic peoples they encountered and subdued. Befogged by the aura of their own remarkable accomplishments—and they were indeed remarkable—they were capable of writing histories that were almost solely records of the impact of the dominant upon the subject peoples. Many of the latter, without written languages, were regarded as history-less, stagnant and underdeveloped in all respects from time immemorial. Knowing little or nothing about the events and processes of "time immemorial" did not prevent them from concluding that these "inferior breeds" were capable only of reacting to, futilely resisting, or childishly accepting the changes imposed on or donated to them by the "superior breeds."

Even such a far-seeing social philosopher as Voltaire, who could find no insurmountable barriers to the growth of the human mind expressing itself in religion, art, science, and philosophy, probably conceived of mankind's future in the categories of thought presented by his own or similarly "advanced cultures." And Kant, who could see no inherent biological difficulties standing in the way of the human race's adjustment to the world through a universal civil society and an international rule of law and order, might well have been surprised at the diversity within the human race, at the difficulties of reconciliation and adjustment, and at the remoteness of the possibility that the human race would ever achieve a common culture that copied his own. These and many shapers of European colonial policies did have a decent respect for the concept of mankind, but in a limited way consistent with their times. Like other normal human beings, most moved with difficulty outside the conceptual bounds of their own social heritage.

Although all observers who have lived in colonies know many colonizers for whom the mankind concept was a guiding principle and who regarded subject peoples as their peers in every respect, the furthest outreach of the majority may be summarized in the concept of "benevolent paternalism." The "native races" were not so much inherently inferior as deprived of opportunity, and essentially in need only of the kindly, patient, civilized trustee who could gradually and eventually nurture them up to the high level of their benefactors. Encumbered in part by an interpretation of evolution which Herbert Spencer and others had projected from Darwin's restricted biological universe into the wider world of human society and culture, Europeans came, consciously or unconsciously, to view their own civilization as that best fitted to survive in the struggle for survival. Had it not gained domination over all those dark and backward parts of the world into which it has expanded? Was it not clearly the ultimate end toward which evolution had been moving, or was it not, at the very least, in the vanguard of human progress? Deviations from Western civilization's designs for living, therefore, could only represent vestigial survivals of early stages of mankind's evolution, stages through which the advanced civilizations long since had passed. And the human carriers of the survivals could only be retarded, if not inherently inferior, specimens of earlier stages of human physical and cultural development.

Some of the events of the century since Darwin, however, have made old, comfortable, ego-strengthening concepts untenable and have made imperative the creation of newer ones—or perhaps the revival of older ones already implicit and explicit in pre-Darwinian thought. Among these events have been the social changes wrought in and by the subject, subordinate, "inferior" peoples. These tended to accept the superior Western technology without accepting the image of the superior Westerner. Now they are demonstrating their inherently human capacities to learn, to adapt, and to create in their changed environments. They are "emerging," as Westerners, plagued by their inherited self-image as "fully emerged," are wont to describe them. "They are adjusting to a changed environment" is perhaps a more objective way to state it. Whatever the phrase, new balances of economic, political and other social forces in the hitherto little known populations of mankind are asserting themselves in such a way as to require new evaluations and greater appreciation of *Homo Sapiens* in all his physical and cultural diversity. The development of the "underdeveloped" no longer permits "developed" men to cherish the errors that have lowered their capacity to deal effectively with these new forces. No longer can men mistakenly attribute social and cultural differences to racial causes on the basis of presumed or imagined evidence; no longer can they regard populations as limited in their possible cultural achievements by inherent physical or psychological traits.

One other significant post-Darwinian development, that to which this paper has primarily been directed, is the clarification of the concept of human evolution. It is consistent with this concept to view mankind as one. Despite the variations in its physical forms, all mankind shares in that unique combination of eyes, hands, feet, brains and other features which makes it a single, unique species. Because of them, even in their diversity, mankind is naturally adapted to survival and satisfaction in the wide gamut of environmental conditions the earth provides. More importantly, because of this unique combination of characteristics, mankind is capable of creating, transmitting and learning a tremendous variety of cultural adaptions that enable it to ameliorate, perhaps even to reverse, the normal processes of natural selection. Mankind can adapt its environments to fit the man.

Homo Sapiens is not outside the processes of evolution, but the time has passed when new species will emerge because of a particular specialized adaptation to a particular local or temporary environment. Because his unique combination of culture-creating characteristics has made him so mobile and ended his earlier isolation, all populations can share in adaptive genetic changes and beneficial cultural innovations that change their environments. Thus the species will evolve while remaining a single species. Furthermore, no populations of mankind have suffered any disadvantages in the inheritance of culture-creating characteristics. If some groups have achieved a lesser degree of control over their environments than others, it is due to their lack of opportunity, broadly conceived, not to their inherent lack of capability. In essence, any population's time may come, and the modern world is witnessing the arrival of that time for many of its lesser known, previously more socially isolated peoples.

Racial ideologies, which divide mankind into forever separate units, will not yield to scientific findings as long as people feel they perform functions that are not better performed by equalitarian ideologies. Nor do racial ideologies necessarily bow before moral assertions about the equality and unity of mankind when they are made by scientists supported by overwhelming evidence. The rational and the non-rational are interwoven in the fabric of cultures, and the non-rational is not easily transformed. Yet mankind is one species, and the human species, *Homo Sapiens*, is uniquely educable. In those scientific findings mankind may itself find some ground of hope for the achievement of greater social unity.

NOTES

1. Infrequently the structure of some gene may be permanently changed or a new gene may appear in a process called mutation. Exposure to certain kinds and intensities of radiation may accomplish such a change. But by and large the original statement stands.

2. Identical twins are a special case. They have identical sets of genes derived from a single-celled new organism which split it into two separate but genetically identical organisms after it had been conceived. Even such twins exhibit phenotypic and behavioral differences despite their great similarities.

3 The draft text was written by physical anthropologists and geneticists at Unesco House, Paris, in June 1951. The final text was approved in May 1952, at a meeting of the International Congress of Anthropological and Ethnological Sciences in Vienna, Austria. The author is indebted to Juan Comas (1961) for the republication of it from which this text is taken.

4. This text has also been published in the *American Journal of Physical Anthropology* 10:363-368; *L'Anthropologie* 56:301-304; *Archives Suisses d'anthropologie générale* 17:81-85; *Qu'est-ce qu'une race?* (Paris: UNESCO, 1952), pp. 83-86; *Le concept de race* (Paris: UNESCO, 1953), pp. 11-16; Juan Comas, *Manual of Physical Anthropology* (Springfield: Charles C. Thomas, 1960), pp. 719-723. It is published here in the expectation that it will reach a wider and different audience.

5. Infertile hybrid forms of animals have occurred in nature or have been artificially bred, but they cannot reproduce themselves and can never "found" a species or a distinctive population or race within a species.

7. See Comas 1961: 307 ff. for a more detailed discussion of the historical development of these ideas.

BIBLIOGRAPHY

American Anthropological Association. "Association Reaffirms its Position on Race," *Fellow Newsletter*, Vol. 2, No. 10 (1961), Washington, D.C.
Boyd, William C. *Genetics and the Races of Man*. Boston: Little, Brown and Co., 1950.

Comas, Juan. "Scientific Racism Again?" *Current Anthropology*, Vol. 2, No. 4(1961), pp. 303-314.

Coon, Carleton S., Stanley M. Garn and Joseph B. Birdsell. *Races: A Study of the Problems of Race Formation in Man.* Springfield, Ill.: C. C. Thomas, 1950.

———. *The Origin of Races.* New York: Alfred A. Knopf, 1962.

Dobzhansky, Theodosius. "Comments," *Current Anthropology*, Vol. 2, No. 4 (1961), p. 315.

———. "Possibility that *Homo Sapiens* Evolved Independently 5 Times is Vanishingly Small," *Current Anthropology*, Vol. 4, No. 4 (1963), pp. 360, 364-366.

Doob, Leonard. "Psychology" in Lystad, Robert A., ed., *The African World: A Survey of Social Research.* New York: Frederick A. Praeger, Inc., 1965.

Labarre, Weston. *The Human Animal.* Chicago: University of Chicago Press, 1954.

Lasker, Gabriel W. *The Evolution of Man.* New York: Holt, Rinehart and Winston, 1961.

Livingstone, Frank B. "Anthropological Implications of the Sickle Cell Gene Distribution in West Africa," *American Anthropologist*, Vol. 60, No. 3 (1958), 533-562.

———. "On the Non-existence of Human Races," *Current Anthropology*, Vol. 3, No. 3 (1962), pp. 279-280.

Montagu, Ashley. *Man's Most Dangerous Myth: The Fallacy of Race.* New York: Columbia University Press, 1942.

———. "What is Remarkable about Varieties of Man is Likenesses, not Differences," *Current Anthropology*, Vol. 4, No. 4 (1963), pp. 361-362.

Nash, Manning. "The Ideology of Race" *Current Anthropology*, Vol. 3, No.3 (1962), pp. 285-288.

Newman, Marshall T. "Geographic and Microgeographic Races" *Current Anthropology*, Vol. 4, No. 2 (1964), 189-205.

Putnam, Carleton. *Race and Reason, a Yankee View.* Washington, D.C.: 1961.

Shuey, Audrey M. *The Testing of Negro Intelligence.* Lynchburg, Va.: J. P. Bell Co., 1958.

Religion, Ideology, and the Idea of Mankind in Contemporary History

W. WARREN WAGAR

Department of History
State University of New York
at Binghamton

FROM THE MIDDLE OF THE EIGHTEENTH CENTURY DOWN TO THE middle of the twentieth, from the first tentative heresies of Voltaire and Rousseau to the suicide of Adolf Hitler in his *Führerbunker* in the ruins of Berlin, the central project of the Western spirit was to find a world-encompassing faith to replace traditional Judaism and Christianity. One ersatz-religion followed another, giving order and direction to Western energies. Under their guidance the Western Powers became the masters of the world. Many good Christians seized the opportunities offered by Western imperialist expansion to establish their faith on alien ground, even while it was declining at home. But the spiritual initiative remained clearly with the ersatz-religions: Enlightenment humanism, the cults of the French Revolution, Positivism, nationalism, the *Volk*-ideologies of central Europe, liberal democracy, socialism, Fascism, Nazism, and Leninism. The rise of these substitute faiths, their struggles with one another and with the surviving spokesmen of Jewish and Christian orthodoxy, gives shape to the intellectual history of the era from 1750 to 1945.

The great fact in the spiritual life of Western man in the years just after the second World War was the apparent suspension of this search for new systems of secular faith. He suddenly found himself living in a post-ideological, anti-utopian, demythologized world in which the will to believe had withered and failed. The emergent nations of Africa and

Asia also experienced great difficulty in creating and sustaining ideological movements, much as they needed doctrines that could unify their peoples and persuade them to make substantial personal sacrifices for the sake of progress. Very recent events suggest that perhaps the post-war ice age of the spirit has already drawn to a close in the Western countries, although we lack the perspective to render a final judgment. In any case, it will be our concern in this chapter to provide a brief overview of the spiritual situation of the world since 1945, and then to consider some of the possibilities open to mankind in the foreseeable future.

We need first some working definitions. These should be as broad as possible. Our theme is man as a spiritual being, seeking to determine what is finally true and good. No form of this quest should be excluded. It may be best to follow Paul Tillich in his definition of religion as "the state of being grasped by an ultimate concern, a concern which qualifies all other concerns as preliminary and which itself contains the answer to the question of the meaning of our life."[1] In true religion the ultimate reality is a transcendental being, power, or principle. But, as we have seen, the same search for final meaning can be pursued in much the same way by secular religions, or ideologies, for which Tillich prefers the term "quasi-religions." The nation, or a given social order, or a type of humanity, is divinized. It becomes the ultimate goal of human aspiration, even when, as sometimes happens, allegiance is still nominally offered to a traditional religious faith. In the present chapter, then, the term "religion" will be used to refer to a system of ultimate meaningfulness grounded in a supernatural or transcendental reality; and the term "ideology" will be used to refer to a system of ultimate meaningfulness grounded in human and this-worldly reality.[2]

What distinguished the period from 1945 down to at least 1965 was the precipitous decline not only of authentic religious faith and not only of the ideologies, but of both together. Decline, to be sure, is not extinction. Reports of the "end" of religion, and the "end" of ideology, were hyperbolic. But all signs pointed to a sharp break with the past. The most telling of these signs was the attitude of the intellectual and artistic leaders of the generation born between 1900 and 1925. They are not, by and large, great theologians, prophets, messiahs, or systematic and programmatic thinkers. They have excelled in analysis, criticism, debunking, and despair. Their art, literature, and theater have expressed all too clearly the alienation of a whole generation from its society and its sense of the meaninglessness of the macrocosm.

Some scholars would insist that, on the contrary, a revival has taken place in the Judeo-Christian tradition. Can we speak of a "decline of faith" in the century of Schweitzer, Barth, Berdyaev, Buber, Tillich, Maritain, Niebuhr, and Bonhoeffer? The answer can only be: yes. The sense of world malaise at the end of the nineteenth century and the horrors of the first World War did in fact call forth a burst of brilliant apologetic thought in the 1920's and 1930's. A reawakening of interest in religion on the part of the sceptical layman could also be observed. As F. L. Baumer pointed out in *Religion and the Rise of Scepticism*, modern man's growing disenchantment with himself forced him to reconsider his assessment of religion. Worry replaced relief; we were no longer triumphant in our unbelief. But, Baumer continued, for many of these same thinkers, "whenever they take it into their heads to 'return,' the shades of all the great sceptics, Pierre Bayle and Voltaire, Ernest Renan and Sigmund Freud and the rest, rise up around them and persuade them, with considerable success, that they cannot go back."[3] Nor did that first impressive generation of apologists inspire a second. After 1945 Protestant theology found itself in the throes of active disintegration, under the impact of existentialism, demythologization, and dekerygmatization, which once again demonstrated its perhaps fatal openness to secular influences.[4] Catholic thought remained more or less intact, but far less vital than during the inter-war years. It is impossible to escape Gerhard Szczesny's conclusion that although aggressive criticism of Christian dogma became almost taboo (outside theological circles!), "the real content of the Christian doctrine of salvation, for a dominant type of modern man, has become completely unacceptable, indeed, a matter of indifference."[5] The "revival of faith" was rather a revival of the social currency of faith, in the face of man's awareness of the failure of ideology; or, at most, a revival of curiosity about the possible uses of religion.

More obvious and more universally agreed upon was the collapse of ideological commitment in the years immediately following World War Two. "For the radical intelligentzia," wrote Daniel Bell, "the old ideologies have lost their 'truth' and their power to persuade." It was "the end of ideology in the West." Judith N. Shklar noted the disappearance of "the urge to construct grand designs for the political future of mankind" and found "the grand tradition of political theory that began with Plato . . . in abeyance." Ours was the age "after Utopia" and reasoned scepticism had become "the sanest attitude for the present." Thomas Molnar addressed himself to the theme of "the decline of the intellectual," who had made himself and his ideologies superfluous, and was being replaced by social engineers.[6]

The briefest glance at the political literature of the post-war period bears out these observations. The number of significant additions to traditional democratic, liberal, nationalist, socialist, Fascist, and communist theory, especially by younger writers, was negligible. For a brief time it appeared that the movement for a federal world government might provide a new focus for ideological passion, but this soon became a casualty of the Cold War.[7] European federalism, Gaullism, American radical conservativism, the civil rights movement, and the programs of the "Fair Deal" and "The New Frontier" failed to generate the sort of quasi-religious faith among intellectuals which our definition of ideology specifies. The United Nations fathered at most a pseudo-ideology, beset with every kind of imaginable ambiguity. The "Isms," wrote John Lukacs in a barely forgivable pun, had become "Wasms."[8]

The reasons for this change in the mental climate cannot be summed up in a phrase or two. Some of them lie deep in the Western spirit, others have little to do with intellectual life as such. Modern analytical philosophy, which strongly emphasizes the arbitrary and non-cognitive character of moral, political, and religious value-propositions, clearly had some effect. The loathing of the Nazis for the Viennese logical positivists (and of Lenin for "empirio-criticism") was well founded. Individual philosophers working in the analytical tradition have been able to take personal stands on public or moral issues, but its long-term influence has been to undermine all forms of unconditional faith. The same sort of impact may be attributed to some varieties of existential philosophy. The existentialist doctrine of the priority of the finite self in the experienced world precludes unconditional attachment to any cause that would rob individual life of its authenticity. Even J.-P. Sartre's ingenious expropriation of Marxism remains fundamentally an existentialist project, unacceptable to party-line communists. The work of Albert Camus, especially influential in the 1950's among young people both in Europe and America, provided perhaps the best illustration of how certain elements of existentialism can be employed to repudiate the collectivistic ersatz-religions.[9]

Another broad movement in thought which contributed to the decline of ideology and religious faith is the relativistic spirit of modern humanistic scholarship. Faiths, whether religious or quasi-religious, need the support of intellectuals, and the majority of twentieth-century intellectuals are academicians, deeply committed to their various specialisms, so deeply that they find it difficult to detach themselves from their point of view as scholars and to become involved in the "real" world. For scholars in the humanities and the social and behavioral sciences, this is not simply a matter of imprisonment in academic ivory towers. Modern humanistic scholarship insists on thoroughness and objectivity. It becomes steadily more thorough and objective. Academicians grow ever more skillful in detecting and extirpating preconceived notions, parochial attitudes, hidden value judgments, and all the rest. The spirit of the exact sciences has been applied with new zest and subtlety to the study of man himself. The result is historical, political, sociological, anthropological, psychological, and, of course, ethical and aesthetic relativism. Nothing is any "better" than anything else: each human phenomenon has its time, its place, its explanation, including the various ideologies and religions themselves. The relativistic spirit dominates the lecture hall, the seminar, and the textbook. Anyone profoundly enough gripped by it cannot commit himself to a system of ultimate meaningfulness of any kind whatsoever.

But the intellectual origins of the decline of faith in the West do not fully explain the change in the climate of opinion between 1945 and the 1960's. One could go on at some length, citing the impact of romantic pessimism, aesthetic revolts from symbolism and Dada to the present day, Freudian anthropology, and much more. But why were so many years required for these intellectual and artistic movements to take full effect? Why the almost sudden change after 1945? To get to the heart of the matter, one must take into account forces and experiences outside the purview of the history of ideas. These forces and experiences, in fact, help to explain the vogue of such movements in thought as historicism, existentialism, and analytical philosophy. It is improbable that any of these movements would have enjoyed the same influence and cachet under different historical circumstances. Ideas and events are at all times interdependent.

The most obvious reason for the exhaustion of ideology in the post-war era was the memory of the historical performance of those regimes in which ideologies had wielded the most pervasive influence. Fascism and Nazism were the official ideologies of totalitarian states repugnant to most men of good will everywhere; these same states led Europe into the debacle of the second World War; their leaders were responsible for unspeakable atrocities against humanity during that war. The ideologies emerged completely discredited in 1945, and the events of the war convinced many sensitive thinking people that ideologies in and of themselves were evil. The same lesson could be learned from an objective scrutiny of the behavior of Soviet Russia. The crimes of the era of the first Five Year Plans, the purges of the late 1930's, the Nazi-Soviet pact of 1939, and the reign of terror and repression reinstated by Stalin in his declining years, blackened the image of communism throughout the world. Even though democratic socialists disowned Stalin and rejected his interpretation of Marxism, the example of socialism in action in the

U.S.S.R. inevitably hurt the cause of socialism elsewhere. It also became impossible to resist comparing the wars of the period 1936 to 1945, in which the chief antagonists were Nazi Germany and Stalinist Russia, with the wars of the period from 1546 to 1648, which had been at least in part wars of religion. As the wars of religion had helped promote a cooling-off of religious fanaticism, so the twentieth-century wars of ideology reduced ideological fervor.

Still more important in the final analysis has been the inexorable drift in all the major Western countries away from politically to technocratically directed societies. Although we are still far from the Utopian visions of Saint-Simon and H. G. Wells, there is no question that in the conduct of public affairs, management by experts in human welfare has tended to replace government by politicians.[10] The welfare state, above all in Western Europe, has become a thoroughly pragmatic sort of polity, without a distinctive ideology, drawing indiscriminately on liberal, democratic, socialist, Christian, nationalist, and internationalist doctrine for whatever guidance it may need. It survives because it works: it defuses class warfare, promotes general prosperity, and abolishes social insecurity. The new dominant type in the Western world is the middle-class organization man, educated, efficient, devoid of political or religious passion, indistinguishable by and large from all his fellows, doing a specialized job well and keeping quiet.

Marx would have been astounded. He predicted that the competitive process of capitalism would end by plunging nearly all the members of the bourgeoisie into the ranks of the proletariat. Instead, by a mindless metamorphosis, the bourgeoisie has benignly absorbed the greater part of the proletariat into its own ranks. Traditional socialism, in particular, has been all but fatally shaken by the new turn of events.[11] The credit for much of the success of the welfare state belongs to trade unionism and socialist political action, but in achieving at least some of their goals, socialists have helped to diminish the appeal to the working man of most of the rest. If one can have meat and potatoes every day without expropriation of the "means of production," why expropriate?

All the most essential tendencies in modern social and economic life militate against the old ideologies. The logic of technology insists on large organizations of highly integrated human units performing the tasks set for them by the machines which serve them. Once the over-all objective of universal well-being is agreed upon, there are no really major political decisions to be taken, apart from foreign affairs. Also, the welfare state through its programs of mass education and redistribution of wealth ensures that as machines replace unskilled workmen, these same workmen—or at any rate their children—can migrate from blue-collar to white-collar occupations, thus actually reducing the size of the old working-class population and further restricting the opportunities for socialist agitation. At the same time, liberal and democratic values suffer as the importance of individual initiative and political action dwindles. Even nationalism—or at least old-fashioned Great Power chauvinism—loses its glamor. The logic of technology and the requirements of welfare engineering rule out intensive national rivalry, encourage free trade, and foster regional economic integration.

Of course for the time being one significant segment of the population has been excluded from the new technocratic synthesis. The literary and artistic avant-garde, which reflects the aspirations and discontents of our culture, which has in its charge the soul of the age, as it does in every age, cannot accept the new order. Avant-gardes rarely do accept civilization just as they find it. They are perfectionists who can never be satisfied with things as they are. But in this instance, the aesthetic avant-garde has been exceptionally unhelpful in picturing credible alternatives to the established order, no doubt because until the last few years, at least, there has been so little constructive visionary thinking on the part of intellectuals. The voices of Edward Albee, Jack Kerouac, William Burroughs, John Osborne, Samuel Beckett, Alain Robbe-Grillet, Jean Genet, Eugène Ionesco, Günter Grass, and Abram Tertz speak a language wholly different from that of Rousseau and Diderot, or Schiller and Goethe, or Ibsen and Zola, or Mann and Malraux. It is the language of escape, alienation, and rootlessness—prefigured, to be sure, by some of the most significant trends in thought, literature, and art in the earlier part of the century, but distilled and purified now, and reduced as it were to an ultimate numbness. All that remains is shapeless indignation, or hollow laughter; the heroin nightmare, or the rattle of the dwarf's tin drum.

In Asia and Africa, everything seemed very different in the early post-war years. Although the traditional religions had failed even more spectacularly than Judaism and Christianity to meet contemporary needs, ideologies flourished as never before. National social, economic, and political integration had not been achieved, as in the West; prosperity and the welfare state were still out of reach. The result was a great search for new faiths that would provide blueprints for national reconstruction. Leninism, as adapted to Eastern needs by Mao Tse-tung, exhibited energies in Asia and Africa which were almost wholly absent in post-war European communism. But many new ideologies also arose, systems of values borrowed in part from Afro-Asian tradition and in part from the West, of which the prototype was Sun Yat-sen's doctrine of the "Three People's

Principles," expounded in a series of lectures in Canton in 1924. In the words of Dr. Sun's biographer, Mrs. Lyon Sharman, "Sun Yat-sen was nothing if not eclectic; he was nobody's exclusive disciple; he picked over foreign ideas, chose what appealed to him and conglomerated what he had selected."[12] His program is usually rendered by the formula "democracy, nationalism, socialism," but in each instance he gave the basically Western idea a Chinese inflection. Democracy, for example, became virtually synonymous with the transfer of sovereign power from emperor to republic, with no provision for direct government by the people. The governing power, in theory and practice, remained in the hands of the superior man, the man of *neng*, or ability. The Kuomintang was to serve somewhat the same function during the period of national "tutelage" as Lenin's Bolshevik party during the period of the dictatorship of the proletariat.[13]

The major ideologies promulgated by the new national leaders of Asia and Africa followed Dr. Sun's example. There was the same preference for what President Nyerere of Tanzania calls "one-party democracy," the same emphasis on independence from Western rule and on national integration, the same devotion to national economic planning and socialism, in principle if nothing more. The needs were everywhere the same, and so was the ideological response. "Arab socialism," as preached by Nasser and Ben Bella; "Nasakom" (nationalism, religion, socialism), the program of Sukarno in Indonesia; and Nkrumah's "consciencism" in Ghana, all belong to the same world of thought. Nkrumah was perhaps the most articulate of the new post-war ideologues, but everything he wrote had its parallels in the pronouncements of the others. Philosophy, he contended, must be intimately allied with action in Africa. Africans could not afford the European luxury of a detached, disengaged philosophy. The people of Africa needed an ideology that combined the best insights of the West with the deepest felt aspirations of Africa herself. Such an ideology would have to express the "African conscience"; it would be an "African ideology." The two fundamental strands of African political tradition that had to be preserved in such an ideology, he continued, were its ancestral egalitarianism and its communalism. Blended with some of the techniques and broader ideas of Western socialism, these elements in the native tradition could produce a genuine African socialism, which alone could meet the needs of the African people today. Nkrumah also favored a union of all the African states, as Nasser has advocated a single Arab republic, and Sukarno dreamed of uniting Malaysia, Indonesia, and the Philippines.[14]

Even where an officially defined ideology did not emerge, the same sort of values have been widely shared by the ruling classes and the intellectuals. Guided democracy by parties of national unity, respect for religious and cultural tradition, national economic planning, some socialist expropriation, fanatical hostility to Western imperialism in all its forms, and projects for regional integration usually on a broad cultural rather than geographical basis have stood out as prominent ingredients of the national political consensus everywhere in non-communist Asia and Africa. Where liberalism and democracy in the Western sense flourish at all, as in India, it is clearly due to the continuing strong influence of Western European and American middle-class culture. Whether that influence can persist in the years ahead remains unclear.

In only one major Afro-Asian country, Japan, has there been a successful transition to modern Western prosperity and freedom. But the psychocultural problems of post-war Japan resemble more the situation elsewhere in Asia than in Europe and North America. If the body has passed over into a developed society, the soul has not. As a result of this spiritual lag, the thirst for faith remains urgent. Some Japanese have learned to live in a vacuum, like Westerners, but for others, especially the young, militant socialism and pacifism are the only answer. A still larger number of Japanese have found solace in the sects and cults of personal salvation which have grown out of modern Shintoism and Buddhism.[15] Their resort to religion, rather than to ideologies, can be explained partly by the failure of the West to provide any sort of ideology to accompany its modern technocratic social order. Japan has the technocratic social order, but those who—unlike the militant socialists—accept it, must look to religion to satisfy their need for faith.

It should be noticed, however, that despite the psychological differences that obviously exist between East and West, the kind of social and political order to which the Afro-Asian countries still aspire is not markedly different from the order already in being in the West. In some respects, and in some countries more than in others, it may resemble the Western European or American welfare state; in other respects, and in some countries more than in others, it may resemble the Soviet or East European socialist state. Local tradition will have its undeniable effect, but the end product is not likely to differ radically. The new ideologies, perhaps not even excluding Maoism, have put their greatest stress on the urgency of directed growth toward economic maturity. As Daniel Bell points out, the new Afro-Asian ideologies were fashioned by political leaders, rather than by intellectuals, in the cause of economic development and national power.[16] We might almost be justified in speaking of them as ersatz-ideologies. The politicians who concocted them may have seen them neither as systems of ultimate meaningfulness nor as Utopian visions, but simply as instruments by which to reach pragmatic ends.

At any rate, since 1965 most of the Afro-Asian politician-ideologues have been replaced by military leaders who pursue similar aims, but who ignore or repudiate the ideological systems of their predecessors: witness the fall of Ben Bella in Algeria, Nkrumah in Ghana, and Sukarno in Indonesia, not to mention the earlier and in some respects comparable depositions of Lumumba in the Congo and U Nu in Burma. It is also clear that the power struggle which erupted openly in China in 1967 represented a life-and-death conflict between the ideologues, led by Chairman Mao, and a rising generation of technocrats who had little use for set doctrines. At the present writing, Maoism has forcibly re-established its hold on public life in China, but the "cultural revolution" of the Maoist Red Guards would not have been necessary if revisionist ideas had not made deep inroads in party and government thinking in the mid-1960's.

As the ideologies begin to founder in Africa and Asia, a new wave of ideological activity appears to be breaking over Europe and the Americas. The most obvious change in the Western mental climate since the early 1960's has been a partial revival of hope, a renewal one might almost say of the Utopian imagination. Judith N. Shklar could write in 1957 that "Utopianism is dead, and without it no radical philosophy can exist."[17] But today, although the state of the world hardly seems less alarming than it did in 1960 or 1950, despair has once again become unfashionable among the younger and more radical minds. The existentialists, even Camus, have lost much of their "relevance," the neo-orthodox theology of original sin and the "wholly otherness" of God has become an embarrassment to religious thinkers, Teilhard de Chardin has replaced Spengler, and even Freud is neglected in favor of such optimistic "neo-Freudian" writers as Erich Fromm and Herbert Marcuse.

In part the new hopefulness of the past few years must be seen as a reaction to decades of unrelieved doom-mongering on the part of the men who achieved prominence during the era of the world wars. In modern history, no mood or trend has endured much longer than twenty or thirty years. As new men come along, they automatically seek their place in the sun by repudiating the values or interests of the preceding generation. In part, optimism has also been generated by the new political heroes and martyrs of the 1960's, from John and Robert Kennedy to Martin Luther King, Fidel Castro, Che Guevara, and Alexander Dubček.

Each owed his reputation for heroism to his opportunity to play the part of liberator in a situation where, for many years past, dramatic change for the better had seemed hopeless.

Whatever its historical bases, the mood of the later 1960's has been in general much brighter than anyone would have predicted a decade before. A variety of so-called "secular" theologies have come forward, theologies of social and political engagement, of hope, of radical dissent, which hark back in many ways to the "social gospel" of the turn of the century.[18] More spectacular have been the new ideologies: black nationalism in the United States, the "New Left" throughout Western Europe and America, *Fidelismo* in Latin America, neo-Marxist humanism in Eastern Europe, and universal revivals of feminism and sexual libertarianism.[19]

It is too early to say whether any of these movements will have a lasting effect or develop a considerable literature and tradition. To date one of their most striking characteristics is a reluctance to dogmatize or to specify a detailed program, which reflects, it would seem, the persistence to some degree of the suspicion of ideology which permeated the first post-war generation. They are ideologies which hesitate to call themselves ideologies or to limit their freedom of movement by becoming too doctrinaire. The tendency is to focus on particular grievances rather than to issue wide-ranging analyses and prescriptions for the future. Nonetheless, it is noteworthy that in practice the adherents of each new creed as it comes forward fall into the historic pattern of using identical language, developing identical rituals of protest, wearing the same clothes and reading the same short list of approved books.

It is time now to turn from analysis to prophecy, and examine the spiritual outlook for man, Eastern and Western alike, in the next century. Barring catastrophe, the material prospect is clear. We must look forward to highly organized societies that will probably evolve in the direction of a unified world civilization, and will guarantee to their citizens a high standard of comfort and security. It will be a world of science and technique, of large-scale industry and government planning, which will demand long years of education, a high degree of social cooperativeness, and much patience and discipline. If we set aside, for the moment, the chance of a third and final world war, its most serious problems will be of two orders: the proximate problem of how to secure human freedom in a society that supplies leisure and welfare but also imposes a vast apparatus of visible and invisible controls over thought and behavior; and the ultimate problem of how to provide an atmosphere in which the spiritual needs of mankind, if such needs still exist, can be definitively satisfied.

Of the first order of problems, it is not our business in this chapter to speak. But we cannot overlook the danger that the coming world society may suffer a kind of spiritual asphyxiation, from lack of freedom, long before it can come to terms with the problem of faith. Without freedom, one may ask whether the question of faith can even be raised. The deep concern of such thinkers as Erich Kahler, C. S. Lewis, Jacques Ellul, and Lewis Mumford that modern man is threatened with radical depersonalization must not be taken lightly.[20] It is imperative to consider with the utmost seriousness how freedom can be safeguarded in a world technocratic order.

But if we may assume for the purposes of argument that the challenge to freedom will be defeated, the way is then cleared for a discussion of how post-modern man will cope with the timeless human need for systems of ultimate meaningfulness.

I think we may expect an acceleration of the warming trend in the life of the spirit that began in the 1960's. But this prophecy involves certain assumptions. Is the need for systems of ultimate meaningfulness, in fact, "timeless"? Is it a perennial need of human nature, or only the form of human spirituality in one passing phase of world history? The simplest solution to the problem of spiritual life in the coming world order would be to suppose that man will outgrow the need for faith altogether. Even if individual men are free to believe what they will, they might choose to believe in nothing. One conjures up the pictures of an endless series of generations waiting for Godot, Nietzschean madmen proclaiming the death of God in the marketplace, Huxleyan agnostics eager to cross swords with ignorant bishops. It need not be so theatrical as all that. Many intelligent men have lived normal lives in our century without the benefit of faith. It involves them in no psychoses, no fear and trembling, no existential anguish. These are perhaps the same kind of people who, in past ages of faith, avowed their allegiance to the ruling orthodoxy—Nazi, Bolshevik, Lutheran, Roman Catholic, Muslim, Homeric, Confucian, or whatever—and in their hearts felt nothing. It would be a mistake to underestimate their numbers.

On the other hand, Tillich is probably right when he protests that "the end of the religious age . . . is an impossible concept. The religious principle cannot come to an end." Whether men choose to adhere to a religion or to an ideology, "the question of the ultimate meaning of life cannot be silenced as long as men are men."[21] Let us add, as long as some men continue to be born who have religious needs which demand satisfaction. Such men have always been with us, and there is no reason to imagine that they will disappear completely in the future. The openly faith-professing man may find himself in a minority in the twenty-first century, but from his point of view at least, he will be the salt of that new earth. If he cannot find a faith that satisfies him, he may be reduced to the role of Kafka's "K.," eternally scheming to make contact with the inscrutable masters of the Castle. But he will go on searching.

At the same time, ideological or religious faith may never again, for most believers, take on that fanatical, dogmatic, self-righteous, and compulsive quality which faith has too often assumed in the past. In the cause of world peace and universal human brotherhood, we may at least devoutly hope that the shattering political events and the intellectual revolutions of our time have imposed certain lasting limitations on the claims to absolute truth of all systems of faith. They will allow themselves, let us suppose, to go only so far. Beyond that, they would risk losing their credibility, and collapse.

One other limitation seems imperative, in a free and peaceful world order. A world resolved not to tear itself apart in further fratricidal wars cannot tolerate faiths that represent the interests of segments of humanity over against humanity itself. Although global conquest by some sort of Hitler *redivivus* cannot be absolutely ruled out, political and military power is now too widely dispersed to give exploits of this kind much hope of success. Hence, the future would seem to belong to faiths that speak for mankind. The actual appeal of such new faiths might fall far short of universality, but they would not attempt to shackle humanity to the service of a particular nation, race, or group. In a world growing in spite of itself toward political, economic, and societal unity, the most relevant faiths will be universalist faiths, pledging fidelity to mankind as a whole.

Of course ideas of mankind differ. There already exists a great constellation of organized ideologies and religions that presume to speak for mankind.[22] Unpromising though their prospects may seem to be in the 1970's, one or more of these faiths may be revitalized and win the world for itself in the next century. The Roman Catholic Church, for example, still openly thinks in terms of such a triumph. Its capacity for resurgence after periods of decline is a fact of history; its faith is universal; and some of its most outstanding thinkers in this century have prophesied a Catholic world civilization. We have Jacques Maritain's project for a "New Christendom," a liberal, democratic, pluralistic society tolerant of all faiths. But the natural order, writes Maritain, cannot maintain itself without divine help, because of man's fallen state. In particular, the Church is charged with responsibility for morals and education, and since these in turn preserve and perfect the natural order, the state will be obliged to "cooperate" with the Church. Legislation would endeavor to direct all men toward the truly virtuous life. The state would give to Christian teaching its "just place" in educational affairs, and the existence of God would be publicly acknowledged. The state would even solicit the prayers of the Church. Other religious bodies, in and out of the Christian confession, would also be asked to do their part. But it is obvious that Maritain has assigned to the Roman Catholic Church a very special place in his New Christendom. Ultimately, he hopes, the Church will receive all humanity back into her bosom, since she alone possesses the true faith. Although this must happen by the free choice of men, and not by coercion, Christian influence over morals and education would no doubt, in practice, dangerously compromise the freedom of conscience which Maritain appears so eager to preserve.[23]

Similar hopes for a Christian world order may be studied in the work of such Catholic writers in Britain as Father Martin D'Arcy and Christopher Dawson. Both agree that the providential mission of the Church and of Christian civilization is to unify mankind. We cannot understand the Church "if we regard her as subject to the limitations of human culture. For she is essentially a supernatural organism which transcends human cultures and transforms them to her own ends. As Newman insisted, the Church is not a creed or a philosophy but an imperial power."[24] Protestants may still be found who share the same hopefulness about the "imperial" role of Christian faith, though not of any one Christian church, in the coming world order. Others prefer to make no prophecy of Christian world conquest or even of a world culture, but insist on the uniqueness and superiority of Christianity. In the "coming dialogue" of the world religions, writes Hendrik Kraemer, the Christian church must reassert its exclusiveness and remain "resolutely the Church of Jesus Christ."[25]

The West is not alone in providing imperial faiths. Islam regards itself as a one-world religion, the one true faith, given by God to all men, and proclaimed for all men by Mohammed in the Koran. Even Buddhism has furnished a contender for world conquest. From the Nichiren Shoshu sect of Buddhism in Japan has come the Soka Gakkai, or Value Creation Society, originally founded in 1937 by two schoolteachers, re-established in 1946, and now one of the most rapidly growing religious movements in the world, with more than fifteen million converts. The values propagated by the Soka Gakkai seem remarkably materialistic, in a faith derived from Buddhism: personal prosperity, good health, happiness, and beauty. The Society preaches a Buddhism of triumph in this world, militant, optimistic, and contemptuous of all other religions. Like Nichiren himself, the thirteenth-century monk whose teachings the Society claims to

follow and fulfill, the leaders of the new movement foresee a special destiny for Japan. From Japan the light of the one true faith will illuminate
the whole world. Soka Gakkai missions have already made some progress
in Southeast Asia, and centers exist in Latin America, the United States,
and Europe. In the end, there will be one world. All men will be saved,
happy, and prosperous, and the Soka Gakkai will then disband itself, its
world-mission completed. One is reminded of the withering away of the
state in Marxism.[26]

Communism is also, for that matter, an imperial faith. Among the
ideologies, as opposed to the religions, it is still the most formidable, although the only significant fields for communist evangelism today lie in
Asia, Africa, and Latin America. The original expectations of Lenin,
Trotsky, and Zinoviev that the world revolution would spread from Russia
to the West have been refuted by history. While the present leadership
of the Soviet Union shrinks from active imperialism on behalf of the one
true faith, except in limited support of "wars of national liberation," the
Asian Marxism formulated by Mao Tse-tung calls for communist revolution throughout the world, vigorously assisted by the parties and peoples
of countries already safely in the socialist fold. Maoism is, again, a faith for
all men and all seasons. It has a sharply defined idea of mankind, a vision
of the future, and a project for world mastery. With increasing prosperity
in Asia and the passing of the older generation of Maoists, Asian communism may in time "soften" after the Soviet example, but the problems
of economic growth are so much greater in Asia and Africa than they were
in Russia that no one should take such a development for granted.

Here, then, we have one conceivable spiritual prospect for twenty-first-
century man—the triumph of a single faith, essentially hostile to its rivals,
although it might in practice allow them to flourish in a limited way
under its wing, as Christianity survives in Soviet Russia. I do not think
that this kind of solution is more than a remote possibility. Nothing
short of supernatural intervention or irresistible military force could
bring the whole world, including the West, under the domination of a
single imperial faith, whether religion or ideology, no matter how universal
its appeal.

One other class of organized faiths should be noted in passing, those
which freely recognize the value and truth of the various historical religions and then insist on the distinctive power of their own historical
faith to effect an integration of all the others. The Baha'i Faith is the
classical example. From its origins in nineteenth-century Persian Islam to
the present day, Baha'i has represented itself as a fresh revelation from
God, fulfilling all past revelations, Eastern and Western, and bringing

them into new unity and harmony. Instead of extirpating its rivals, Baha'i proposes to absorb and encompass them. The ultimate end in view is a Baha'i world order, but the way of the Baha'i true-believer is compassionate and unfanatical.[27]

The Indian equivalent of the Baha'i movement, also founded in the nineteenth century, is the Ramakrishna Vedanta Society, a missionary order well known in Europe and America, which looks benevolently on all religious faiths, sees truth in all of them, and then encloses them all in the higher truth of Hindu monism and the traditional doctrine of *neti neti*: the truth is not this, not that.[28] From the point of view of the Western confessional faiths, Ramakrishna's formula is no less imperialistic in its own subtle way than Christianity, Islam, or Baha'i. Both Baha'i and Ramakrishna Vedanta offer a unity achieved from the perspective of a single tradition, Islamic or Hindu, very much as the efforts of some Unitarian-Universalists in the United States to suggest a world religion have their origins in the fundamental insights of nineteenth-century liberal Protestantism.[29]

Among secular faiths, the clearest parallel is the international Humanist movement, centered in the English-speaking countries and in the Netherlands. Its spiritual roots lie in the Enlightenment and in Victorian agnosticism and positivism. Although Humanism offers itself as a unifying world faith, it is unmistakably the expression of a particular kind of post-Christian, liberal, rationalist, sceptical, progressivist Western mentality.[30] It may be as well qualified to unite the ideologies as Baha'i or Ramakrishna Vedanta to unite the religions, but it does so from an historically limited and local perspective. Again, however, it does meet one crucial test for a possible world faith: it ministers to all mankind.

Many individual prophets, not attached at least in their prophetic capacity to an organized movement, have devoted their attention since 1945 to the question of religious and ideological commitment in the coming world civilization. They divide, roughly, into two camps—those who foresee a unitary world culture, developing through a process of synthesis and coalescence from compatible elements in the existing local cultures, and those who foresee a pluralistic culture-pattern, marked by dialogue and communication among the several surviving traditions, but without integration. Their work provides us with a framework of ideas for discussing the possibilities that remain. The shape of things to come, I suspect, lies somewhere within the range of their speculations.

The thinking of one such prophet, F. S. C. Northrop, in a sense joins the two positions, although ultimately coming down on the side of a unitarian solution. He sees the future of humanity in two stages: the amalgamation of national cultures and polities into regional systems, such as Europe, Africa, and the Arab world; and their final integration in a world civilization uniting the basic premises of both Eastern and Western thought. In the era of the national and supra-national regional state, a strengthened United Nations Organization would undertake to guarantee the values of each separate culture, as it would guarantee the integrity of political frontiers, except that no state could enter the world community whose ruling ideology or religion rejected the norm of "living law pluralism." There could be no toleration of the intolerant. After the achievement of a genuinely tolerant and pluralist world society, Northrop anticipates steady further growth toward world ideological and religious synthesis, culminating in a rich unitary culture true for all mankind. Through philosophical analysis, the truths, values, and methodologies of each tradition will be brought into concert. To ensure that the powers of science and technology are harnessed for the welfare of humanity and not for world destruction, "a truly global, as opposed to a provincially Eastern or a provincially Western, morality and religion are essential."[31]

The philosophical approach to synthesis has also found able exponents in Oliver L. Reiser and Lancelot Law Whyte. Both insist on the need for a single world culture, with a planetary ideology or doctrine capable of uniting the world-outlooks of East and West. Western science and Eastern religion will fuse in a higher, unitary system of thought.[32] In the same vein, Erich Fromm predicts the emergence of a new religion of humanity. "The most important feature of such a religion would be its universalistic character, corresponding to the unification of mankind which is taking place in this epoch; it would embrace the humanistic teachings common to all great religions of the East and West."[33] The approach of Reiser, Whyte, and Fromm is purely humanistic, but the prophetic literature of our time also abounds in proposals for a synthetic world religion more intimately linked to religious tradition, such as Charles Morris's conception of a "Maitreyan" world religion in his book Paths of Life and Gerald Heard's project for a new world faith in The Human Venture.[34]

The most prestigious apostle of the unitarian approach is the late Father Pierre Teilhard de Chardin. His debt to Catholicism and to evolutionary philosophy goes without saying. Yet he somehow transcended both. His sense of the growing oneness of humanity has all the vividness of a mystical vision. Evolution since the beginning of time has labored, he wrote, to produce the most complex and individual of all existing things, the human personality. But as mankind multiplies and civilization grows, the planet becomes enveloped in a "noösphere," an atmosphere of thought, a world community of minds in ever closer dependence on one another, initiating the evolution of a still more complex being. The goal of history, in Teilhard's vision, is the emergence of a "hyper-person," an organic synthesis of minds each retaining its personality but achieving fulfillment in spiritual union with all of humanity. When and if the entire human species constitutes such a collective personality, all hitherto unreconciled differences of faith and aspiration will be resolved in unanimity. Man will enjoy a unity akin to that of God himself, the ultimate hyper-person outside of space and time from whom the cosmos takes its being. The gulf between science and religion will close, eugenics will replace reproduction by chance, research will be fully organized at last, the human mind will enter upon its true inheritance of knowledge and power.[35]

Despite the great success of Teilhard's writings, the majority of prophets who have given attention to the problem of spiritual life in the coming world order prefer to think in terms of a pluralist solution. The "pluralism" of the past, with its wars of religion and ideology, finds few defenders. But a world sheltering a wide variety of free faiths which respect one another's rights and engage in friendly dialogue, eager to learn and teach, is another matter altogether. The key word is "dialogue." In an age when religions and ideologies have lost much of their dynamism, when intolerance and dogmatism have resulted in so much misery in recent memory, the idea of a continuing exchange of thoughts across carefully respected boundary lines has much appeal. The integrity of each body of true-believers is protected, but missionary zeal need no longer be sustained. Peace talks between undefeated rivals take the place of demands for unconditional surrender.

Most of the prophetic literature committed to an enlightened pluralism centers its attention on the religions.[36] William Ernest Hocking in his Hibbert Lectures, Living Religions and a World Faith, has made one of the most impressive contributions. Although published thirty years ago, their relevance to the spiritual problem of contemporary man has, if anything, increased since they first appeared. Hocking rejects both imperialism and synthesis in favor of what he terms "the way of reconception." The positive religions must come to understand that their historically conditioned particularity, although inevitable, has deprived them of much wisdom. Underlying all religions are the same basic human needs and the same ultimate spiritual reality, but historical accidents result in different formulations of truth, growing from different fundamental options and utilizing different systems of symbols. As the various traditions come into ever more intimate communication with one another, Hocking suggests that they will be challenged not merely to incorporate compatible insights from other faiths but also to reconceive their basic premises. The broadening of outlook achieved by reconception will enable them to make use of hitherto incompatible insights, as well. The religions will retain their organic and historical identities, but they will ultimately stand together on the same broad foundations. "Retaining the symbols of their historic pieties," as Hocking writes in a more recent book, "the great faiths will grow in their awareness of a unity more significant than the remaining differences." In the process each faith will become more, rather than less, true to itself, by reaching a deeper understanding of its fundamental point of view in relation to other approaches.[37]

This is somewhat the position taken by Tillich in his *Christianity and the Encounter of the World Religions*. Conversion, he argues, must give way to dialogue. The religions of the world have much to learn from one another, just as Christianity and Platonism enjoyed fruitful interaction throughout the Middle Ages and the Renaissance. At the same time, a mixture of religions would destroy in each of them the "concreteness" from which they draw their "dynamic power." The way to reach universal spiritual truth "is not to relinquish one's religious tradition for the sake of a universal concept which would be nothing but a concept. The way is to penetrate into the depth of one's own religion, in devotion, thought and action. In the depth of every living religion there is a point at which the religion itself loses its importance, and that to which it points breaks through its particularity, elevating it to spiritual freedom and with it to a vision of the spiritual presence in other expressions of the ultimate meaning of man's existence."[38] Unity must be sought, as it were, in the timeless depths of religious experience, while preserving the historically dynamic uniqueness of each living faith. Every formulation of truth is historically finite and concrete, but the truth to which it points is for all faiths the same.

Arnold Toynbee carries the argument a step further in one of the "annexes" of his *A Study of History*, suggesting that each of the major world religions has evolved from premises which answer the needs of a fundamentally different personality type. Following the typology of Jung, he sees Christianity as the religion pre-eminently of the "feeling" extravert, Islam as the religion of the "sensing" extravert, Hinduism as the religion of the "thinking" introvert, and Buddhism as the religion of the "intuiting" introvert.[39] In a world civilization, it should be possible not only for peoples of a given cultural background to remain in the historical faith which has given rise to that culture, but also for individuals, if they choose, to transfer their allegiance to the religion of another culture which happens to meet their spiritual needs more fully. A Frenchman for whom Buddhism can reveal the cosmos better than Christianity will become a Buddhist. A Burmese whose personality inclines him toward a more extraverted faith than East Asian tradition allows, may choose Christianity. "The divers higher religions must resign themselves to playing limited parts, and must school themselves to playing these parts in harmony, in order, between them, to fulfill their common purpose of enabling every human being of every psychological type to enter into communion with God the Ultimate Reality."[40] Each living faith is, therefore, an experiment directed to the same end, and each has its own value. Even if one religion does ultimately prevail, the victorious faith "will not eliminate the other religions that it replaces. Even if it does replace them, it will achieve this by absorbing into itself what is best in them."[41]

In the same spirit, Toynbee also anticipates the development of many sub-cultures in the coming world civilization patterned after the Jewish world diaspora. Local cultures will survive, but with continuing improvements in communication and transport, and the abolition of national sovereignties in a freely formed universal state (here Toynbee and Hocking disagree), the local unit will "come to play a progressively less important part by comparison with units whose principle of association is, not physical neighbourhood, but a community of beliefs, ideas, aspirations, interests, or activities." Just as in great cities, friendships are formed with people from all over the metropolitan area, so in the world order. "Now that the World is becoming one city, we may expect to see associations based on neighbourhood overshadowed by others based on spiritual affinity: that is to say, by diasporas in the broadest sense of the term."[42] As the authority of the traditional local community is, by degrees, surrendered to the community of all mankind, the freedom of the individual is correspondingly enhanced.

The one possible flaw in all these prophetic visions lies in their assumption that the existing religions and ideologies, despite the decline that most have undergone since 1945, still possess enough energy to evolve toward synthesis or interdependence, and that they will be able to respond creatively to the demands of mankind in the coming world order. The spiritual ferment of the late 1960's suggests that perhaps the future belongs instead to systems of faith not yet defined, or to older systems so radically changed as to be virtually unrecognizable.

Let us also bear in mind that no benevolent providence assures us of the years of peace necessary for the eventual achievement of a secure world society. It is entirely conceivable that the unifying tendencies in world history will be overwhelmed by the tendencies toward disaggregation, and that holocausts are in the making without precedent in the long history of human folly. If the emphasis here falls on the spiritual prospects for man in a world that has been spared future total wars, it is only because I seriously doubt that mankind can have any sort of higher spiritual life at all in a disunited and warring world, given the potentialities for tyranny and genocide of modern technology. To gain a conception of the spiritual life of humanity in the aftermath of Armageddon, we would be well advised to ignore the speculations of the prophets discussed above and return with Frazer, Lévy-Bruhl, and Malinowski to a study of the mind of the Stone Age.

These are some of the possibilities in store for humanity in the twenty-first century and beyond. But one vital and overarching concept has been somewhat neglected in the discussion thus far. What place can we assign to the idea of mankind itself, as opposed to the particularized ideas of mankind in living faiths? Here the work of the Council for the Study of Mankind, under whose auspices this book has been written, deserves the most careful attention.

As between the unitarian and the pluralist positions, the Council has generally expressed its solidarity with pluralism. In the words of Gerhard Hirschfeld, describing the consensus which developed among the scholars who first met in Chicago to plan the work of the Council, "We felt that the unity of mankind in cooperative action does not depend on a unity in ideas and beliefs; on the contrary, it depends on a pluralism that would provide the energy and diversity of ideas to constitute an active and ever-growing unity."[43] The Council has no desire to become a pressure group or sect promoting a determinate doctrine of world order. Nonetheless, it has always insisted upon the need to see problems and to think out solutions in terms of the interests of mankind as a whole, and not in terms of what it calls "segmental" interests. In effect, the idea of mankind becomes an unconditional value, a center of ultimate meaningfulness, although the way is left open for the individual believer to adhere to many other compatible values and meanings as well. The Council has not arrived at a formal definition of mankind, and disclaims a messianic role, but most of its members are not in favor merely of "seeing" problems from the point of view of mankind: they also ask us to solve them *ad majorem humanitatis gloriam*. A commitment is demanded, as in any religion or ideology.

At the same time, the Council has refrained from defining what it means by "mankind," and this carries with it certain profound advantages, in addition to obvious disadvantages. As soon as a particular direction of human evolution, a particular conception of human nature, or a particular code of ethical values is specified, a new sect springs into being. This would not run contrary to the human spiritual experience down to the present time. Indeed, one of the strongest arguments for seeking to preserve already existing historical faiths and urging the formation of new ones, is that most of the advances recorded by the human spirit have been made by messiahs, prophets, and ideologues, and not by committees of scholars steeped in the dispassionate relativism of modern science. But the peculiar nature of the spiritual condition of contemporary man may well preclude any simple repetition of the patterns of the past. Although we may need the historic faiths, and new faiths as well, they cannot easily escape serious infection by modern academic relativism. Without such infection, for that matter, unitarian synthesis or pluralist dialogue would be impossible. But then what can ensure that synthesis will be achieved in peace and harmony? Or what can ensure that dialogue will not degenerate into chaos, confusion, and strife? Can there be a unifying absolute, a spiritual pole star, to guide humanity in its voyage on the ever-changing seas of relativism?

It is here that the idea of mankind, conceived as a moral and spiritual commitment, but not precipitated into history, as it were, by a creedal definition, can play a decisive role in the coming world civilization. We may agree, at least, on this much: one overarching value, which must find its place in all religions and ideologies, although it is not the premise necessarily of any system of faith of its own. It may, and I think must, have its prophets and messiahs, but they will not be prophets and messiahs on the traditional model. They may not choose to come before us with a full-blown religion or ideology, replete with symbols, myths, creeds, and churches. Their *kerygma* will consist of the simple but profound insistence that we must always strive to think and act in terms of the welfare of the single, universal family of mankind. Mankind is an ultimate, an absolute good. There may be other ultimate and absolute goods. But none of them can be allowed to conflict in any way with our unconditional loyalty to mankind.

Since the freedom to believe is valueless without the freedom to disbelieve, we must also expect great numbers of agnostics in the coming world society. They, too, can be asked—in exchange for fellowship and citizenship—to make at least this one commitment. The only true heretics in the world civilization will be criminal minds who plot the murder or mutilation or impoverishment of the human race, or any fraction of it, for the sake of personal or segmental profit.

This, then, is the conclusion to which we are led by the present inquiry. It should come as no surprise. As a supreme value and a spiritual commitment, the idea of mankind informs most of the efforts made by contemporary prophets of world order to forecast the spiritual life of the future. Their interest is not to determine what kind of future will be best for the Christian faith, or for Buddhism, or for Marxism-Leninism, or for liberal democracy, but for mankind. If this feeling of ultimate concern for mankind can pervade all efforts to direct and unify the spiritual life of our nascent world civilization, then the nascent world civilization has an excellent chance of surviving the hazards of birth and growth, and of reaching a dynamic, life-fulfilling maturity.

In those years of maturity, the time may come when mankind will be able, after all, to define itself. A broad consensus on aims and purposes may be achieved, even if the pluralist pattern of individual cultures, nationalities, and faiths persists indefinitely. But that time is not yet here. It may not arrive until mankind has encountered other intelligent species of life elsewhere in the universe. Meanwhile, a world is waiting to be made here on earth. Whether it will collapse in violence and despair, or whether it will grow to the fullness of years which we can all see in our mind's eye, depends in some not inconsiderable measure on the decisions that we, as individuals, make to believe or not to believe in the human cause. Who is for mankind—unconditionally? Who is not? This is the central question of our time.

NOTES

1. Paul Tillich, *Christianity and the Encounter of the World Religions* (New York, 1963), p. 4.

2. Of course some political programs are called "ideologies" which in no sense serve as surrogates for religion: the "ideology" of European Christian Democracy, for example, attempts to import into secular politics the alleged social message of the Christian faith. One thinks also of the "ideology" of nudism, or feminism, or vegetarianism, none of which pretends, as a rule, to supply a system of ultimate values. Even a full-fledged ideology, such as socialism or nationalism, may have little religious meaning to the individual adherent, if he chooses to accept it only conditionally and partially.

3. Franklin Le Van Baumer, *Religion and the Rise of Scepticism* (New York, 1960), p. 20.

4. See Peter L. Berger, "Demythologization—Crisis in Continental Theology,"

Review of Religion, 20 (November 1955), 5-24. Berger's article is also reprinted in W. Warren Wagar, ed., *European Intellectual History since Darwin and Marx* (New York, 1967), pp. 237-261.

5. Gerhard Szczesny, *The Future of Unbelief* (New York, 1961), p. 12.

6. Daniel Bell, *The End of Ideology* (Glencoe, Ill., 1960), p. 373; Judith N. Shklar, *After Utopia: The Decline of Political Faith* (Princeton, N.J., 1957), pp. vii, 272-273; Thomas Molnar, *The Decline of the Intellectual* (Cleveland, 1961). Political philosophy, too, as distinguished from ideology, has fallen into rapid decay. Consult Alfred Cobban, "The Decline of Political Theory," *Political Science Quarterly*, 68 (September 1953), 321-337 (reprinted in Wagar, *European Intellectual History since Darwin and Marx*, pp. 184-202); David Easton, "The Decline of Modern Political Theory," *Journal of Politics*, 13 (February 1951), 36-58.

7. See Frederick L. Schuman, *The Commonwealth of Man* (New York, 1952) and W. Warren Wagar, *The City of Man: Prophecies of a World Civilization in Twentieth-Century Thought*, rev. ed. (Baltimore, 1967), pp. 221-235.

8. John Lukacs, *Decline and Rise of Europe* (Garden City, N.Y., 1965), p. 261.

9. See especially Camus's *The Rebel: An Essay on Man in Revolt* (New York, 1956). For Sartre's Marxism see his *Critique de la raison dialectique* (Paris, 1960) and Wilfrid Desan, *The Marxism of Jean-Paul Sartre* (Garden City, N.Y., 1965).

10. I may seem here to be inconsistent with my argument, in *H. G. Wells and the World State* (New Haven, Conn., 1961), p. 201, that Wells's hope for world de-politicization has not been realized. I pointed out that politicians, and not engineers are managers, still decide what is to be done. There has been no Wellsian revolution against the political order by the "experts." This is quite true. On the other hand, although the politician has not relinquished his power, the range of decisions which he can reasonably make and enforce is severely limited by technological requirements, as specified by the experts. In place of a crude Wellsian revolution, what we are seeing is the gradual erosion of the politician's effective freedom of choice, which may in time amount to much the same thing. But the experts can take no credit for this expansion of their power—it has come to them willy-nilly.

11. See, for example, Kurt Shell, "The Crisis of Modern Socialism," *World Politics*, 9 (January 1957), 295-305. Symptomatic is the explicit public repudiation of the ties of ideology by Pietro Nenni, the veteran leader of the once pro-communist Italian Socialist party. Italian socialists, he declared in 1966, "want a party not the slave of ideological fetishes, but based on a policy and a program, without dogmas, without an internal or external 'Church.'" *New York Times*, November 5, 1966.

12. Lyon Sharman, *Sun Yat-sen* (New York, 1934), p. 281.

13. Sun's teachings are translated into English by Leonard Shihlien Hsu in *Sun Yat-sen: His Political and Social Ideals* (Los Angeles, 1933). See also N. Gangulee, ed., *The Teachings of Sun Yat-sen* (London, 1945), and Paul M. A. Linebarger, *The Political Doctrines of Sun Yat-sen* (Baltimore, 1937).

14. For Nkrumah, see his books *I Speak of Freedom: A Statement of African Ideology* (New York, 1961); *Africa Must Unite* (New York, 1963); and *Consciencism* (New York, 1965).

15. See Clark B. Offner and Henry Van Straelen, *Modern Japanese Religions* (New York, 1963).

16. Bell, *The End of Ideology*, p. 373.

17. Shklar, *After Utopia*, p. 268.

18. See John Macquarrie, *God and Secularity* (Philadelphia, 1967). Some of the

more important primary sources include John Robinson, *Honest to God* (Philadelphia, 1963); Harvey Cox, *The Secular City* (New York, 1964); Thomas J. J. Altizer and William Hamilton, *Radical Theology and the Death of God* (Indianapolis, 1966); and Jürgen Moltmann, *The Theology of Hope* (New York, 1967).

19. Consult, e.g., Malcolm X with Alex Haley, *The Autobiography of Malcolm X* (New York, 1965); Stokely Carmichael and Charles V. Hamilton, *Black Power* (New York, 1967); Paul Jacobs and Saul Landau, *The New Radicals* (New York, 1966); Phillip Abbott Luce, *The New Left* (New York, 1966); Carl Oglesby and Richard Shaull, *Containment and Change* (New York, 1967); Herbert Marcuse, *One-Dimensional Man* (Boston, 1964) and *An Essay on Liberation* (Boston, 1969); and Kenneth Keniston, *Young Radicals: Notes on Committed Youth* (New York, 1968). Cf. Keniston's earlier book, *The Uncommitted: Alienated Youth in American Society* (New York, 1965). For Castro, Guevara, and revolutionary socialism in Latin America, see Régis Debray, *Revolution in the Revolution?* (New York, 1967). The new "humanistic" tendencies in Marxism in the West and in Eastern Europe are discussed in Erich Fromm, ed., *Socialist Humanism: An International Symposium* (Garden City, N.Y., 1965). For neo-feminism and the sexual revolution, see Betty Friedan, *The Feminine Mystique* (New York, 1963); Albert Ellis, *Sex Without Guilt* (New York, 1958); and Lars Ullerstam, *The Erotic Minorities* (New York, 1966).

20. See Erich Kahler, *The Tower and the Abyss* (New York, 1957); C. S. Lewis, *The Abolition of Man* (New York, 1947); Jacques Ellul, *The Technological Society* (New York, 1964); and Lewis Mumford, *The Transformations of Man* (New York, 1956) and *The City in History* (New York, 1961).

21. Tillich, *Christianity and the Encounter of the World Religions*, p. 96.

22. See my *The City of Man*, pp. 112-125, for a fuller discussion of the established world faiths in relation to the problem of world order.

23. Jacques Maritain, *The Range of Reason* (New York, 1952), chs. 14-15; see also *True Humanism* (New York, 1938) and *Man and the State* (Chicago, 1951). Maritain's prophetic thought is conveniently anthologized by Joseph W. Evans and Leo R. Ward in their *Social and Political Philosophy of Jacques Maritain: Selected Readings* (New York, 1955). See in particular chs. 18-19 and 21-22.

24. Christopher Dawson, *The Historic Reality of Christian Culture: A Way to the Renewal of Human Life* (New York, 1960), p. 117. See also Dawson, *The Dynamics of World History*, ed. John J. Mulloy (New York, 1956); and Martin C. D'Arcy, "Is There a Nascent World Culture?" in A. William Loos, ed., *Religious Faith and World Culture* (New York, 1951), pp. 259-277.

25. Hendrik Kraemer, *World Cultures and World Religions: The Coming Dialogue* (Philadelphia, 1960). For an example of "imperialism," see John Baillie, *The Belief in Progress* (London, 1950), ch. 5.

26. For an introduction to the Soka Gakkai, see Offner and Van Straelen, *Modern Japanese Religions*, pp. 98-109.

27. See Shoghi Effendi, *The World Order of Bahá'u'lláh* (New York, 1938) and John Ferraby, *All Things Made New* (London, 1957).

28. See Swami Nikhilananda, *Hinduism: Its Meaning for the Liberation of the Spirit* (New York, 1958). See also Sri Aurobindo, *The Ideal of Human Unity* (New York, 1950); and Sarvepalli Radhakrishnan, *Religion and Society* (London, 1947), *Recovery of Faith* (New York, 1955), *East and West* (New York, 1956), and "The Religion of the Spirit and the World's Need" in Paul Arthur Schilpp, ed., *The Phil-*

osophy of *Sarvepalli Radhakrishnan* (New York, 1952), pp. 5-82. An able study of "Hindu relativism" is available in R. L. Slater, *World Religions and World Community* (New York, 1963), ch. 3.

29. See Kenneth L. Patton, *A Religion for One World* (Boston, 1964).

30. For an introduction to the Humanist movement, see the article by the British Humanist, H. J. Blackham, "Modern Humanism," *The Journal of World History*, 8 (1964), pp. 100-122; reprinted in Guy S. Métraux and François Crouzet, eds., *Religions and the Promise of the Twentieth Century* (New York, 1965), pp. 156-182. See also Corliss Lamont, *Humanism as a Philosophy* (New York, 1949); Sir Julian Huxley, ed., *The Humanist Frame* (New York, 1961); and A. J. Ayer, ed., *The Humanist Outlook* (London, 1968).

31. F. S. C. Northrop, *The Logic of the Sciences and the Humanities* (New York, 1948), p. 364. The chief sources for Northrop's philosophy of world order are his books, *The Meeting of East and West* (New York, 1946) and *The Taming of the Nations* (New York, 1952). His thinking is summarized in Wagar, *The City of Man*, pp. 136-138, 142-145, 167, and 231-233.

32. Oliver L. Reiser, *The Promise of Scientific Humanism* (New York, 1940); *The Integration of Human Knowledge* (Boston, 1958): and *Cosmic Humanism* (Cambridge, Mass., 1965). Lancelot Law Whyte, *Accent on Form* (New York, 1954) and *The Next Development in Man* (New York, 1950).

33. Erich Fromm, *The Sane Society* (New York, 1955), p. 352.

34. Charles Morris, *Paths of Life: Preface to a World Religion* (New York, 1942); Gerald Heard, *The Human Venture* (New York, 1955).

35. Pierre Teilhard de Chardin, *The Phenomenon of Man* (New York, 1959).

36. See Wagar, *The City of Man*, pp. 155-172.

37. William Ernest Hocking, *Living Religions and a World Faith* (New York, 1940). See also Hocking's *The Coming World Civilization* (New York, 1956), from which the quotation is taken, p. 170.

38. Tillich, *Christianity and the Encounter of the World Religions*, p. 97. This idea of an ultimate oneness in the "depths" is discussed insightfully by R. L. Slater in his chapter on "Depth Religion" in *World Religions and World Community*. Slater also foresees a continuing pluralism, accompanied by serious and open-minded dialogue.

39. Arnold J. Toynbee, *A Study of History* (New York, 1934-61), VII, pp. 716-736.

40. Ibid., VII, p. 374.

41. Arnold J. Toynbee, *Christianity among the Religions of the World* (New York, 1957), p. 110.

42. Toynbee, *A Study of History*, XII, pp. 216-217.

43. Gerhard Hirschfeld, "Foreword: On the History of the Council for the Study of Mankind" in Bert F. Hoselitz, ed., *Economics and the Idea of Mankind* (New York, 1965), p. x. But see also W. Warren Wagar, *Building the City of Man* (New York, 1971), where cultural pluralism comes under severe criticism.

Index